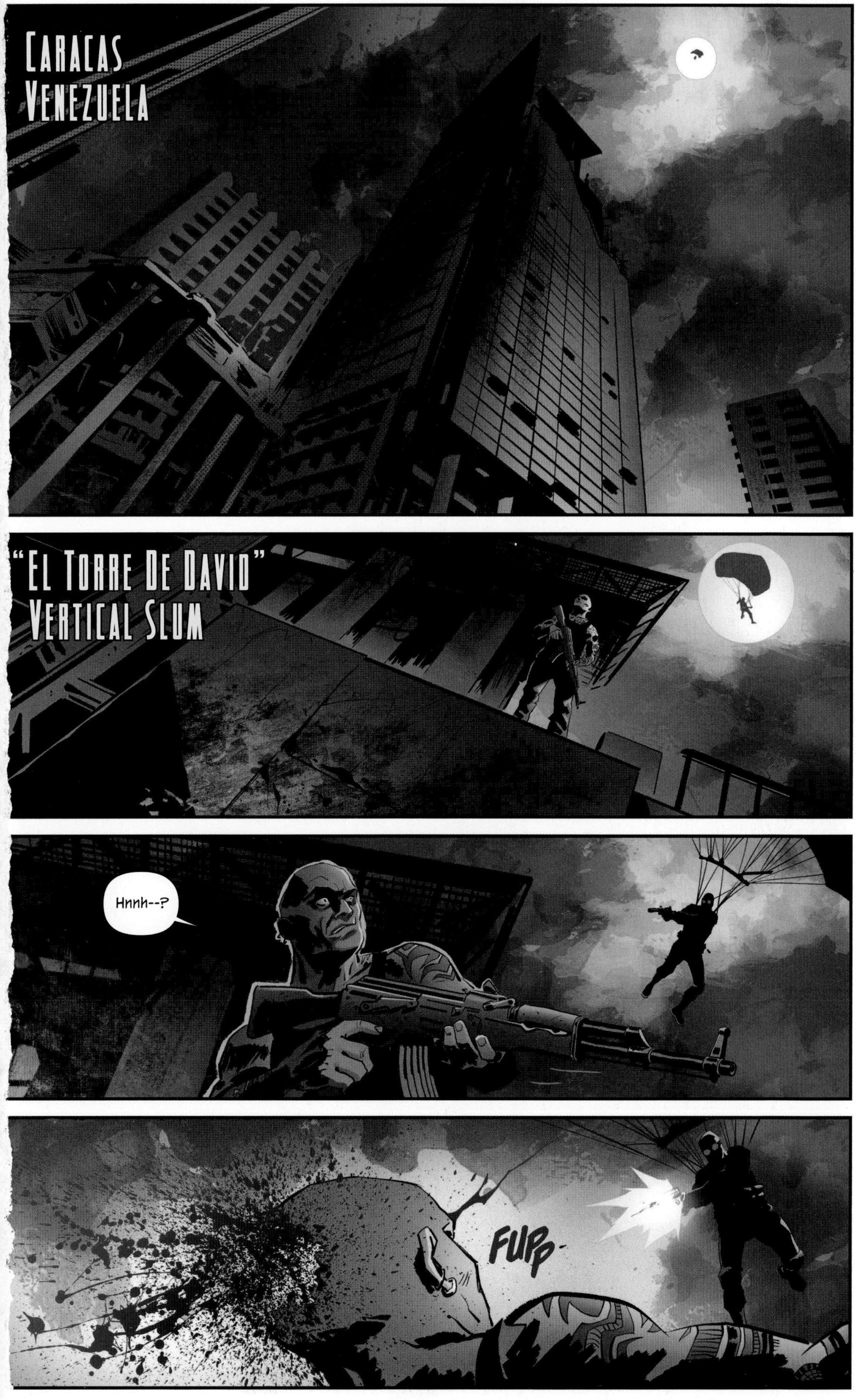
Caracas
Venezuela
"El Torre De David"
Vertical Slum
Hnnh--?
FUPP

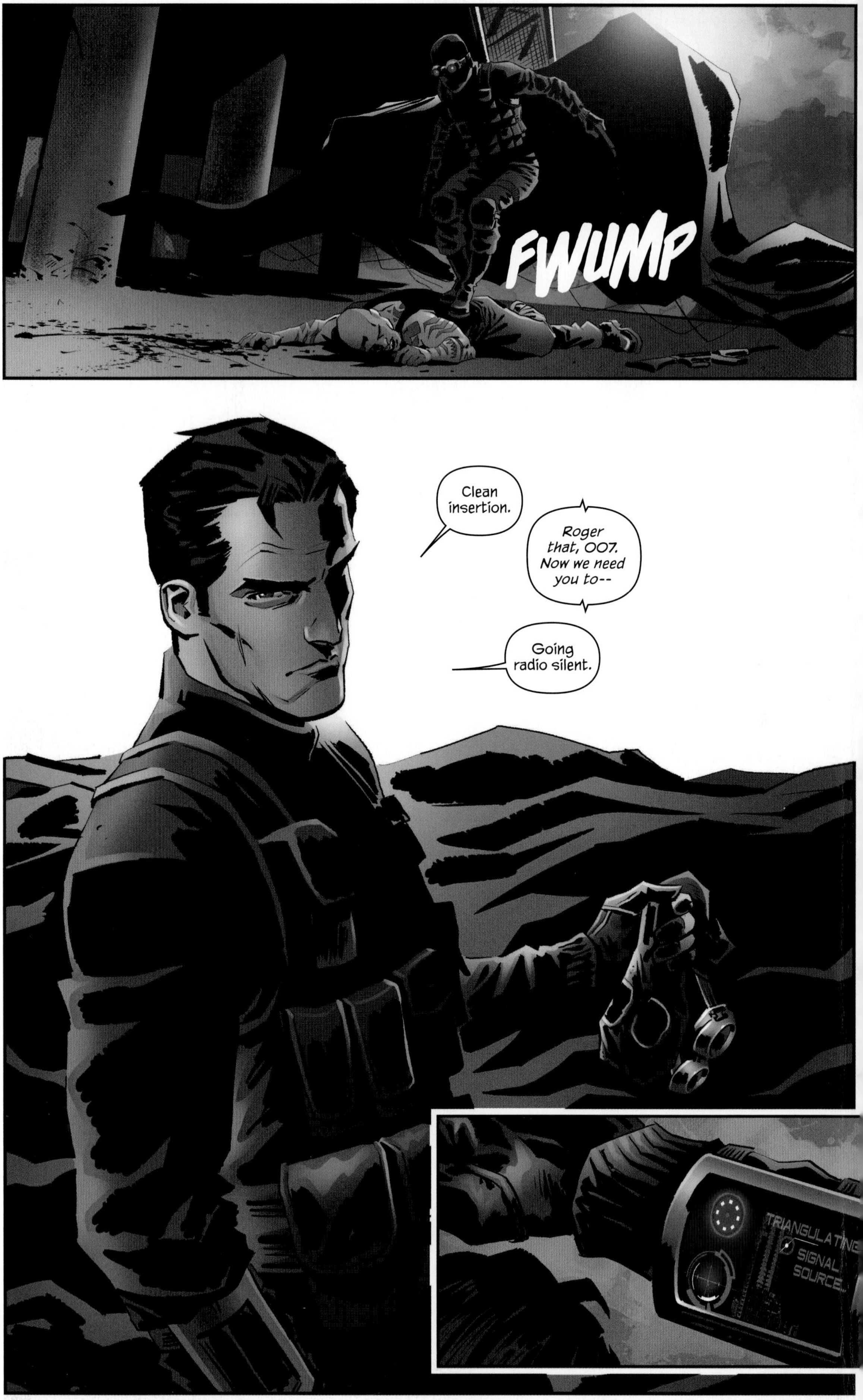
FWUMP
Clean insertion.
Roger that, 007. Now we need you to--
Going radio silent.
TRIANGULATING SIGNAL SOURCE...

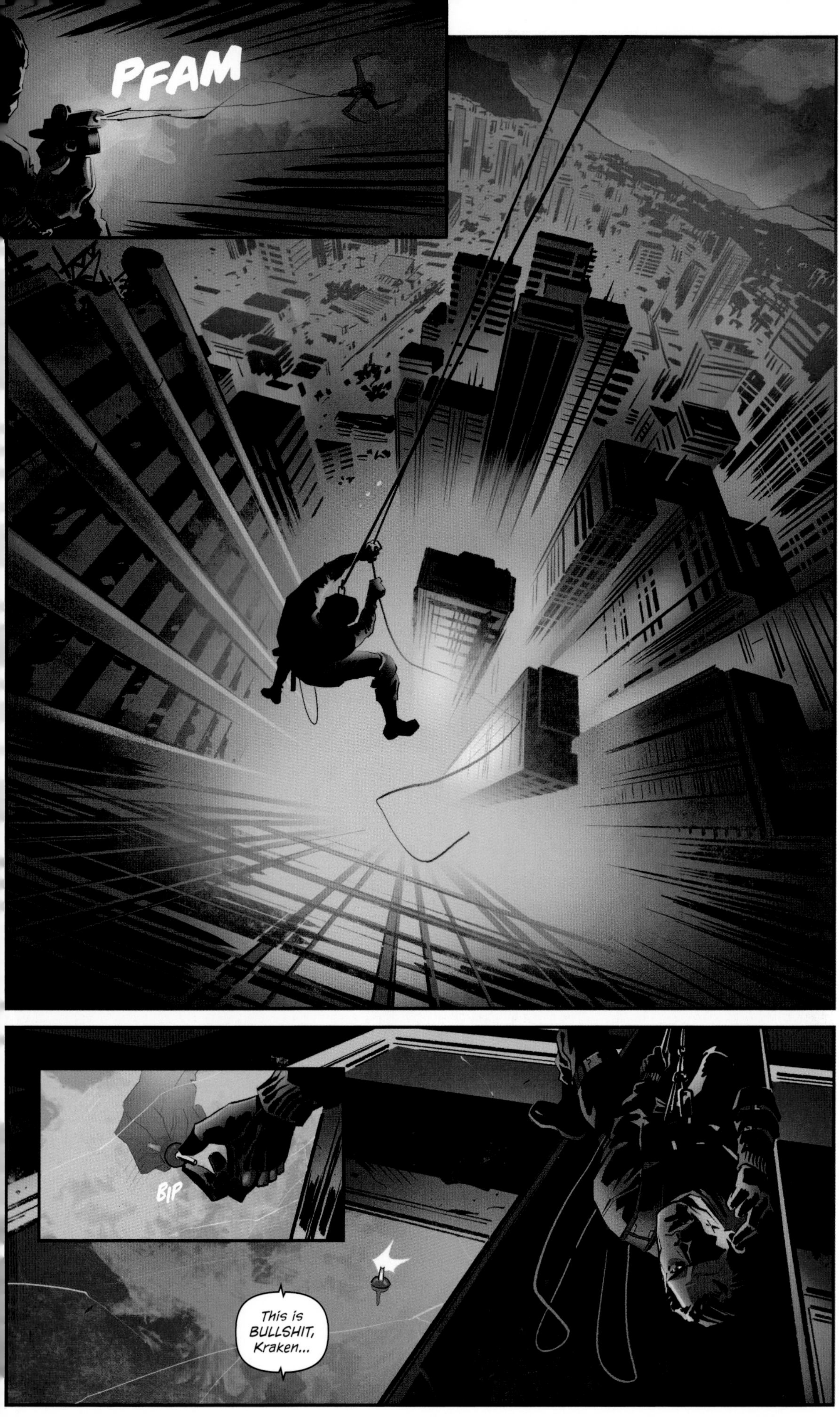
PFAM
BIP
This is BULLSHIT, Kraken...

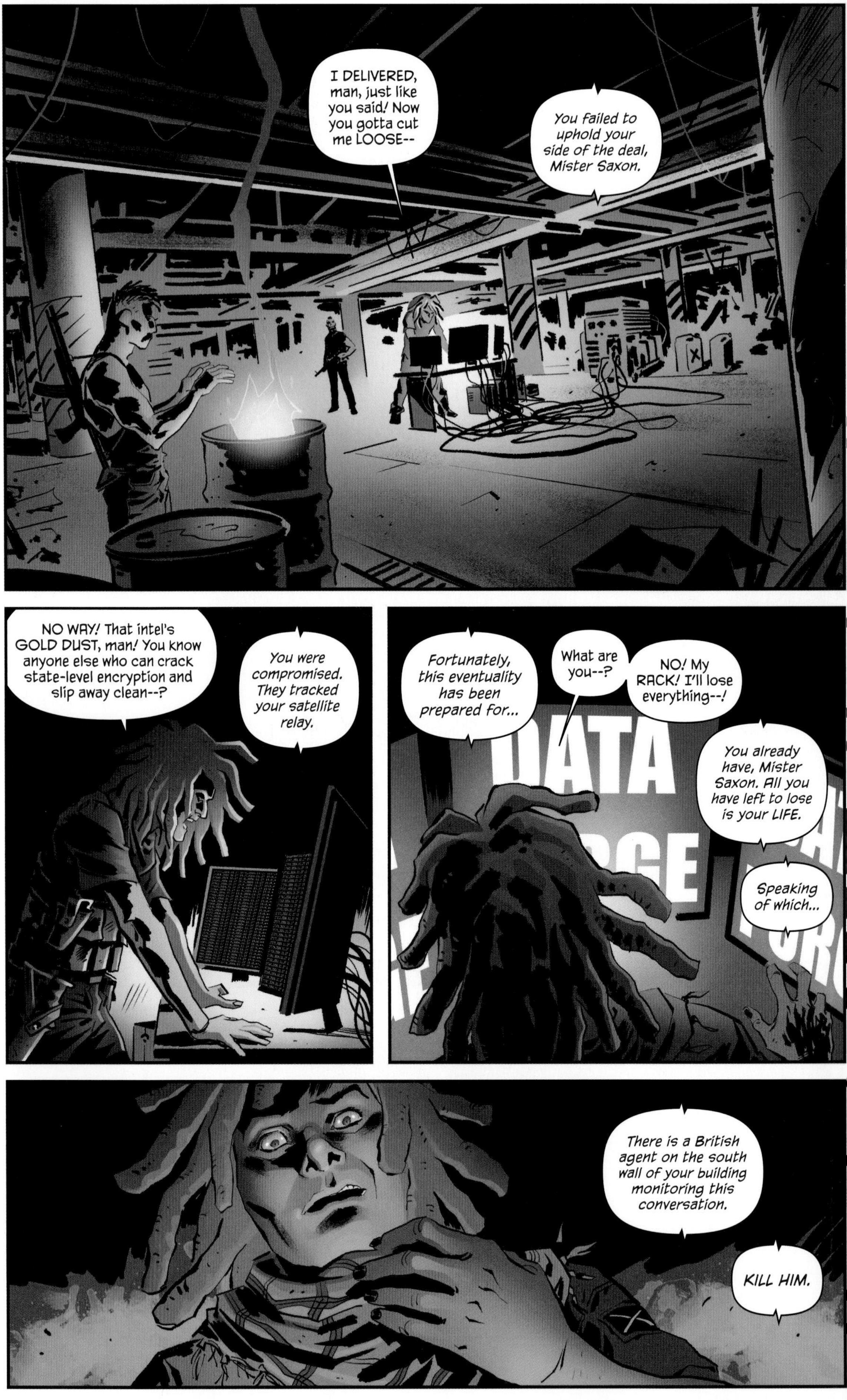
I DELIVERED, man, just like you said! Now you gotta cut me LOOSE--
You failed to uphold your side of the deal, Mister Saxon.
NO WAY! That intel's GOLD DUST, man! You know anyone else who can crack state-level encryption and slip away clean--?
You were compromised. They tracked your satellite relay.
Fortunately, this eventuality has been prepared for...
What are you--?
NO! My RACK! I'll lose everything--!
DATA
You already have, Mister Saxon. All you have left to lose is your LIFE.
Speaking of which...
There is a British agent on the south wall of your building monitoring this conversation.
KILL HIM.

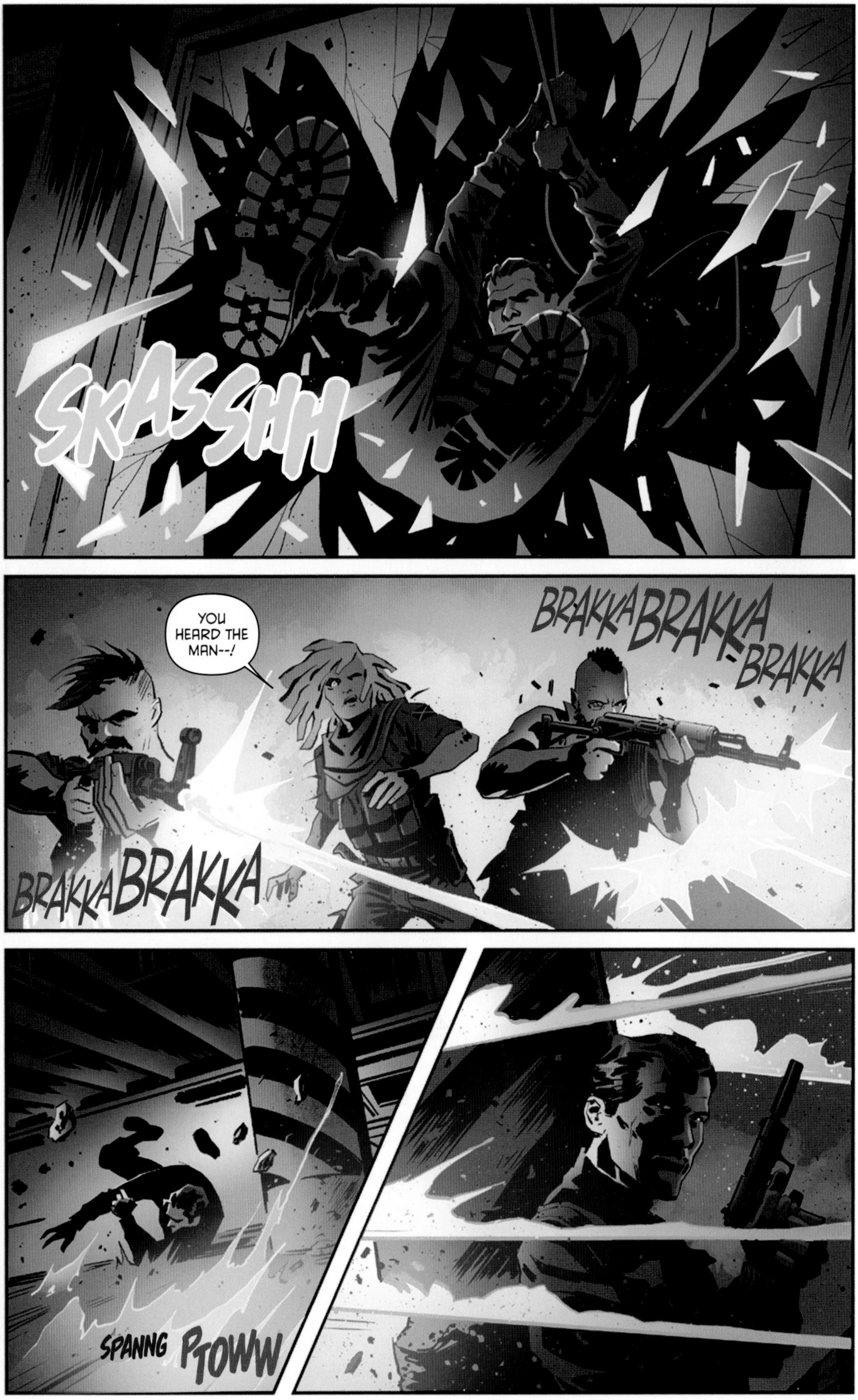
SKASSHH
YOU HEARD THE MAN--!
BRAKKA BRAKKA BRAKKA
BRAKKA BRAKKA
SPANNG
PTOWW

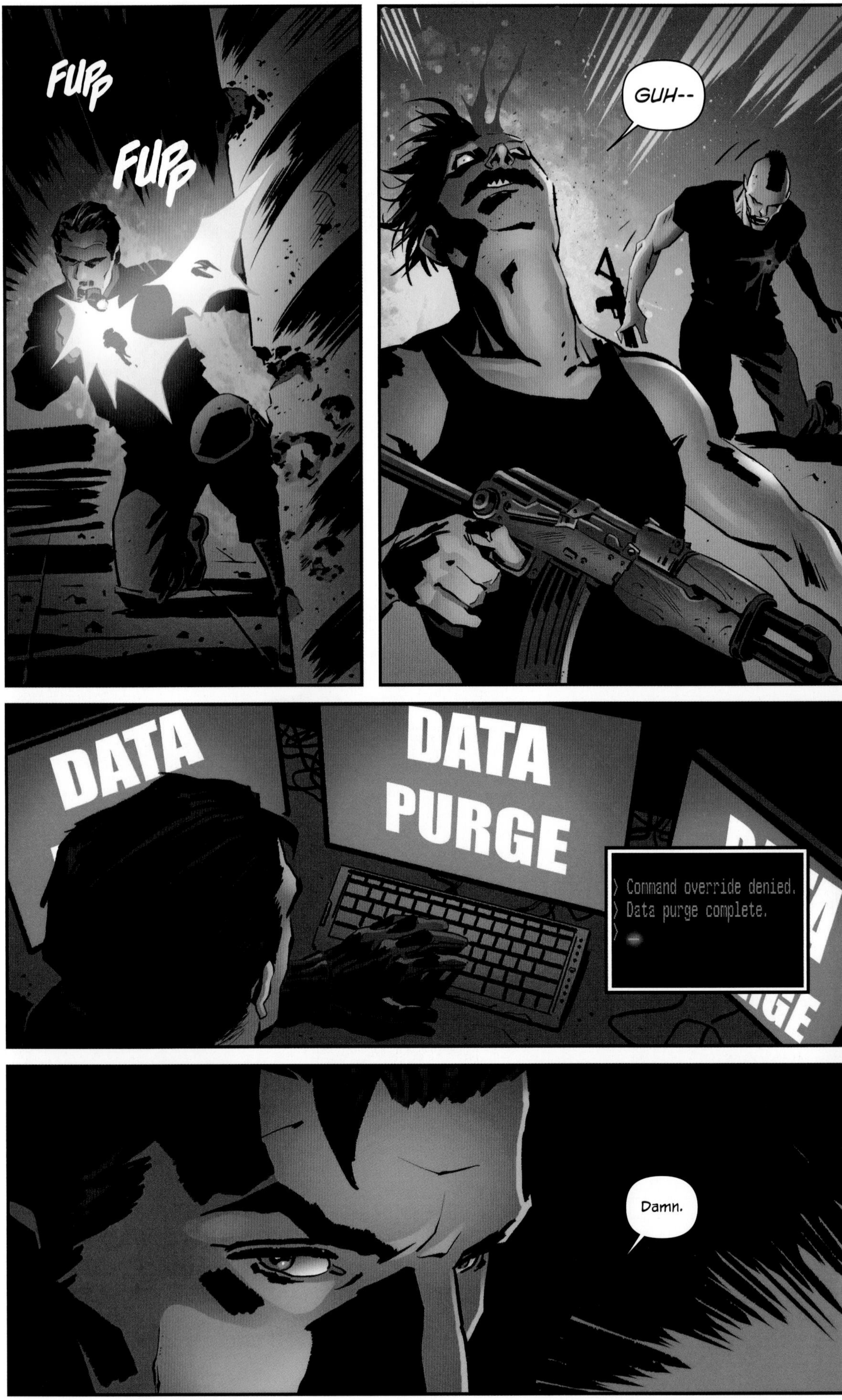
FUPP
FUPP
GUH--
DATA
DATA
PURGE
> Command override denied.
> Data purge complete.
>
Damn.

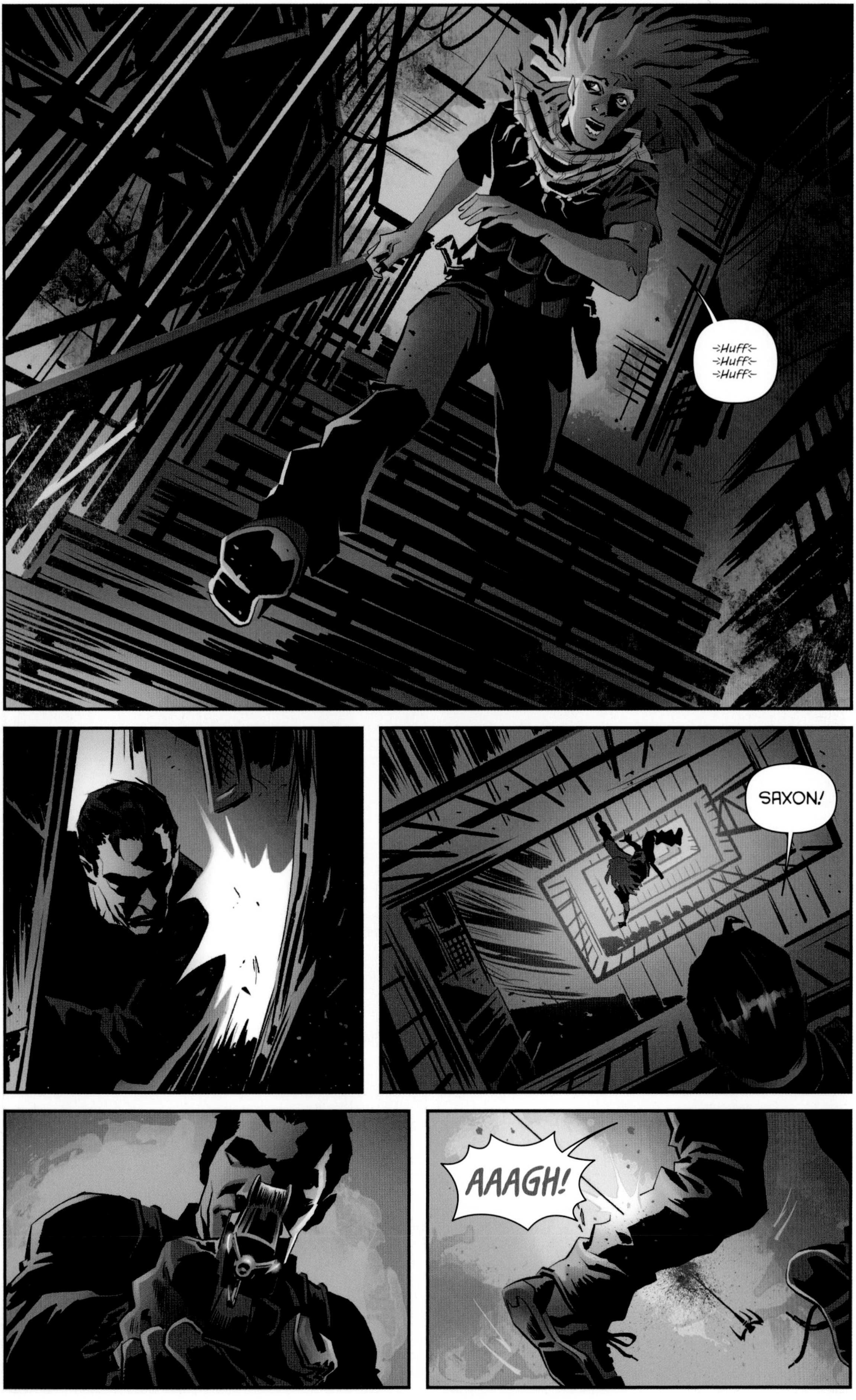
~Huff~
~Huff~
~Huff~
SAXON!
AAAGH!

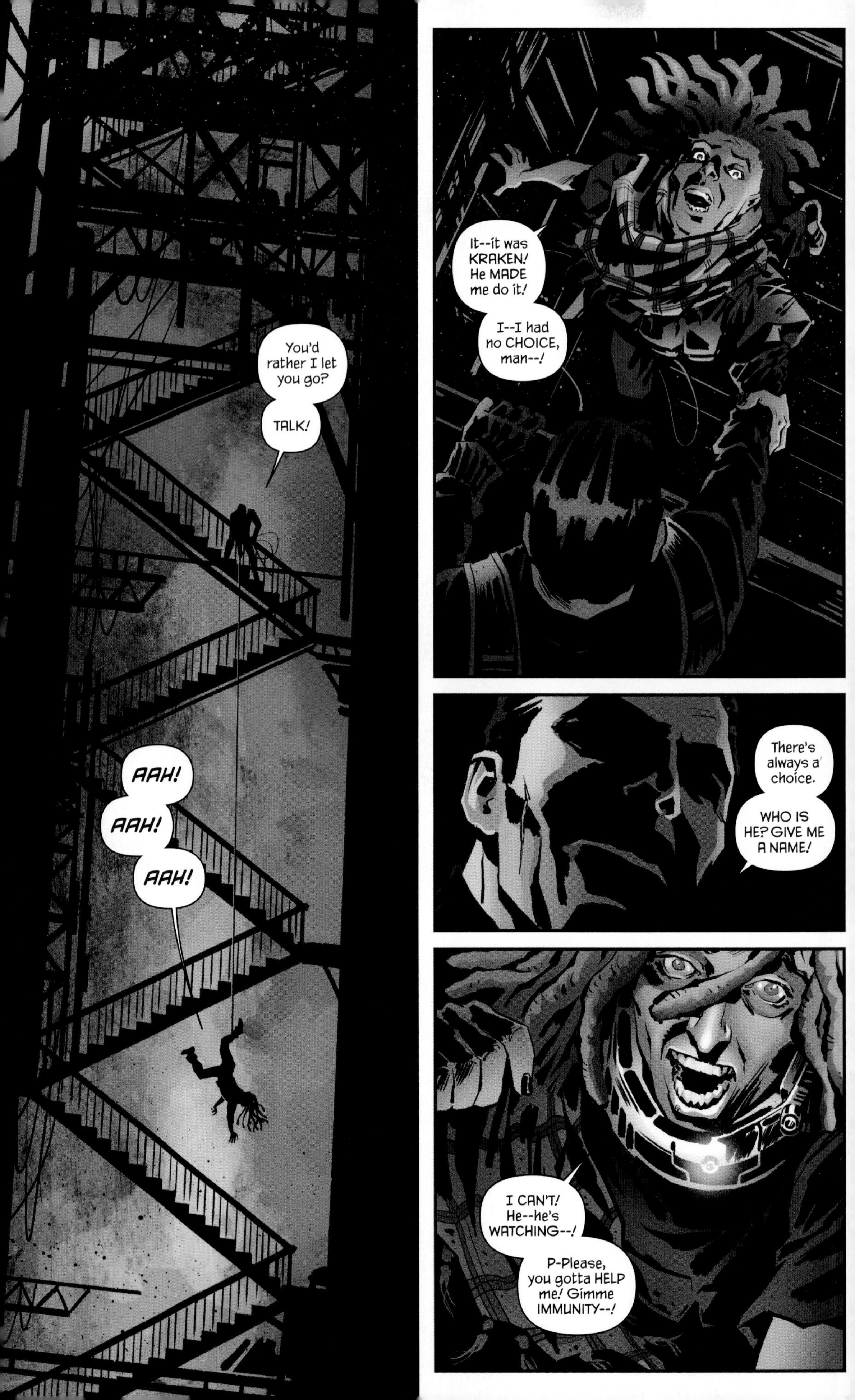
You'd rather I let you go?
TALK!
AAH!
AAH!
AAH!
It--it was KRAKEN! He MADE me do it!
I--I had no CHOICE, man--!
There's always a choice.
WHO IS HE? GIVE ME A NAME!
I CAN'T! He--he's WATCHING--!
P-Please, you gotta HELP me! Gimme IMMUNITY--!

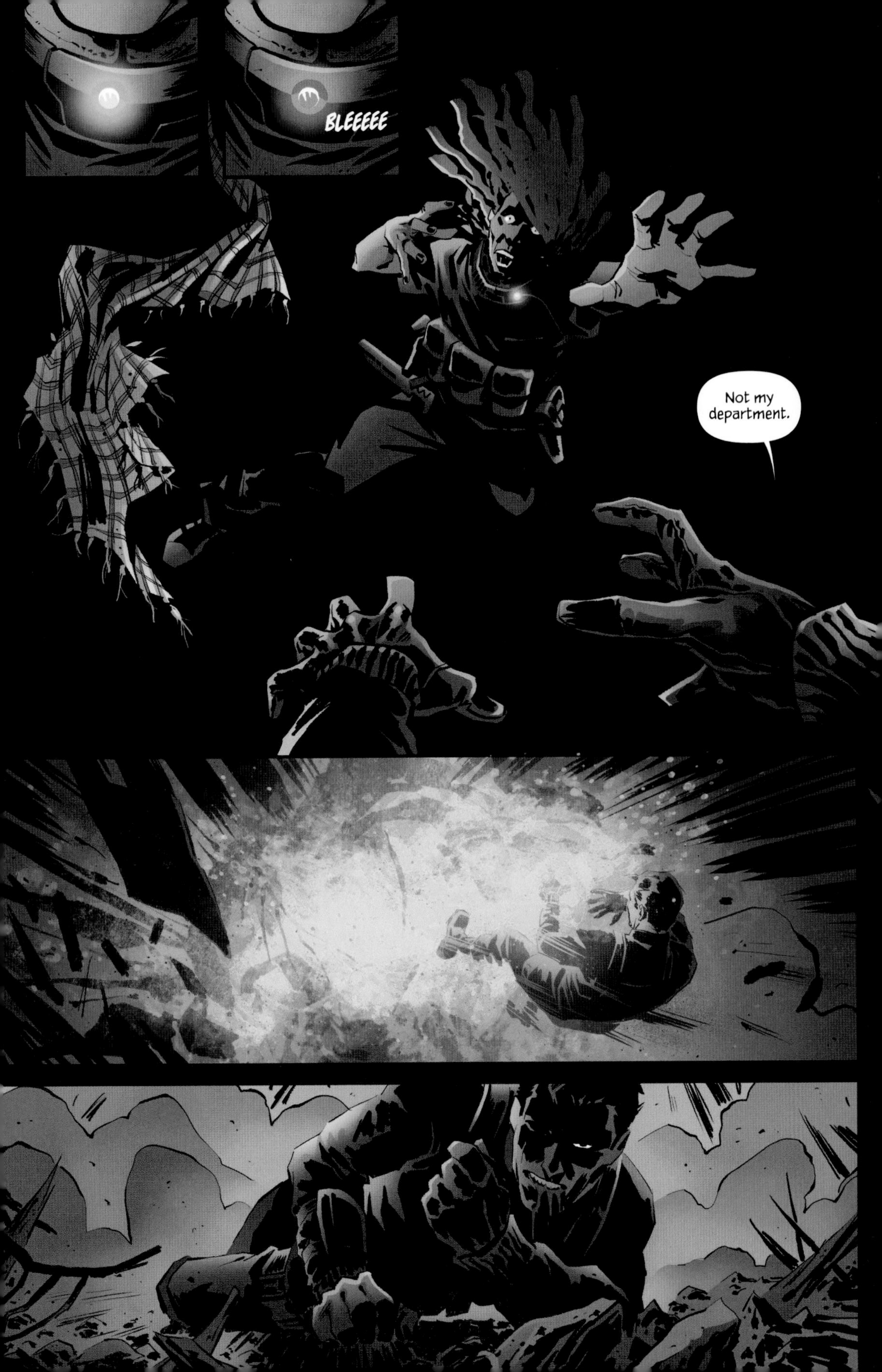
BLEEEEE
Not my department.

JAMES BOND 007

IN:
HAMMERHEAD

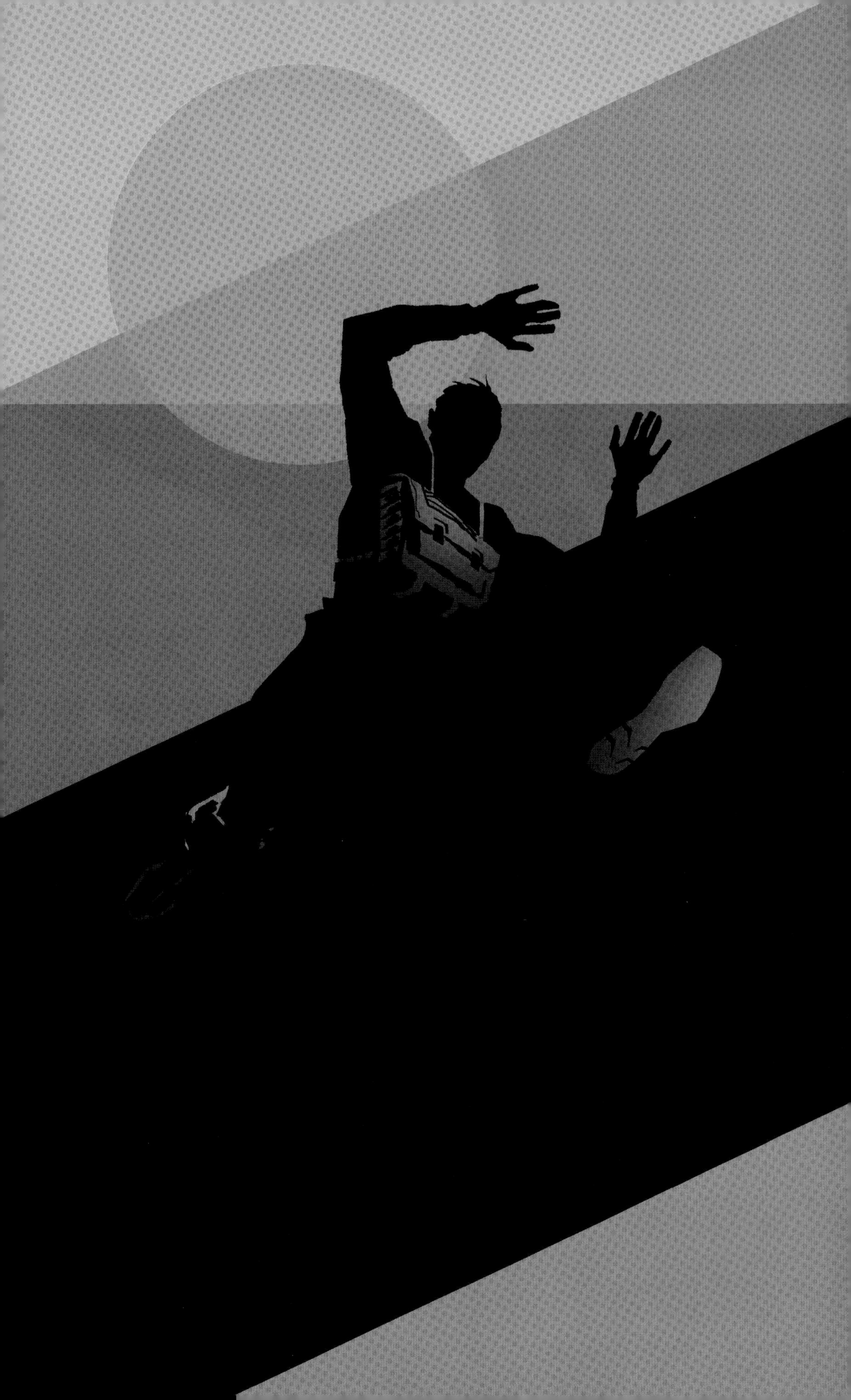

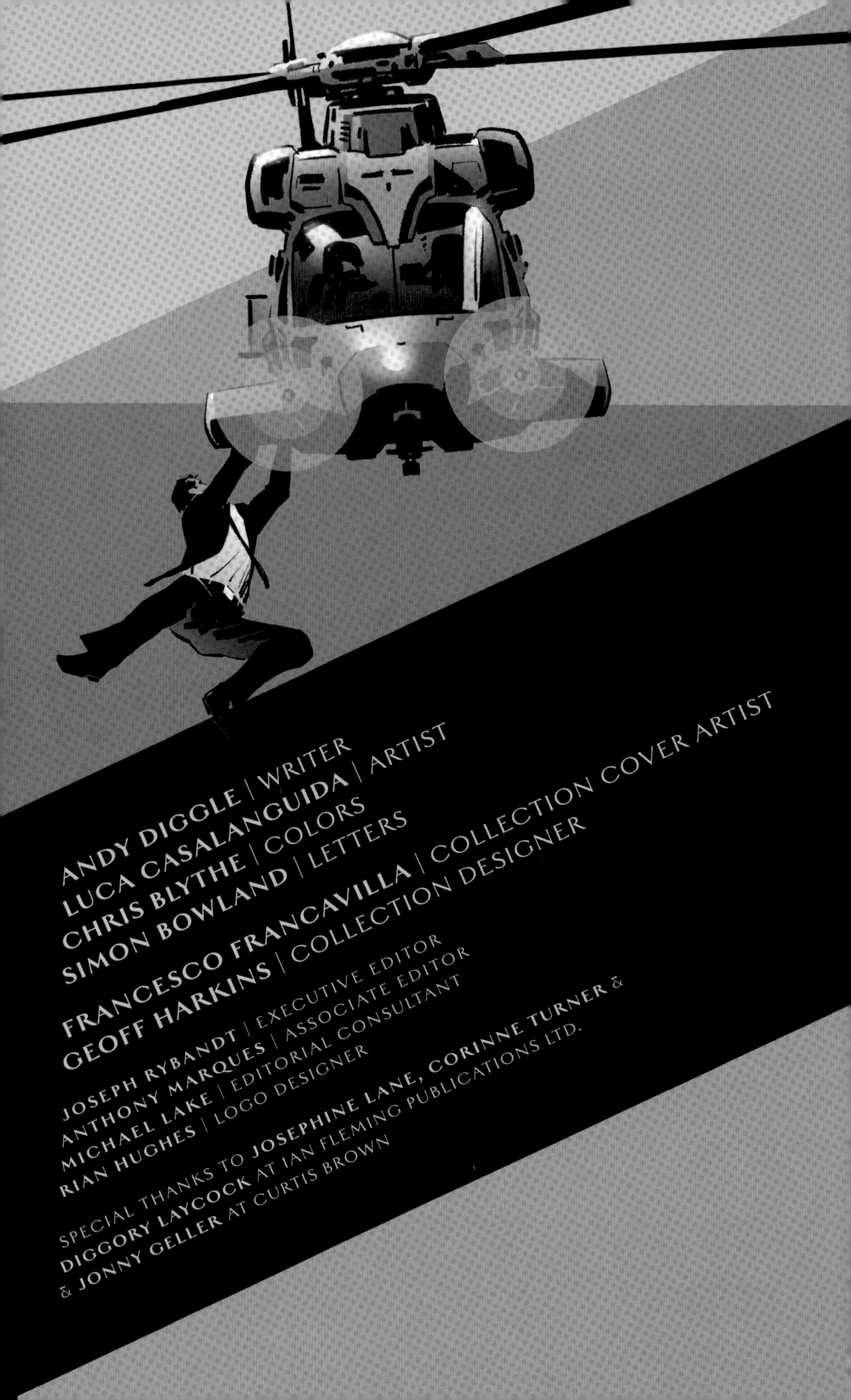

ANDY DIGGLE | WRITER
LUCA CASALANGUIDA | ARTIST
CHRIS BLYTHE | COLORS
SIMON BOWLAND | LETTERS

FRANCESCO FRANCAVILLA | COLLECTION COVER ARTIST
GEOFF HARKINS | COLLECTION DESIGNER

JOSEPH RYBANDT | EXECUTIVE EDITOR
ANTHONY MARQUES | ASSOCIATE EDITOR
MICHAEL LAKE | EDITORIAL CONSULTANT
RIAN HUGHES | LOGO DESIGNER

SPECIAL THANKS TO **JOSEPHINE LANE, CORINNE TURNER** &
DIGGORY LAYCOCK AT IAN FLEMING PUBLICATIONS LTD.
& **JONNY GELLER** AT CURTIS BROWN

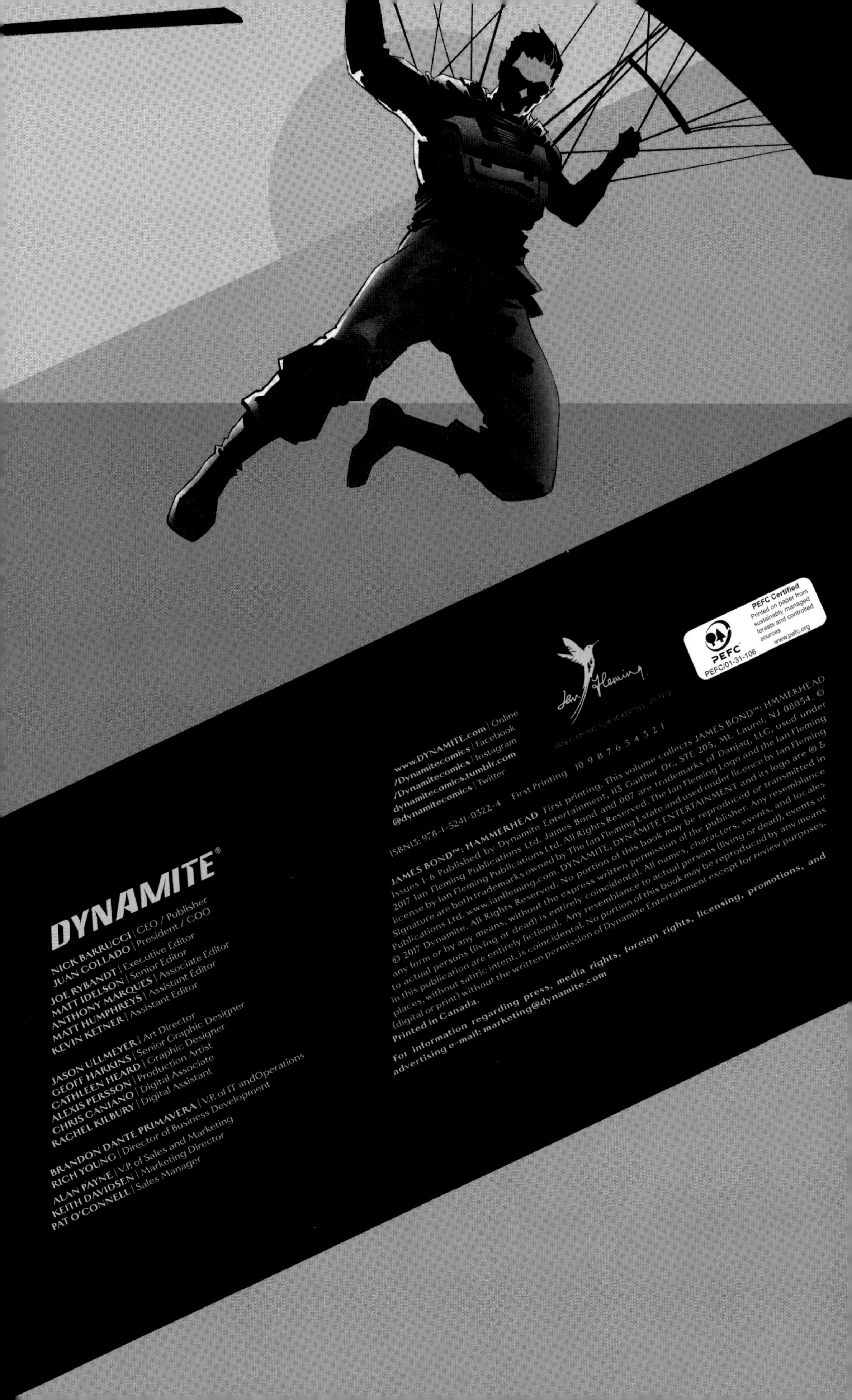

DYNAMITE®

www.DYNAMITE.com | Online
/Dynamitecomics | Facebook
/Dynamitecomics | Instagram
dynamitecomics.tumblr.com
@dynamitecomics | Twitter

Ian Fleming

IAN FLEMING PUBLICATIONS LIMITED

ISBN13: 978-1-5241-0322-4 First Printing 10 9 8 7 6 5 4 3 2 1

Printed in Canada.

For information regarding press, media rights, foreign rights, licensing, promotions, and advertising e-mail: marketing@dynamite.com

PEFC Certified
Printed on paper from sustainably managed forests and controlled sources
www.pefc.org
PEFC/01-31-106

ISSUE 1

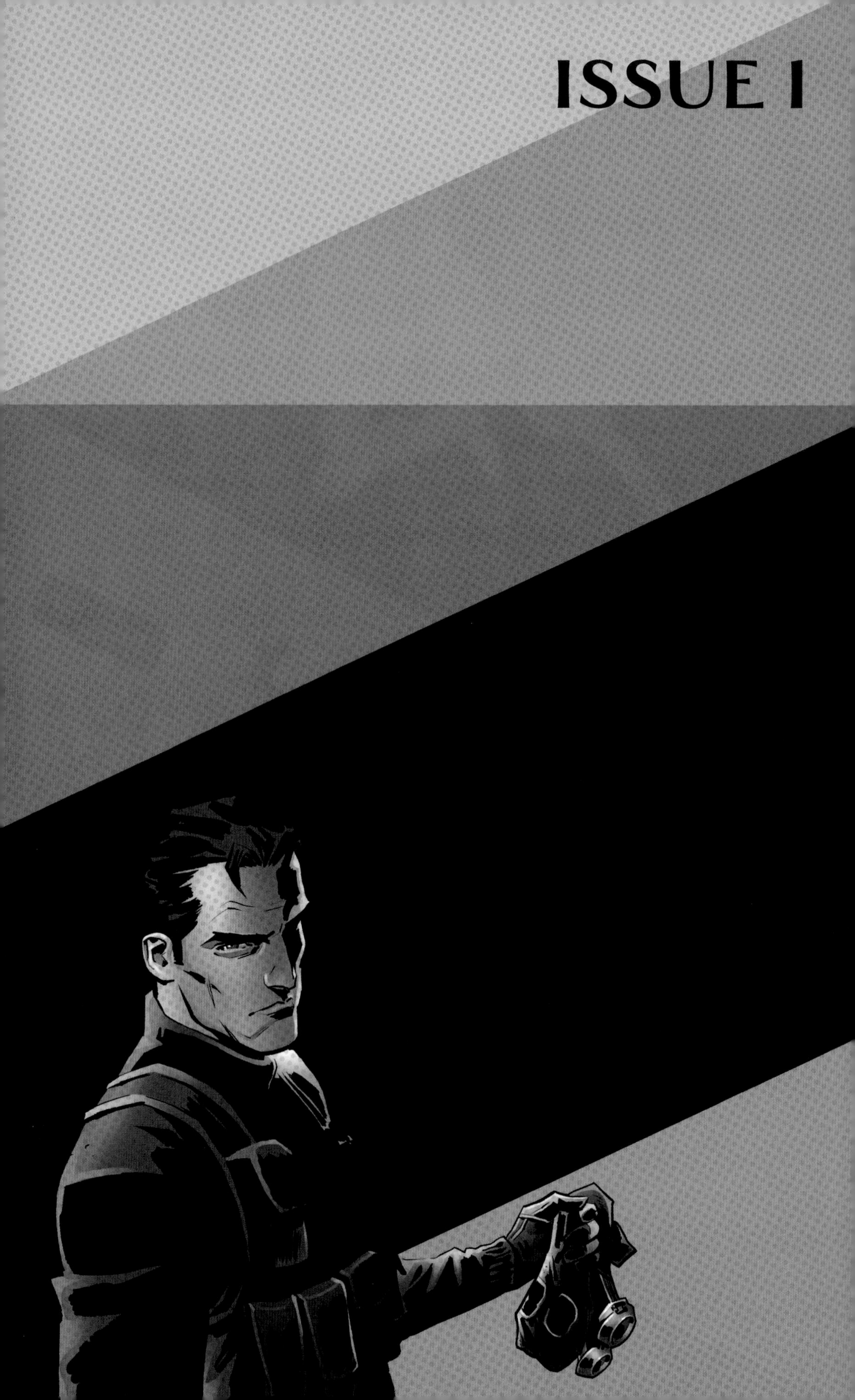

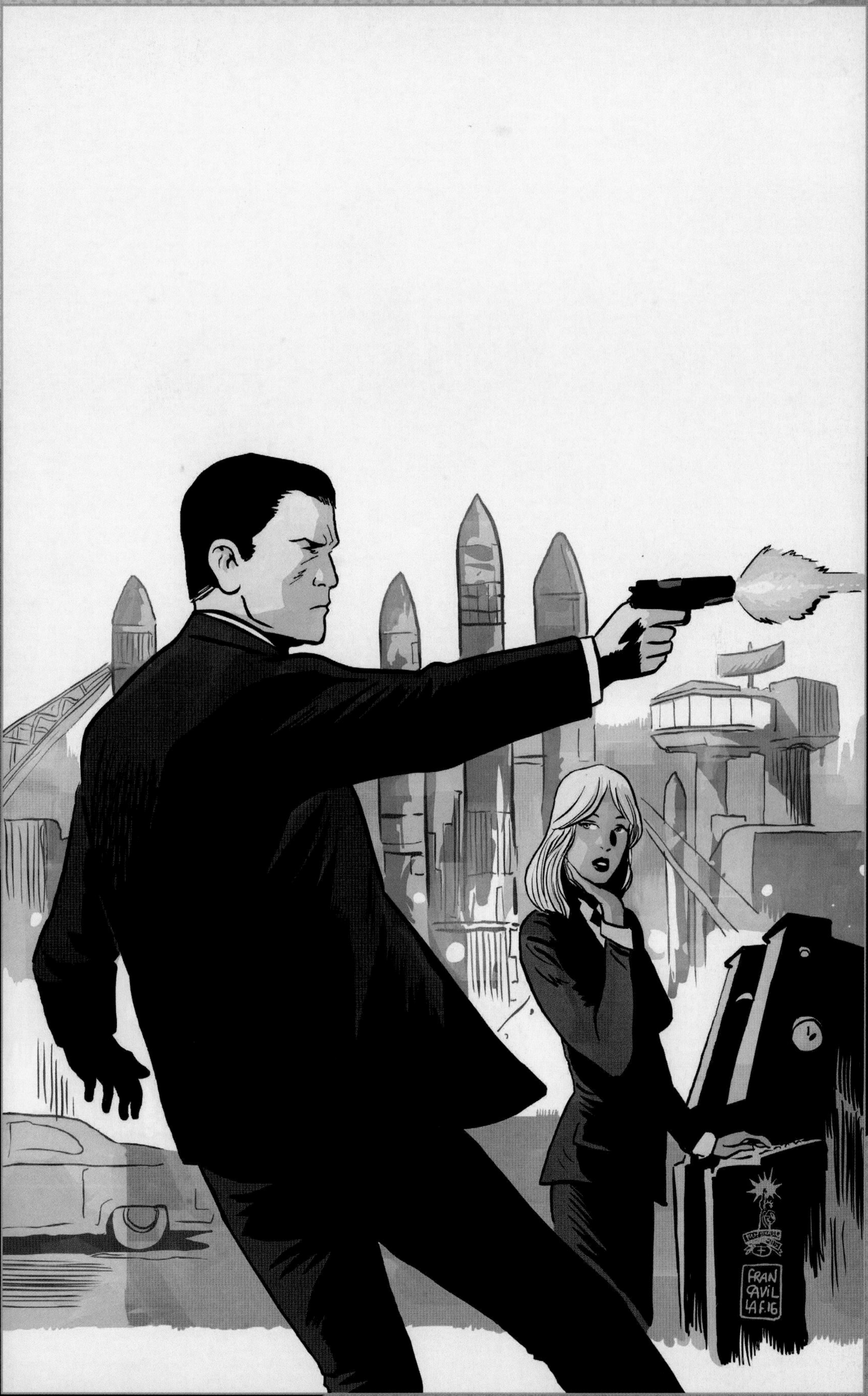

ISSUE 1 COVER
BY FRANCESCO FRANCAVILLA

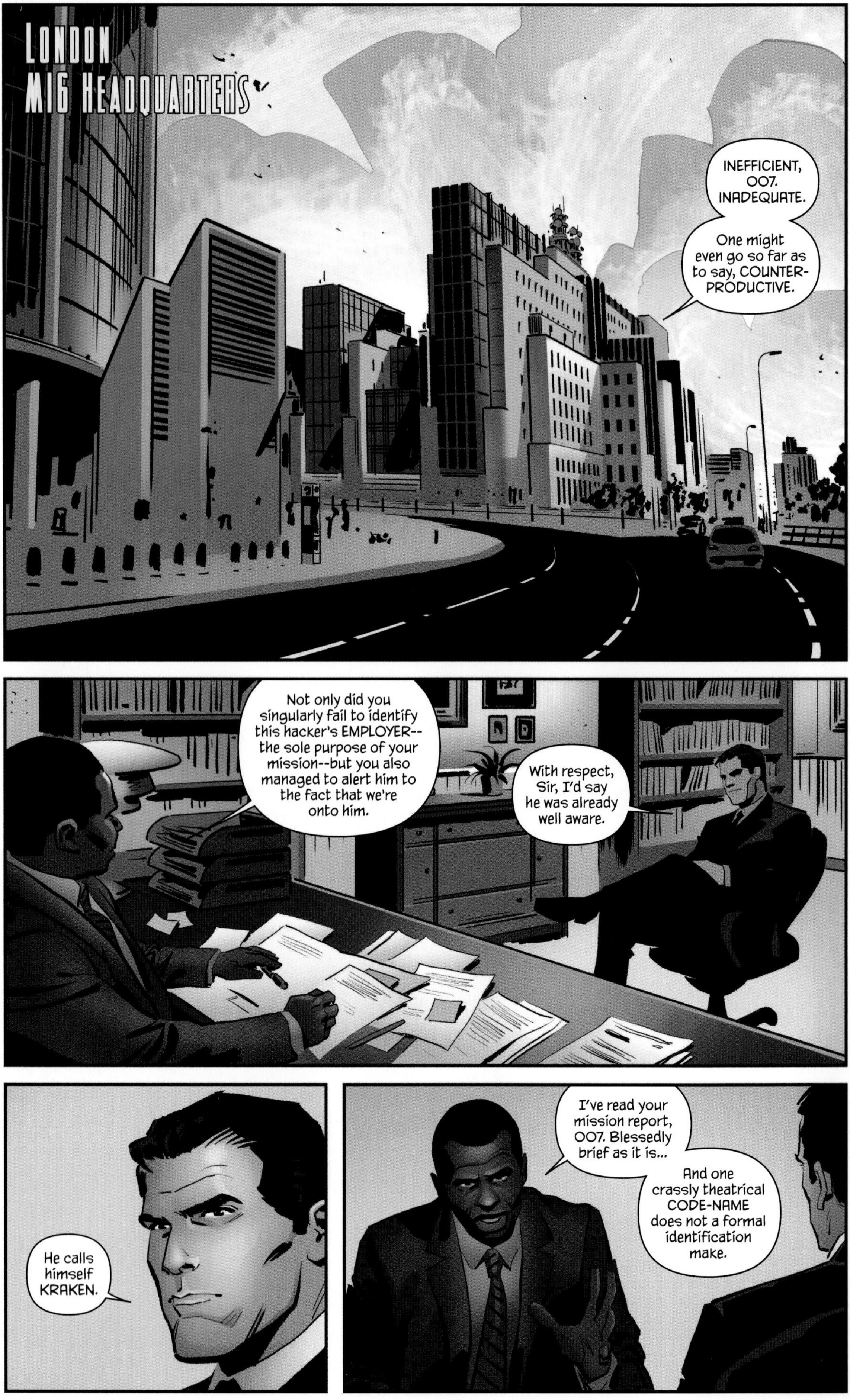
LONDON
MI6 HEADQUARTERS
INEFFICIENT, 007. INADEQUATE.
One might even go so far as to say, COUNTER-PRODUCTIVE.
Not only did you singularly fail to identify this hacker's EMPLOYER--the sole purpose of your mission--but you also managed to alert him to the fact that we're onto him.
With respect, Sir, I'd say he was already well aware.
He calls himself KRAKEN.
I've read your mission report, 007. Blessedly brief as it is...
And one crassly theatrical CODE-NAME does not a formal identification make.

Kraken's voice was synthesized, so your intercept was biometrically useless.

Still, G.C.H.Q.* have been able to dig up a few scraps...

*Government Communications Headquarters

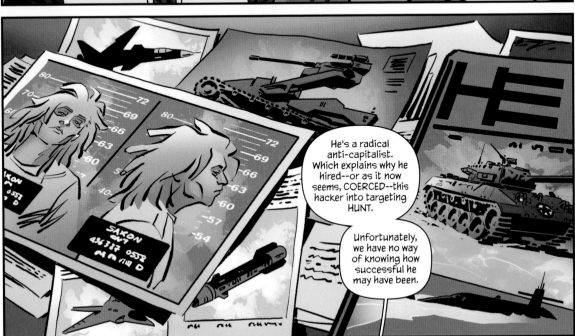

He's a radical anti-capitalist. Which explains why he hired--or as it now seems, COERCED--this hacker into targeting HUNT.

Unfortunately, we have no way of knowing how successful he may have been.

Hunt, Sir?

HUNT ENGINEERING, 007. As in Britain's leading ARMS MANUFACTURER.

I do assume you've heard of them.

Of course, Sir. Responsible for billions of pounds in exports to our allies in the Middle East and elsewhere.

I understand the C.E.O., LORD HUNT, is a close personal friend of the PRIME MINISTER.

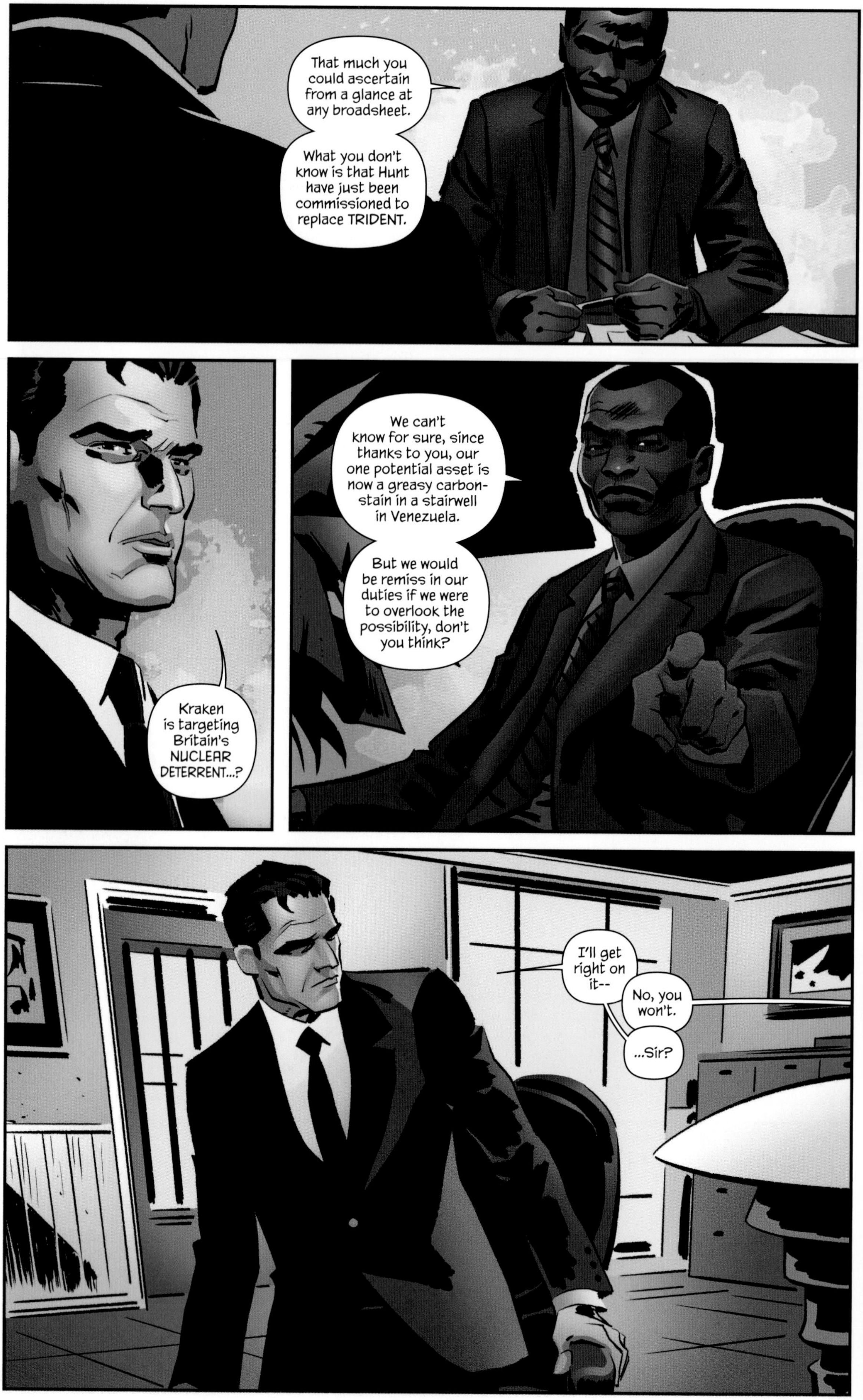
That much you could ascertain from a glance at any broadsheet.
What you don't know is that Hunt have just been commissioned to replace TRIDENT.
Kraken is targeting Britain's NUCLEAR DETERRENT...?
We can't know for sure, since thanks to you, our one potential asset is now a greasy carbon-stain in a stairwell in Venezuela.
But we would be remiss in our duties if we were to overlook the possibility, don't you think?
I'll get right on it--
No, you won't.
...Sir?

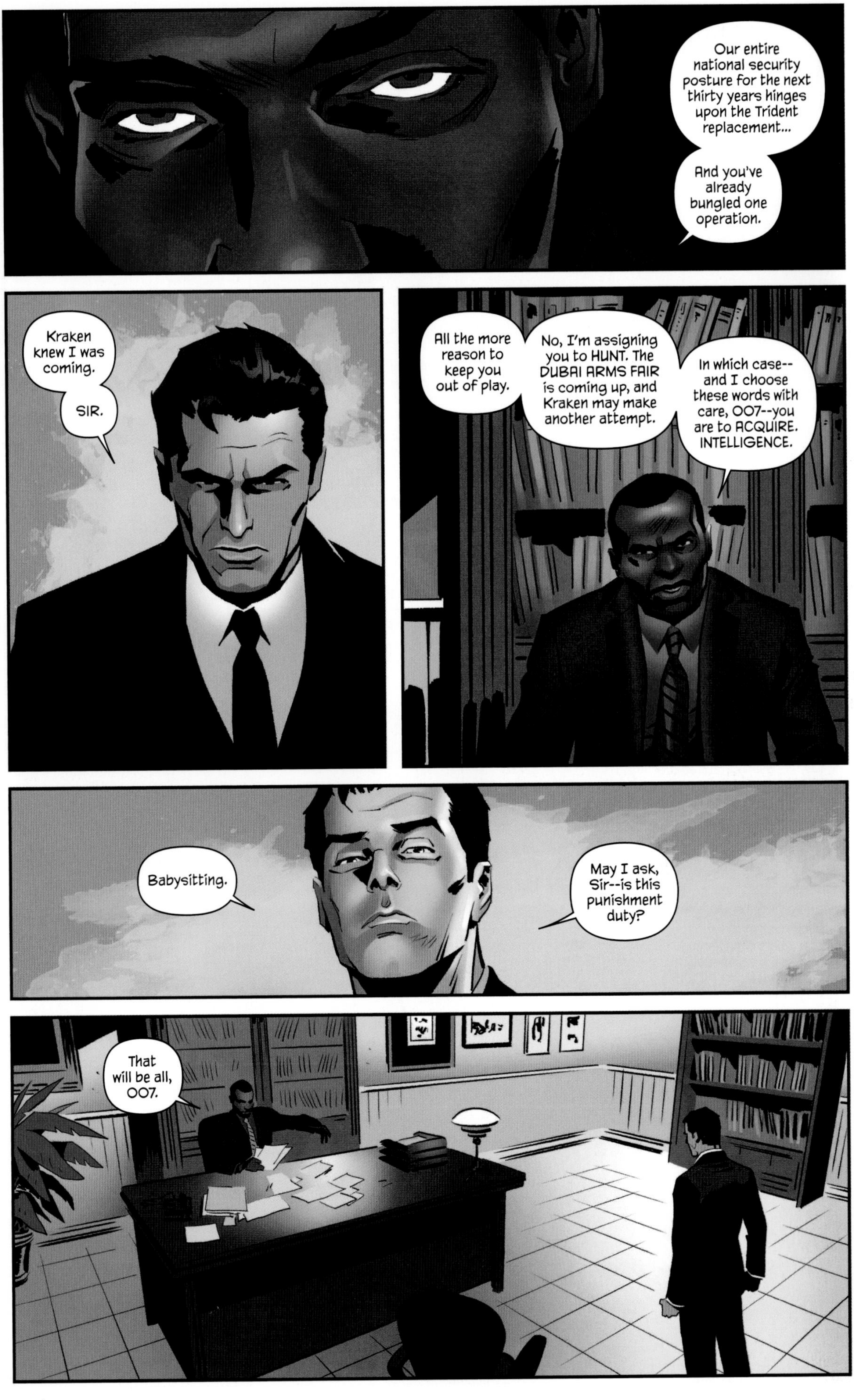
Our entire national security posture for the next thirty years hinges upon the Trident replacement...
And you've already bungled one operation.
Kraken knew I was coming.
SIR.
All the more reason to keep you out of play.
No, I'm assigning you to HUNT. The DUBAI ARMS FAIR is coming up, and Kraken may make another attempt.
In which case--and I choose these words with care, 007--you are to ACQUIRE. INTELLIGENCE.
Babysitting.
May I ask, Sir--is this punishment duty?
That will be all, 007.

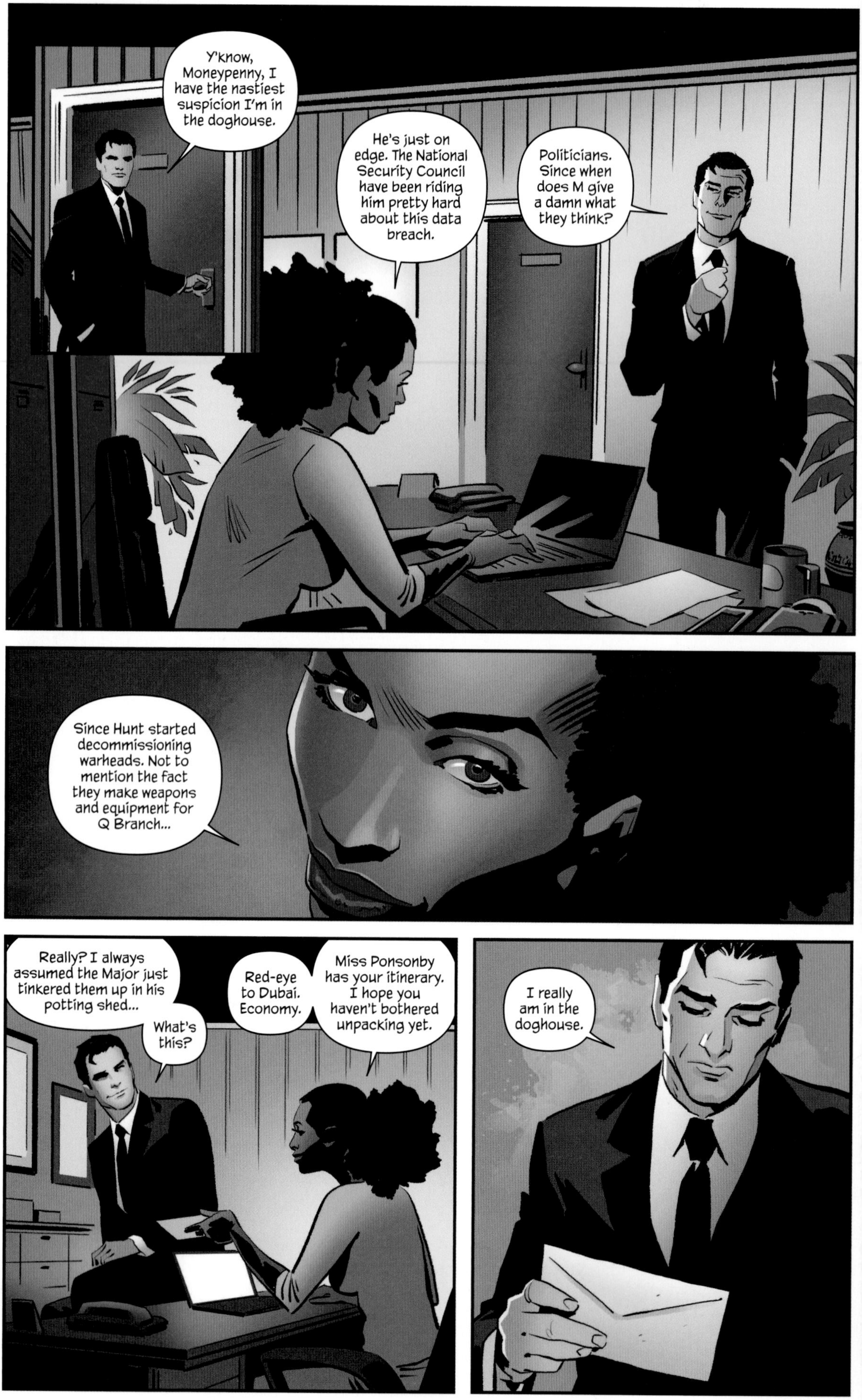
Y'know, Moneypenny, I have the nastiest suspicion I'm in the doghouse.
He's just on edge. The National Security Council have been riding him pretty hard about this data breach.
Politicians. Since when does M give a damn what they think?
Since Hunt started decommissioning warheads. Not to mention the fact they make weapons and equipment for Q Branch...
Really? I always assumed the Major just tinkered them up in his potting shed...
What's this?
Red-eye to Dubai. Economy.
Miss Ponsonby has your itinerary. I hope you haven't bothered unpacking yet.
I really am in the doghouse.

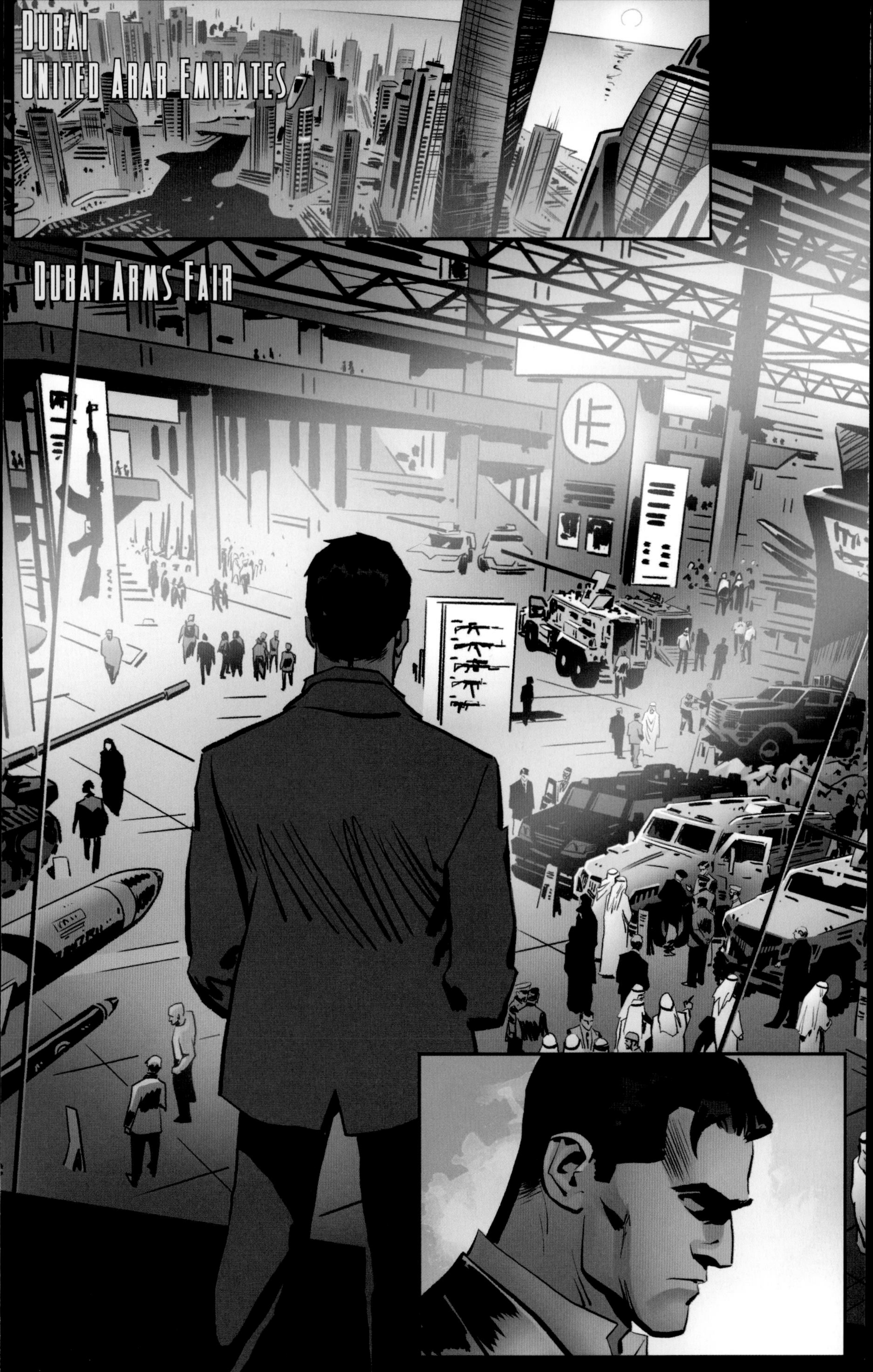
DUBAI
UNITED ARAB EMIRATES
DUBAI ARMS FAIR

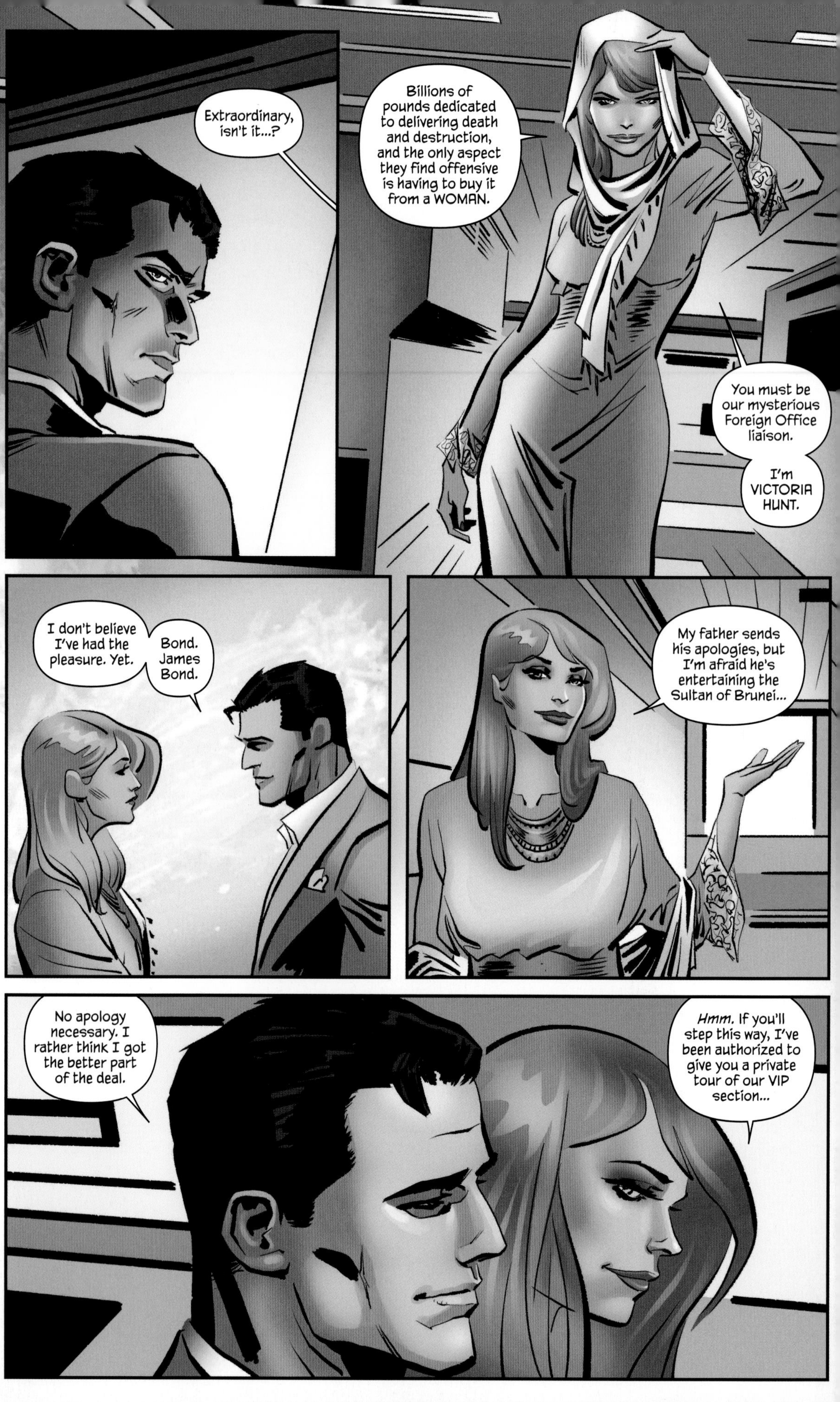

Extraordinary, isn't it...?
Billions of pounds dedicated to delivering death and destruction, and the only aspect they find offensive is having to buy it from a WOMAN.
You must be our mysterious Foreign Office liaison.
I'm VICTORIA HUNT.
I don't believe I've had the pleasure. Yet.
Bond. James Bond.
My father sends his apologies, but I'm afraid he's entertaining the Sultan of Brunei...
No apology necessary. I rather think I got the better part of the deal.
Hmm. If you'll step this way, I've been authorized to give you a private tour of our VIP section...

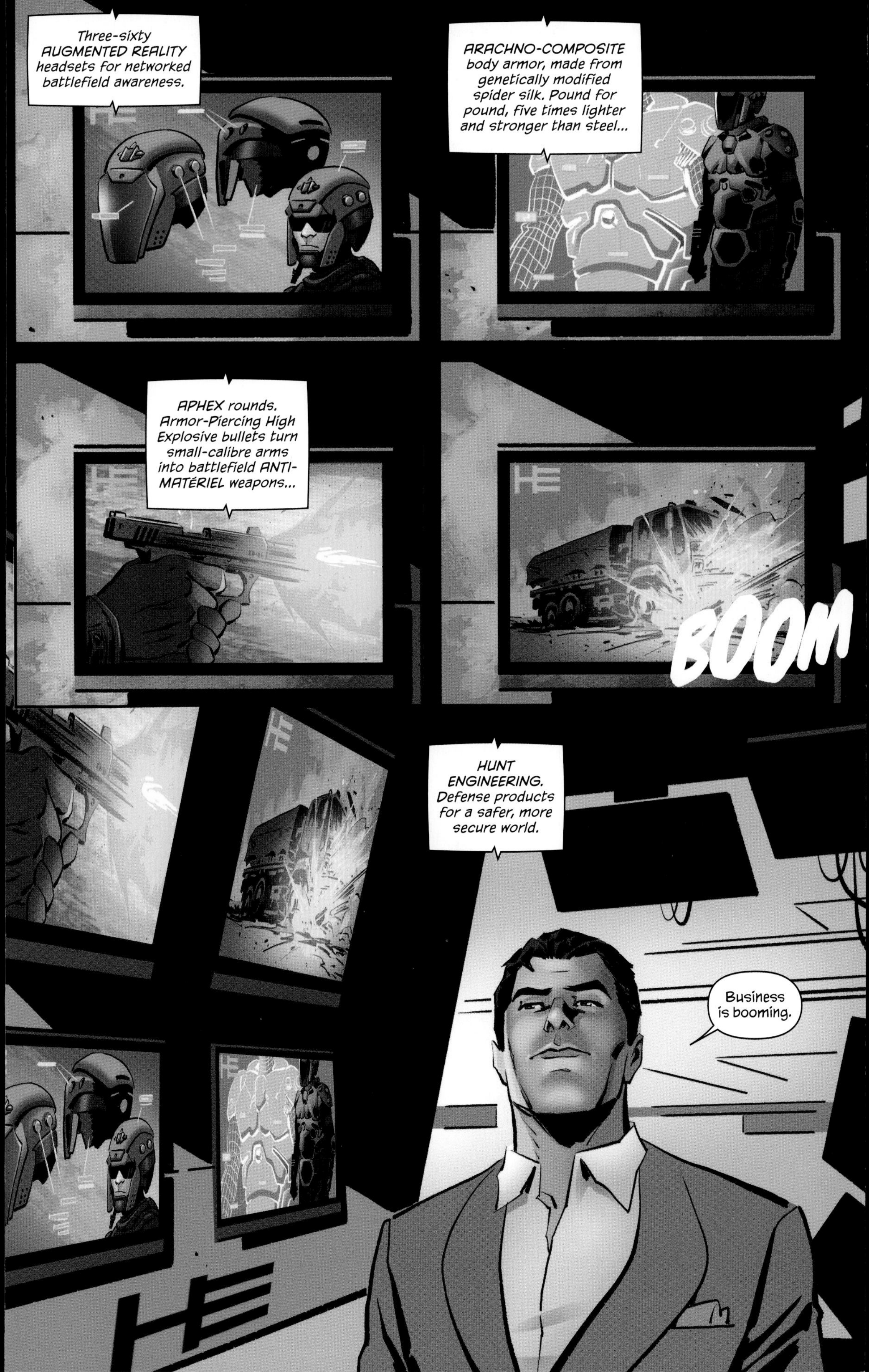
Three-sixty AUGMENTED REALITY headsets for networked battlefield awareness.
ARACHNO-COMPOSITE body armor, made from genetically modified spider silk. Pound for pound, five times lighter and stronger than steel...
APHEX rounds. Armor-Piercing High Explosive bullets turn small-calibre arms into battlefield ANTI-MATÉRIEL weapons...
BOOM
HUNT ENGINEERING. Defense products for a safer, more secure world.
Business is booming.

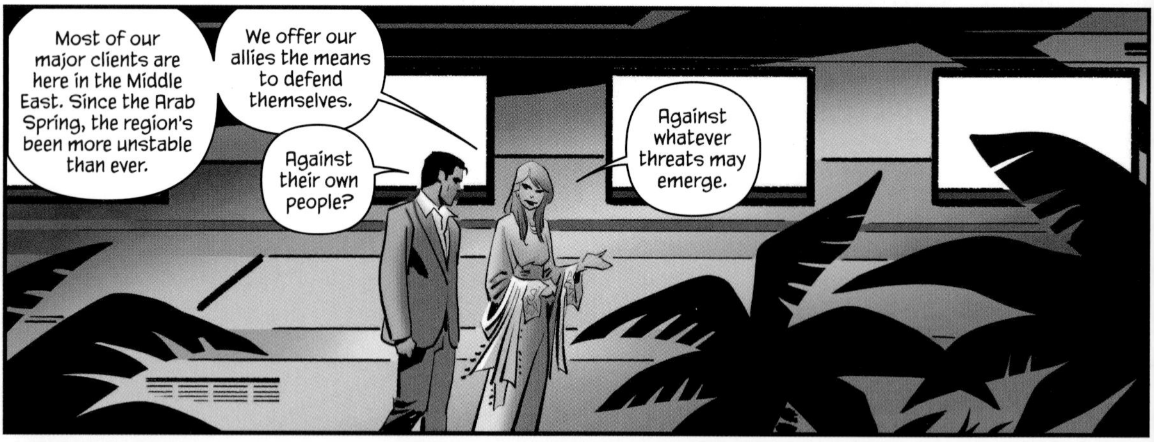
Most of our major clients are here in the Middle East. Since the Arab Spring, the region's been more unstable than ever.
We offer our allies the means to defend themselves.
Against their own people?
Against whatever threats may emerge.

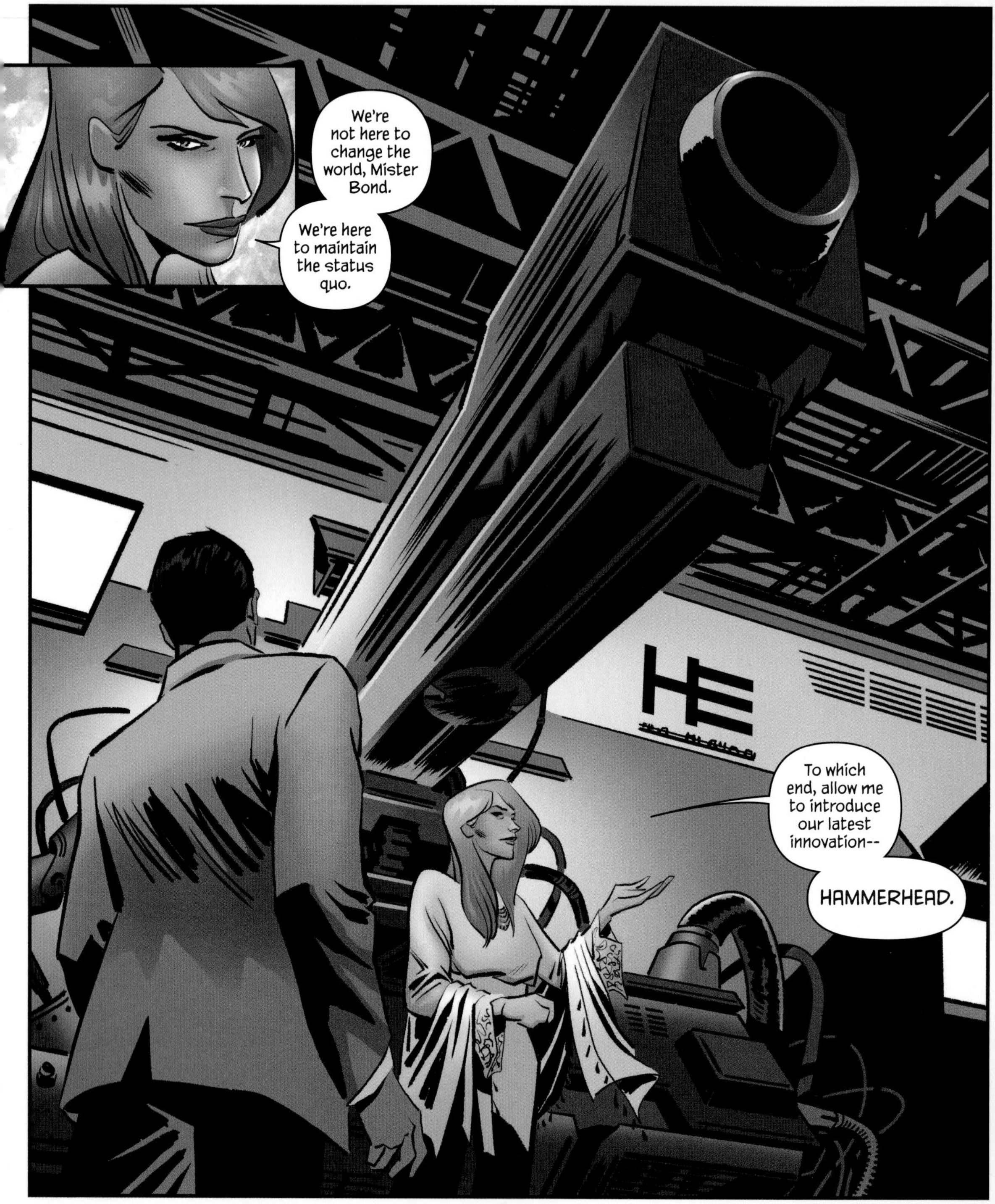
We're not here to change the world, Mister Bond.
We're here to maintain the status quo.
To which end, allow me to introduce our latest innovation--
HAMMERHEAD.

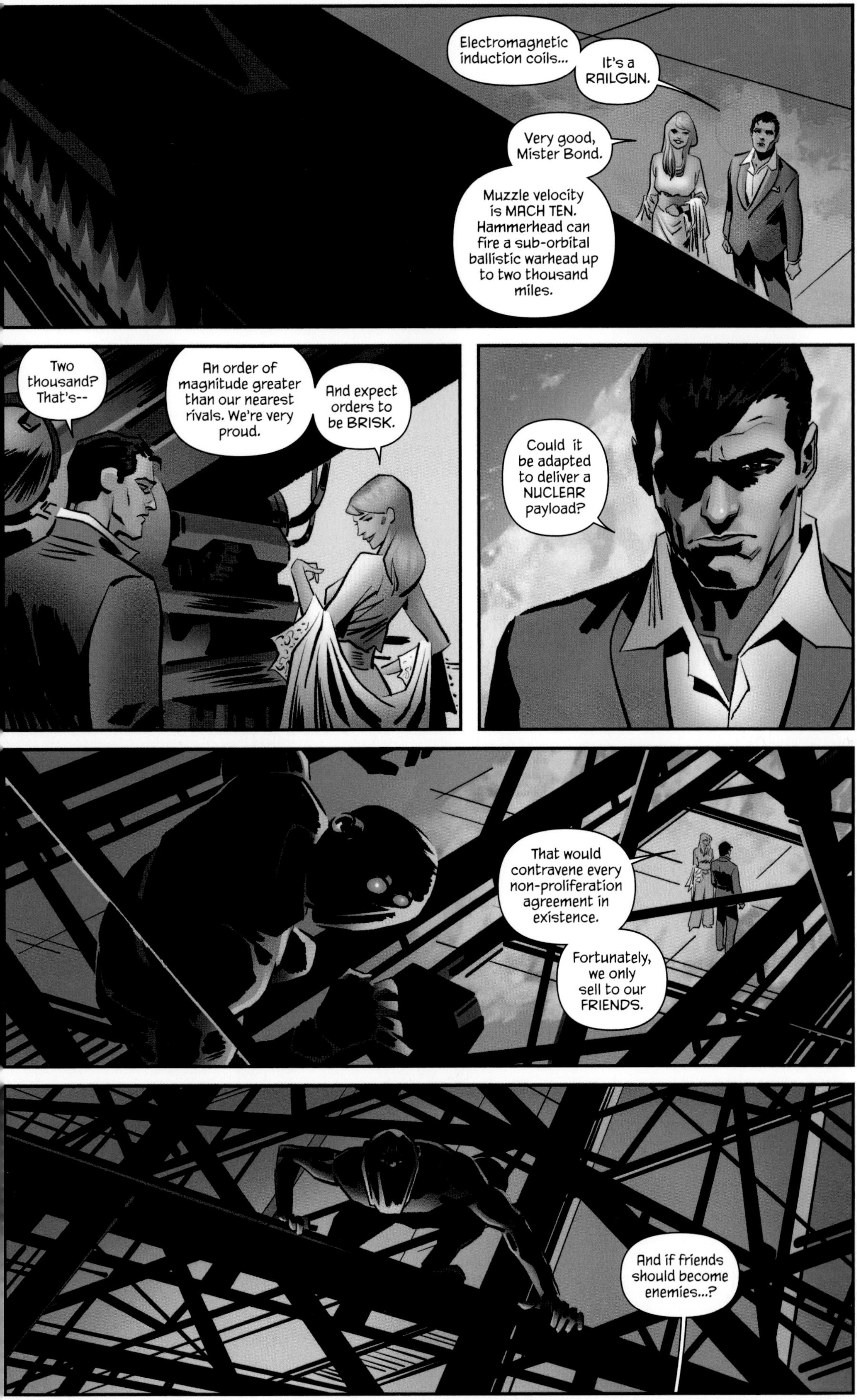
Electromagnetic induction coils...
It's a RAILGUN.
Very good, Mister Bond.
Muzzle velocity is MACH TEN. Hammerhead can fire a sub-orbital ballistic warhead up to two thousand miles.
Two thousand? That's--
An order of magnitude greater than our nearest rivals. We're very proud.
And expect orders to be BRISK.
Could it be adapted to deliver a NUCLEAR payload?
That would contravene every non-proliferation agreement in existence.
Fortunately, we only sell to our FRIENDS.
And if friends should become enemies...?

Actually, Mister Bond, I rather think that's YOUR department.

OND, JAMES
ECRET INTELLIGENCE SERVICE, UK
SECTION
CENSED TO KILL
REAT LEVEL: HIGH
EIGHT: 1.83M
EIGHT: 76KG
AIR: BLACK
ES: BLUE-GREY
CAR: RIGHT CHEEK
CAR: RIGHT HAND
DUCATION: ETON COLLEGE, FETTES, EDINBURGH
RVICE HISTORY: ROYAL NAVY
BOAT SQUADRON...

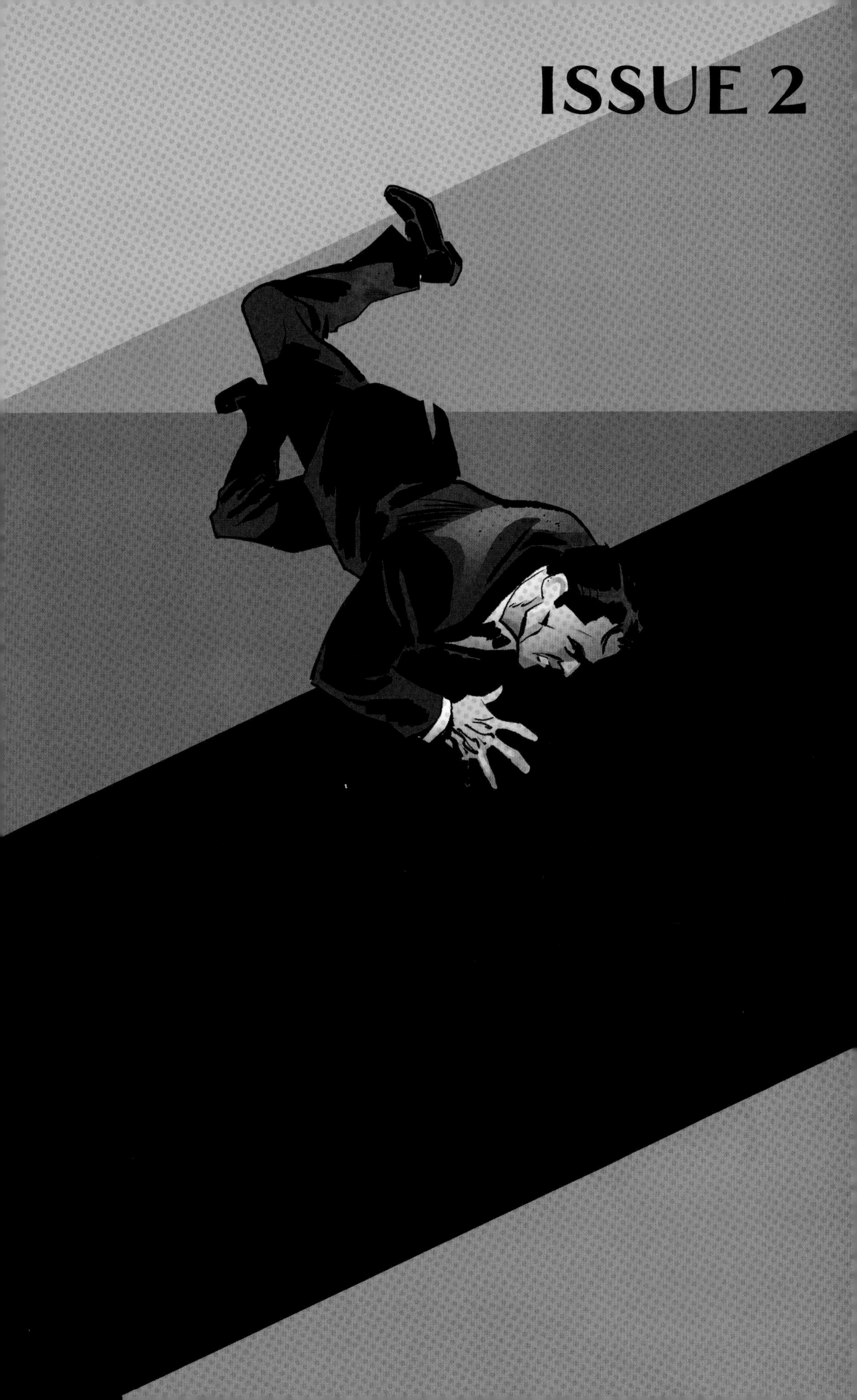
ISSUE 2

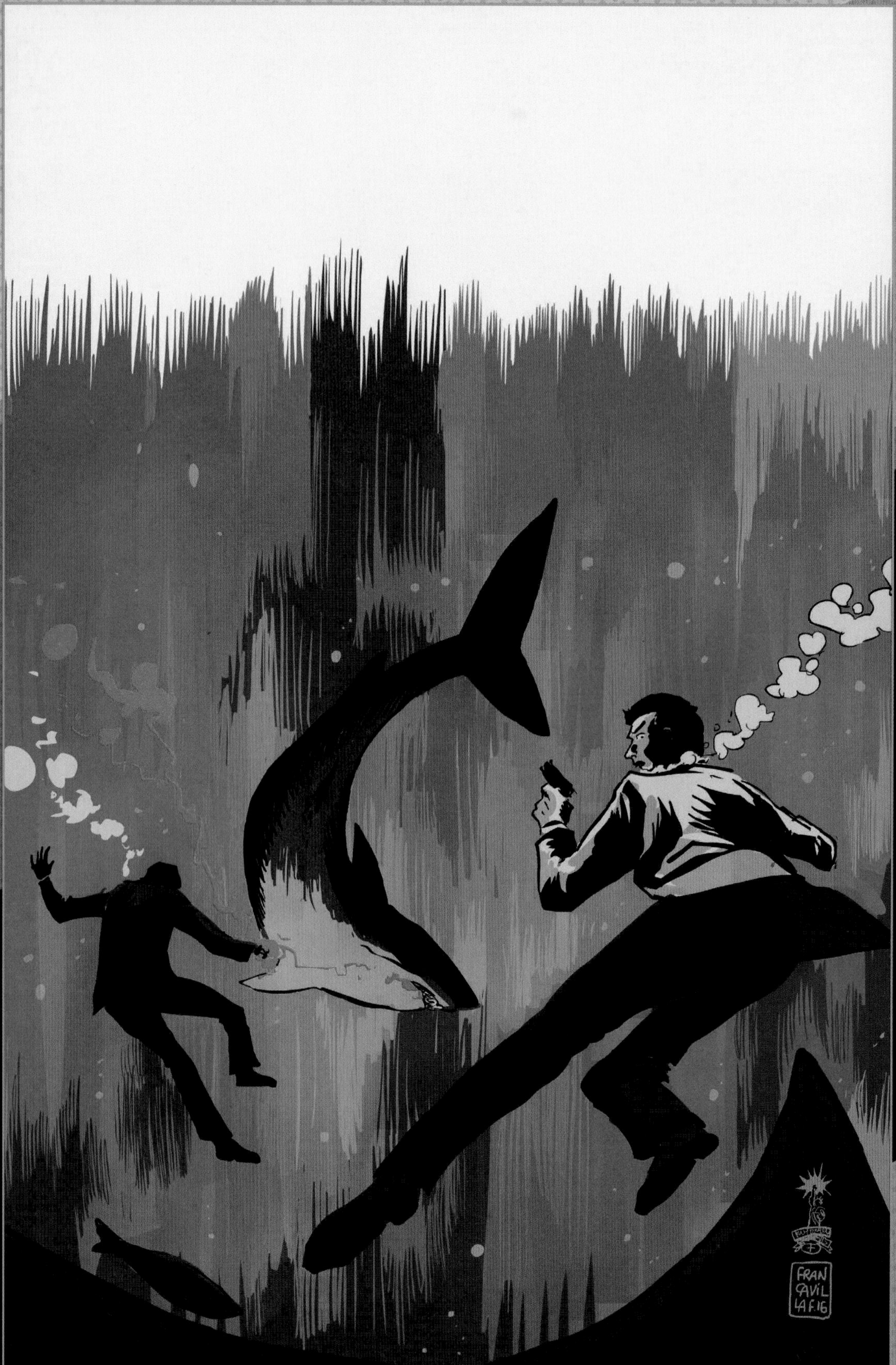
FRAN
CAVIL
LA F.16

ISSUE 2 COVER
BY FRANCESCO FRANCAVILLA

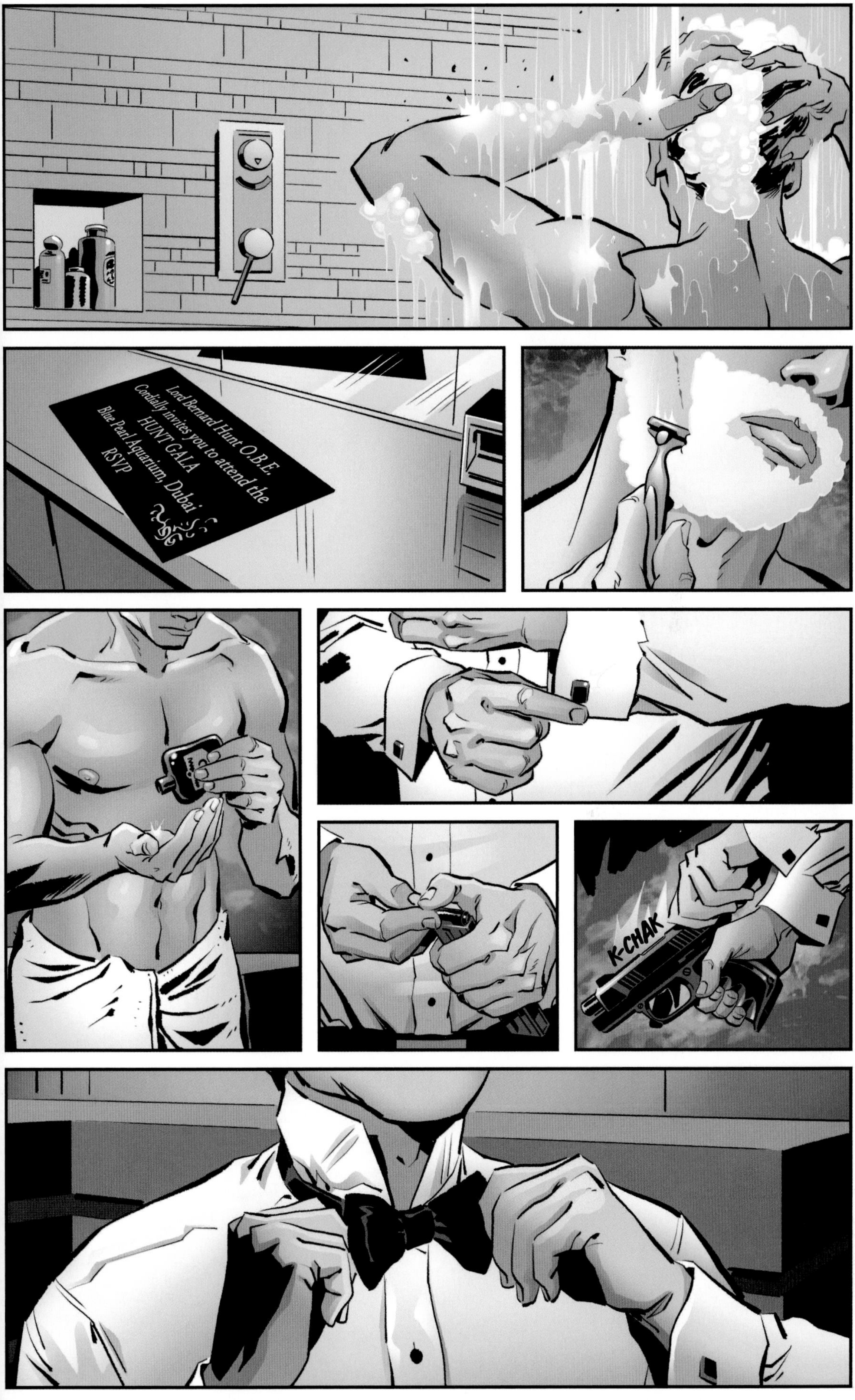
Lord Bernard Hunt O.B.E.
Cordially invites you to attend the
HUNT GALA
Blue Pearl Aquarium, Dubai
RSVP
K-CHAK

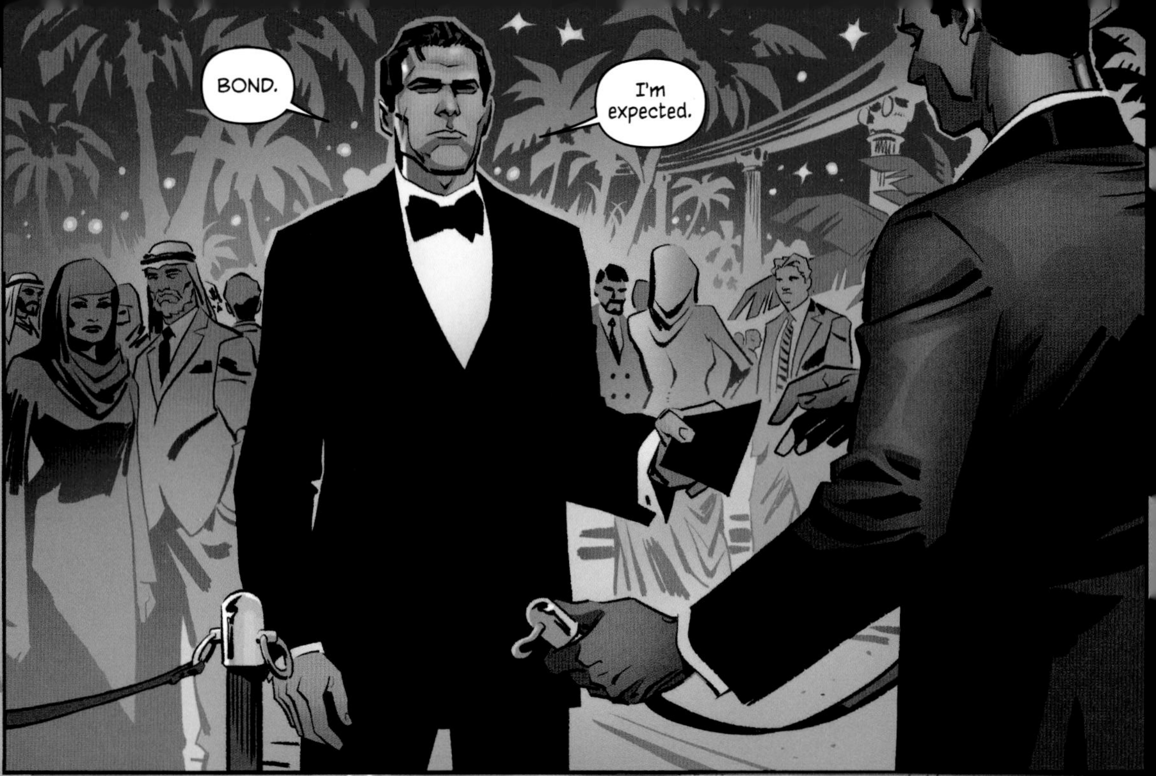
BOND.
I'm expected.

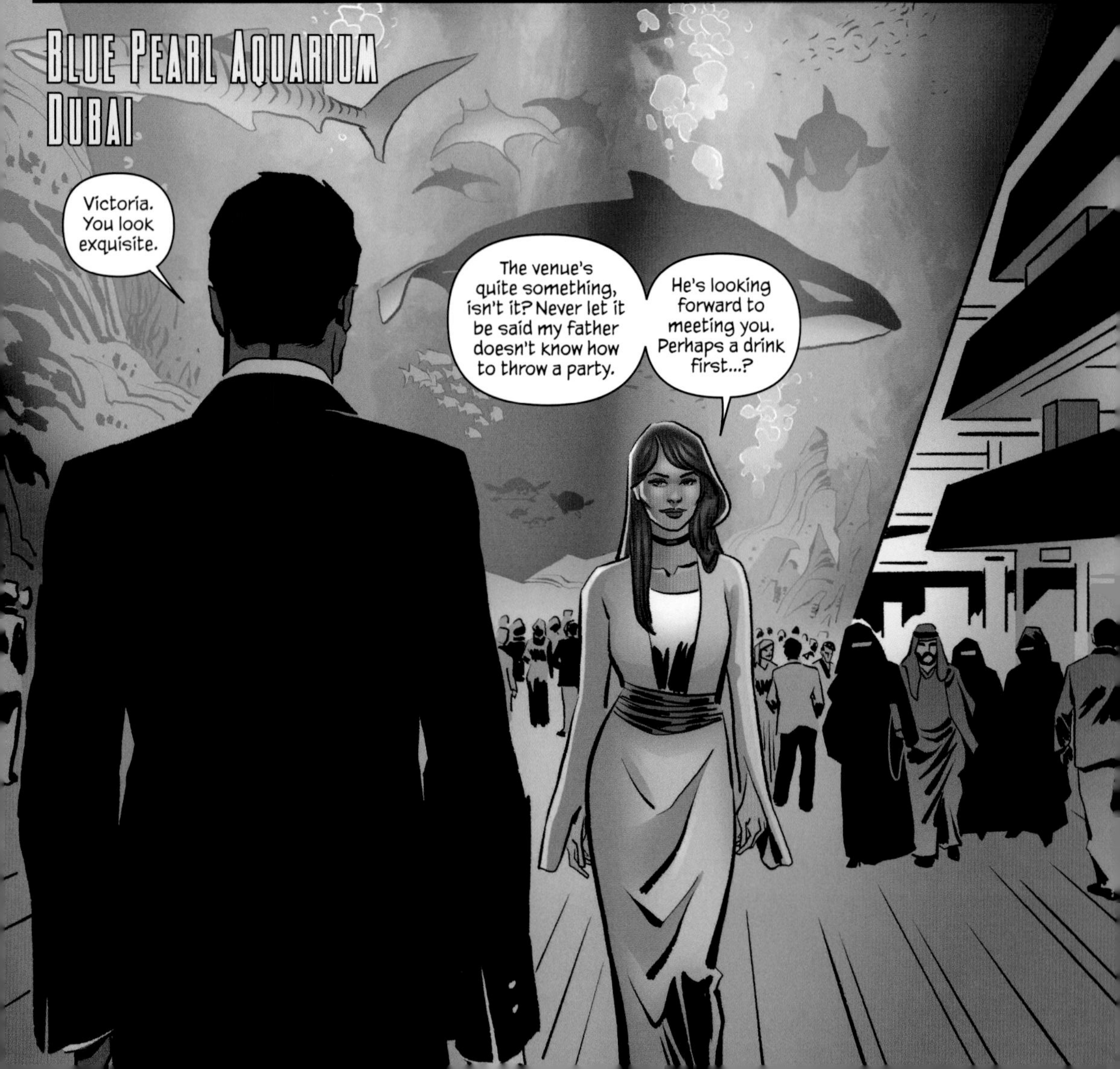
BLUE PEARL AQUARIUM
DUBAI
Victoria. You look exquisite.
The venue's quite something, isn't it? Never let it be said my father doesn't know how to throw a party.
He's looking forward to meeting you. Perhaps a drink first...?

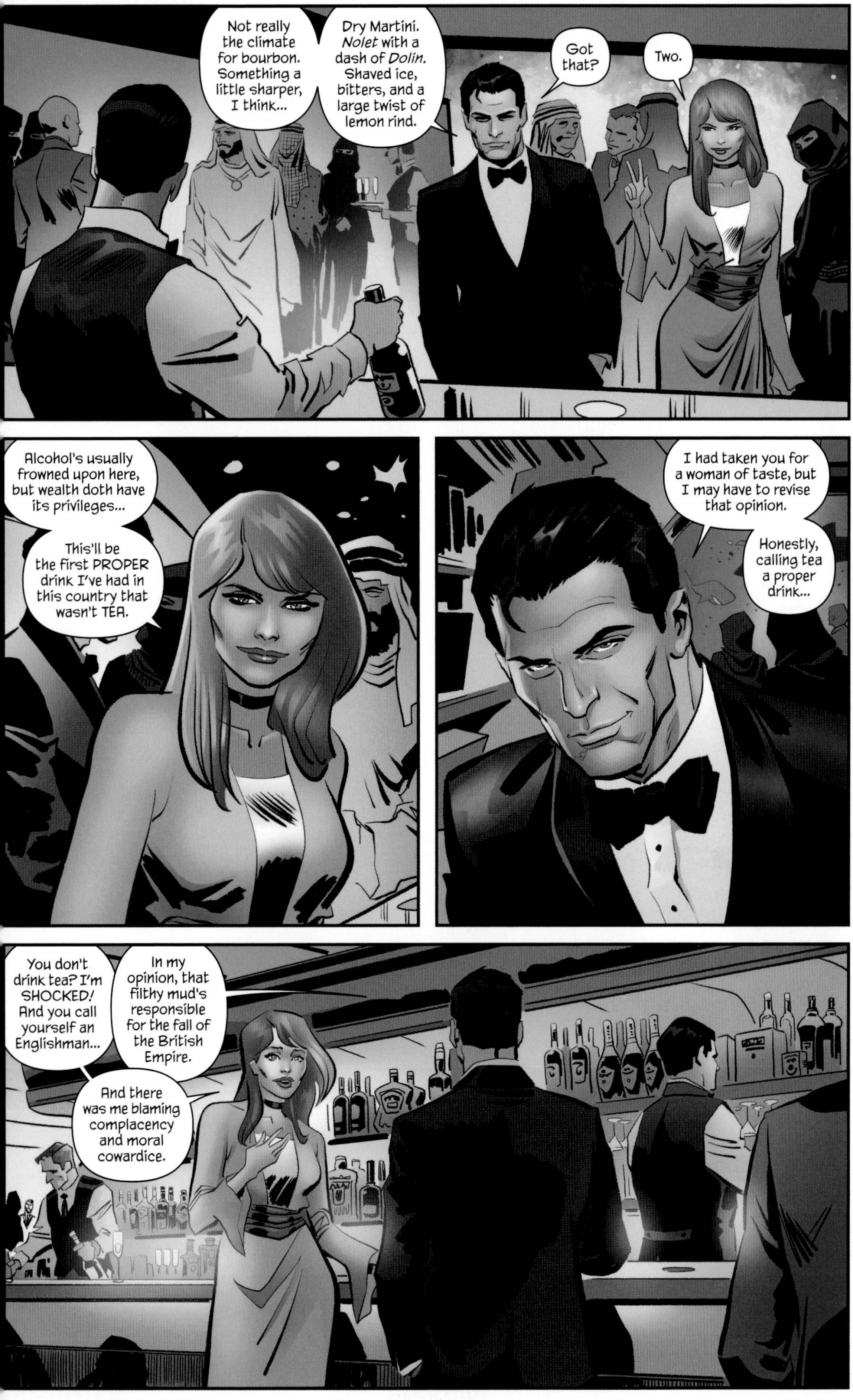
Not really the climate for bourbon. Something a little sharper, I think...
Dry Martini. *Nolet* with a dash of *Dolin.* Shaved ice, bitters, and a large twist of lemon rind.
Got that?
Two.
Alcohol's usually frowned upon here, but wealth doth have its privileges...
This'll be the first PROPER drink I've had in this country that wasn't TEA.
I had taken you for a woman of taste, but I may have to revise that opinion.
Honestly, calling tea a proper drink...
You don't drink tea? I'm SHOCKED! And you call yourself an Englishman...
In my opinion, that filthy mud's responsible for the fall of the British Empire.
And there was me blaming complacency and moral cowardice.

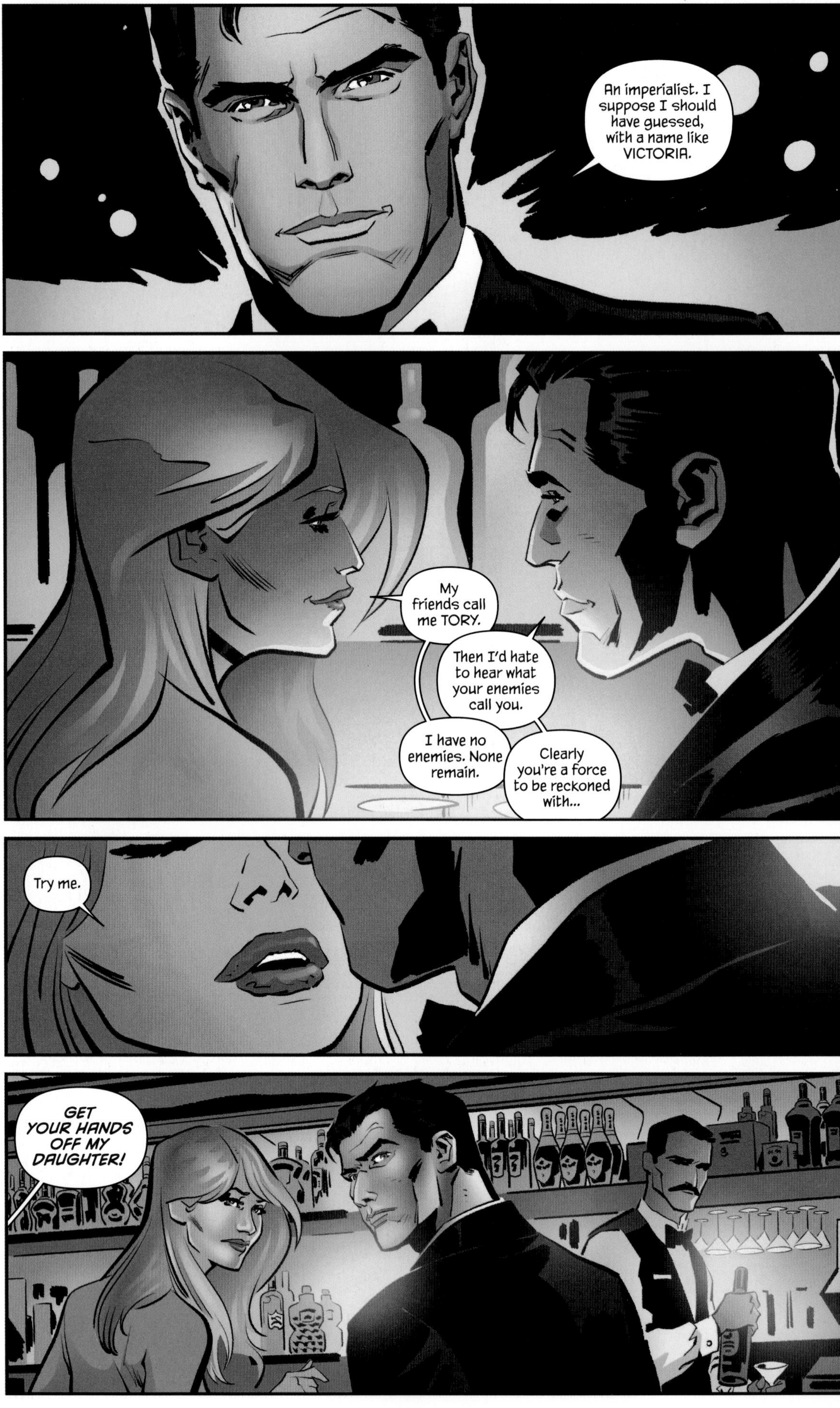
An imperialist. I suppose I should have guessed, with a name like VICTORIA.
My friends call me TORY.
Then I'd hate to hear what your enemies call you.
I have no enemies. None remain.
Clearly you're a force to be reckoned with...
Try me.
GET YOUR HANDS OFF MY DAUGHTER!

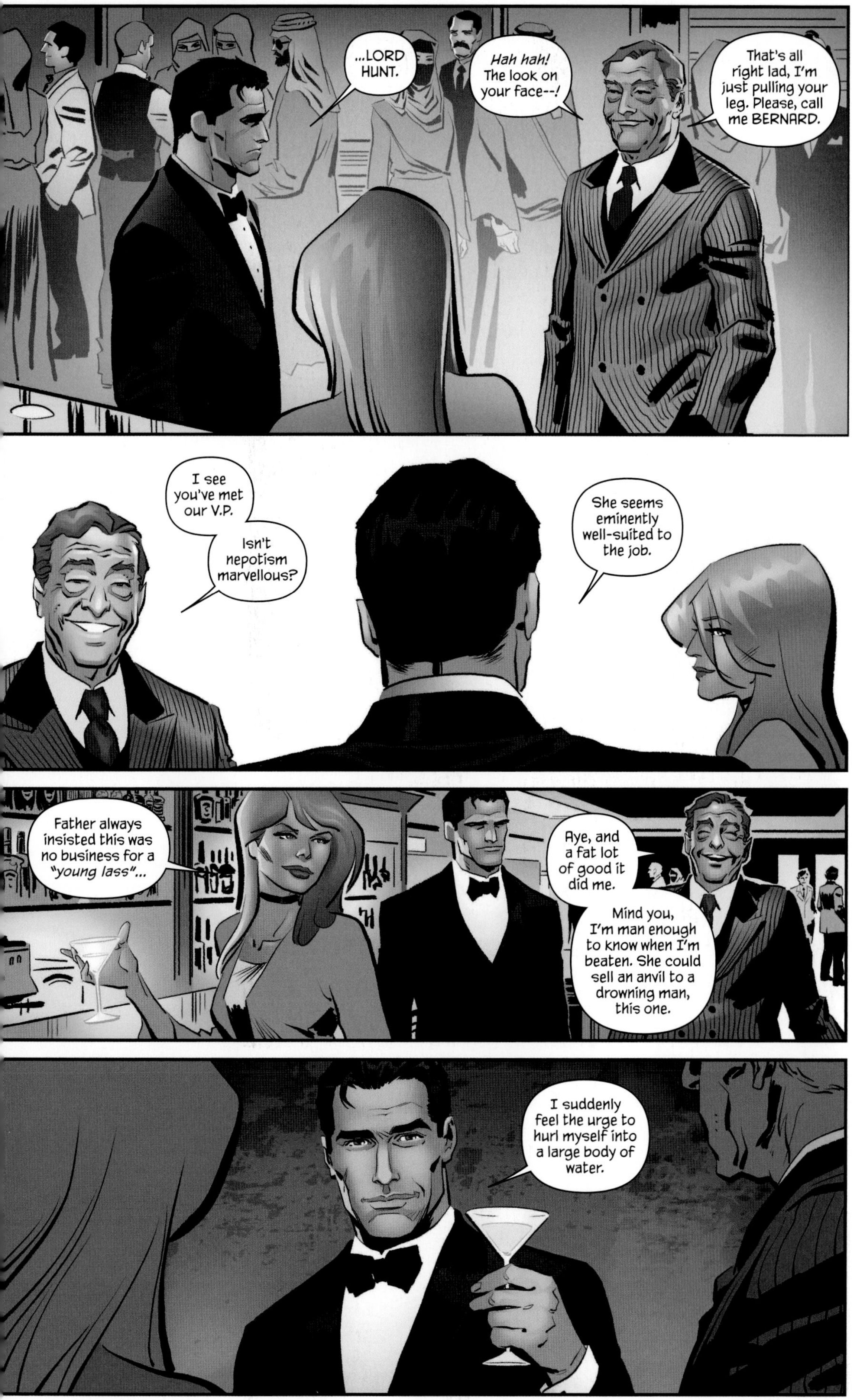
...LORD HUNT.
Hah hah! The look on your face--!
That's all right lad, I'm just pulling your leg. Please, call me BERNARD.
I see you've met our V.P.
Isn't nepotism marvellous?
She seems eminently well-suited to the job.
Father always insisted this was no business for a *"young lass"*...
Aye, and a fat lot of good it did me.
Mind you, I'm man enough to know when I'm beaten. She could sell an anvil to a drowning man, this one.
I suddenly feel the urge to hurl myself into a large body of water.

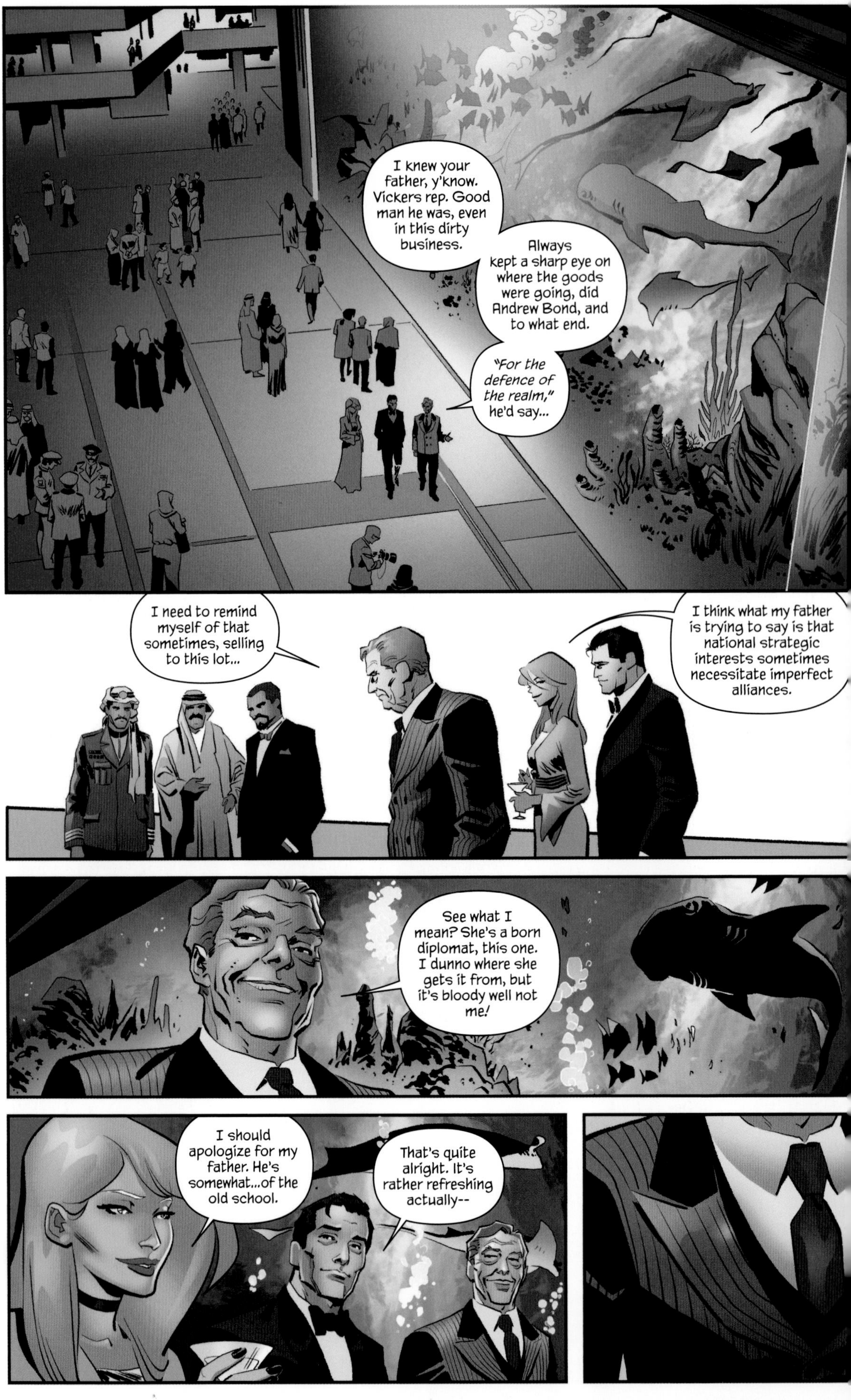
I knew your father, y'know. Vickers rep. Good man he was, even in this dirty business.
Always kept a sharp eye on where the goods were going, did Andrew Bond, and to what end.
"For the defence of the realm," he'd say...
I need to remind myself of that sometimes, selling to this lot...
I think what my father is trying to say is that national strategic interests sometimes necessitate imperfect alliances.
See what I mean? She's a born diplomat, this one. I dunno where she gets it from, but it's bloody well not me!
I should apologize for my father. He's somewhat...of the old school.
That's quite alright. It's rather refreshing actually--

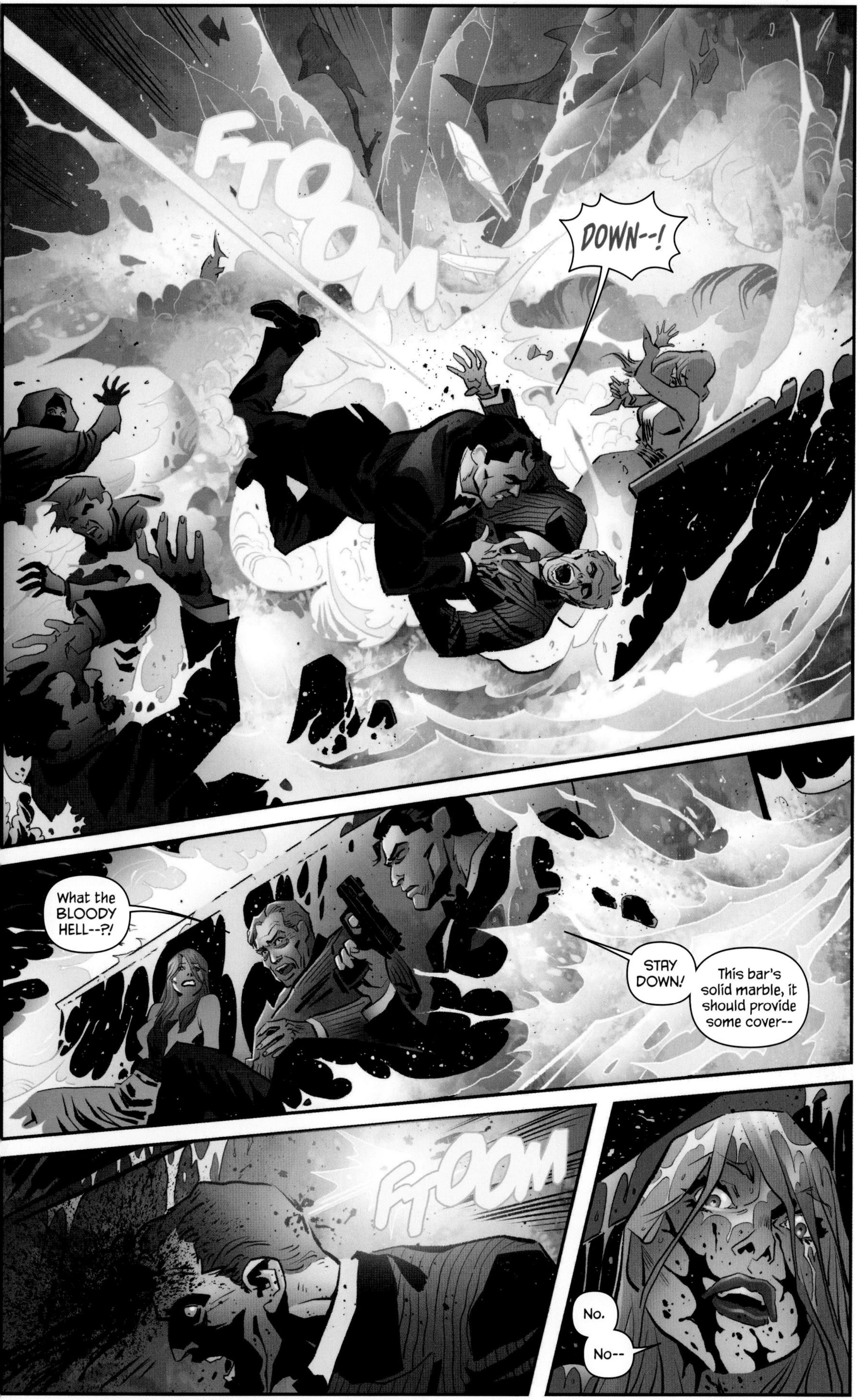
FTOOM
DOWN--!
What the BLOODY HELL--?!
STAY DOWN!
This bar's solid marble, it should provide some cover--
FTOOM
No.
No--

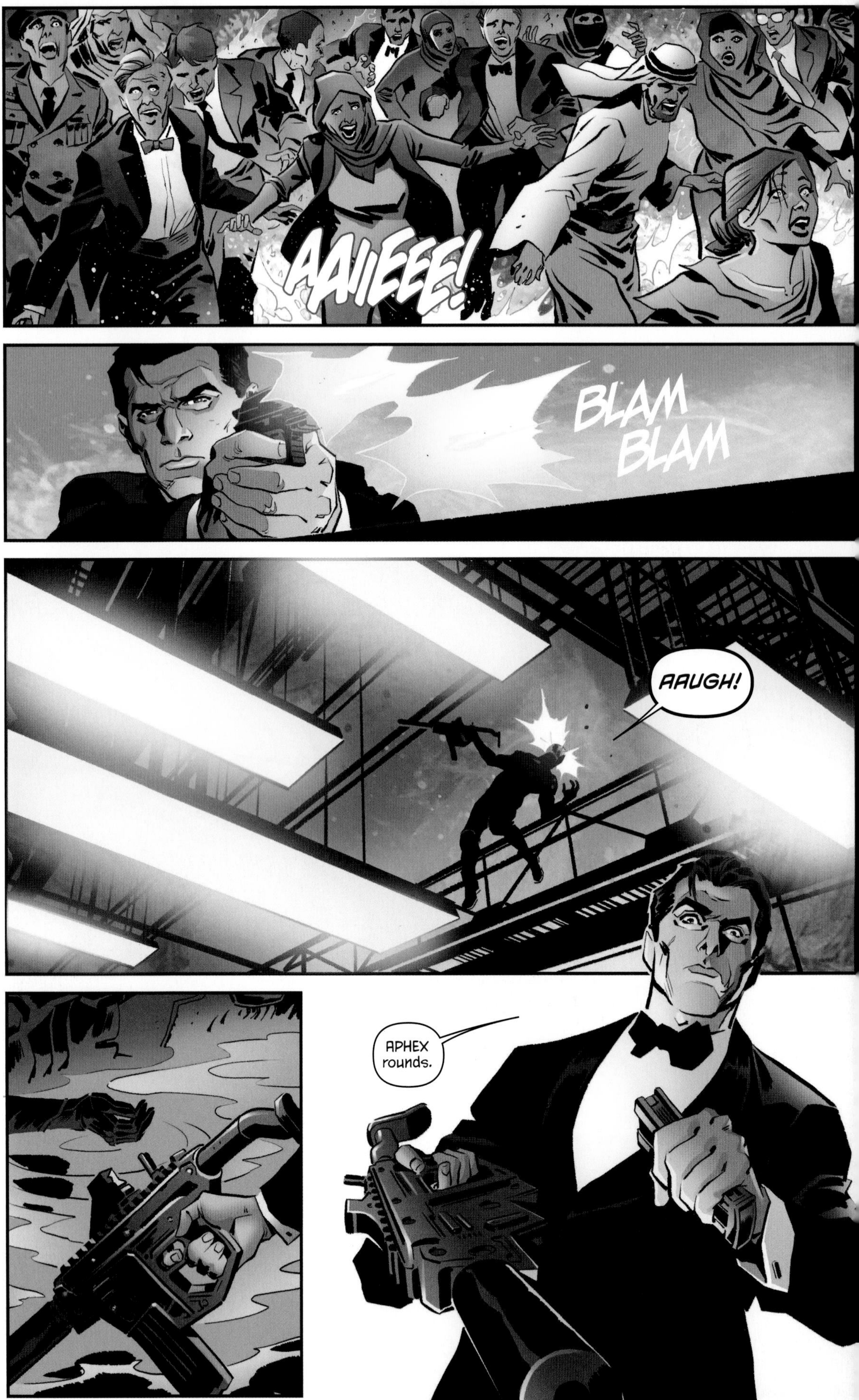
AAIIEEEE!
BLAM
BLAM
AAUGH!
APHEX rounds.

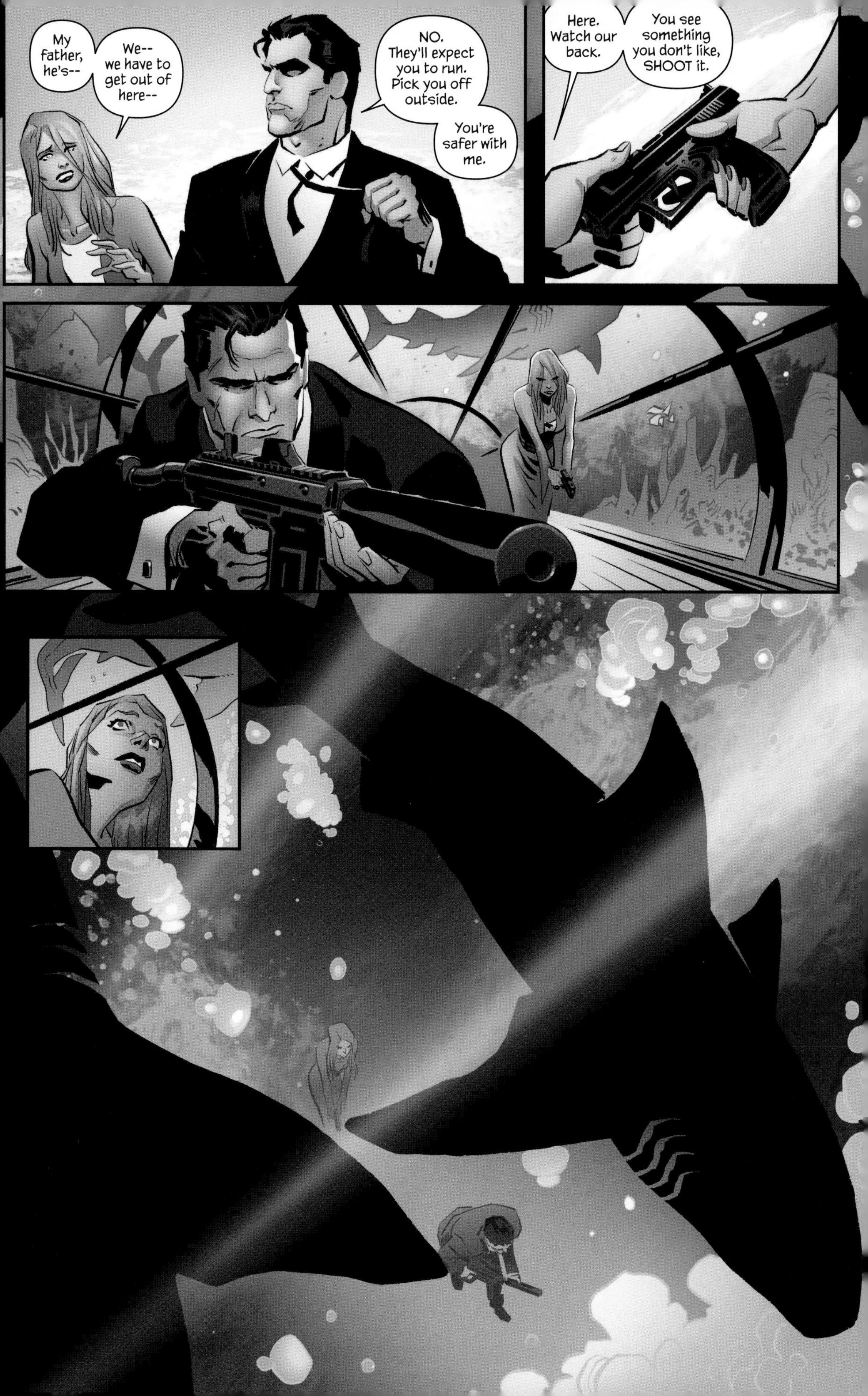
My father, he's--
We-- we have to get out of here--
NO. They'll expect you to run. Pick you off outside.
You're safer with me.
Here. Watch our back.
You see something you don't like, SHOOT it.

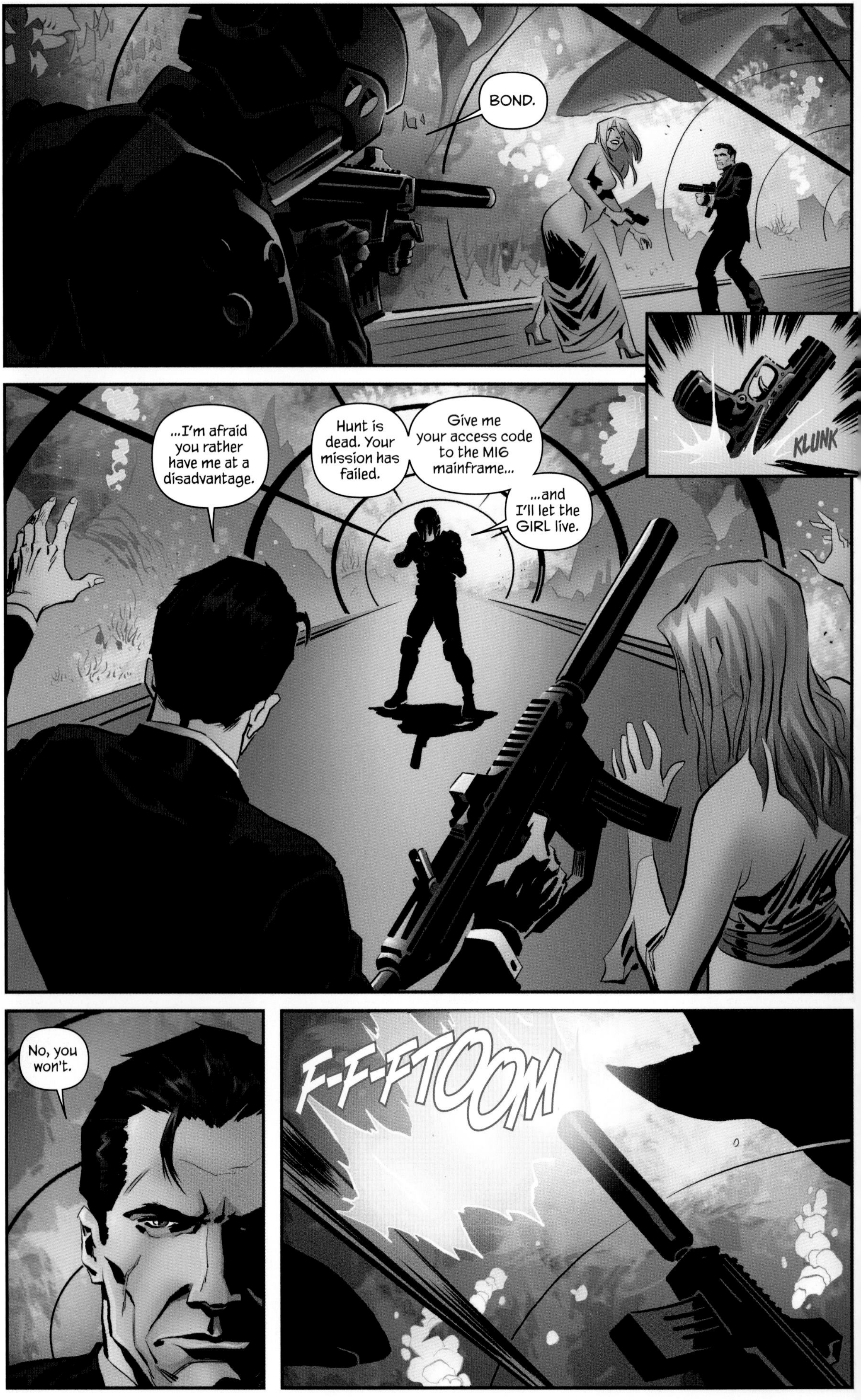
BOND.
KLUNK
...I'm afraid you rather have me at a disadvantage.
Hunt is dead. Your mission has failed.
Give me your access code to the MI6 mainframe...
...and I'll let the GIRL live.
No, you won't.
F-F-FTOOM

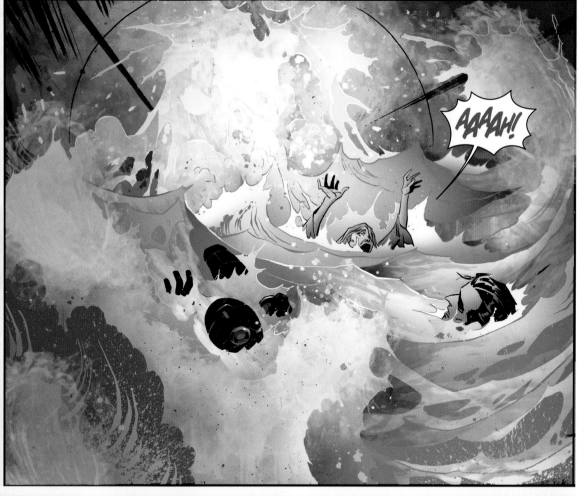

AAAAH!

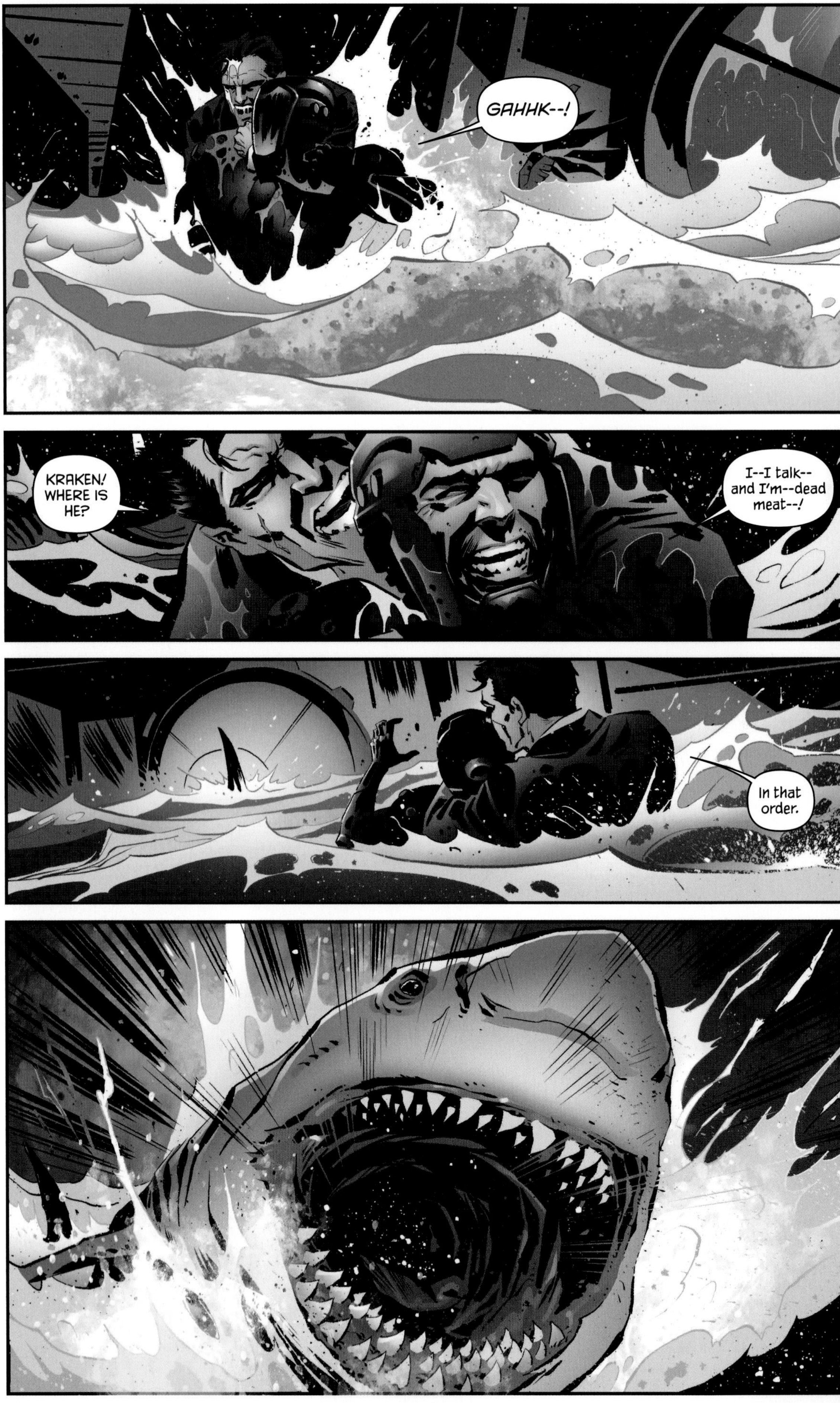
GAHHK--!
KRAKEN! WHERE IS HE?
I--I talk-- and I'm--dead meat--!
In that order.

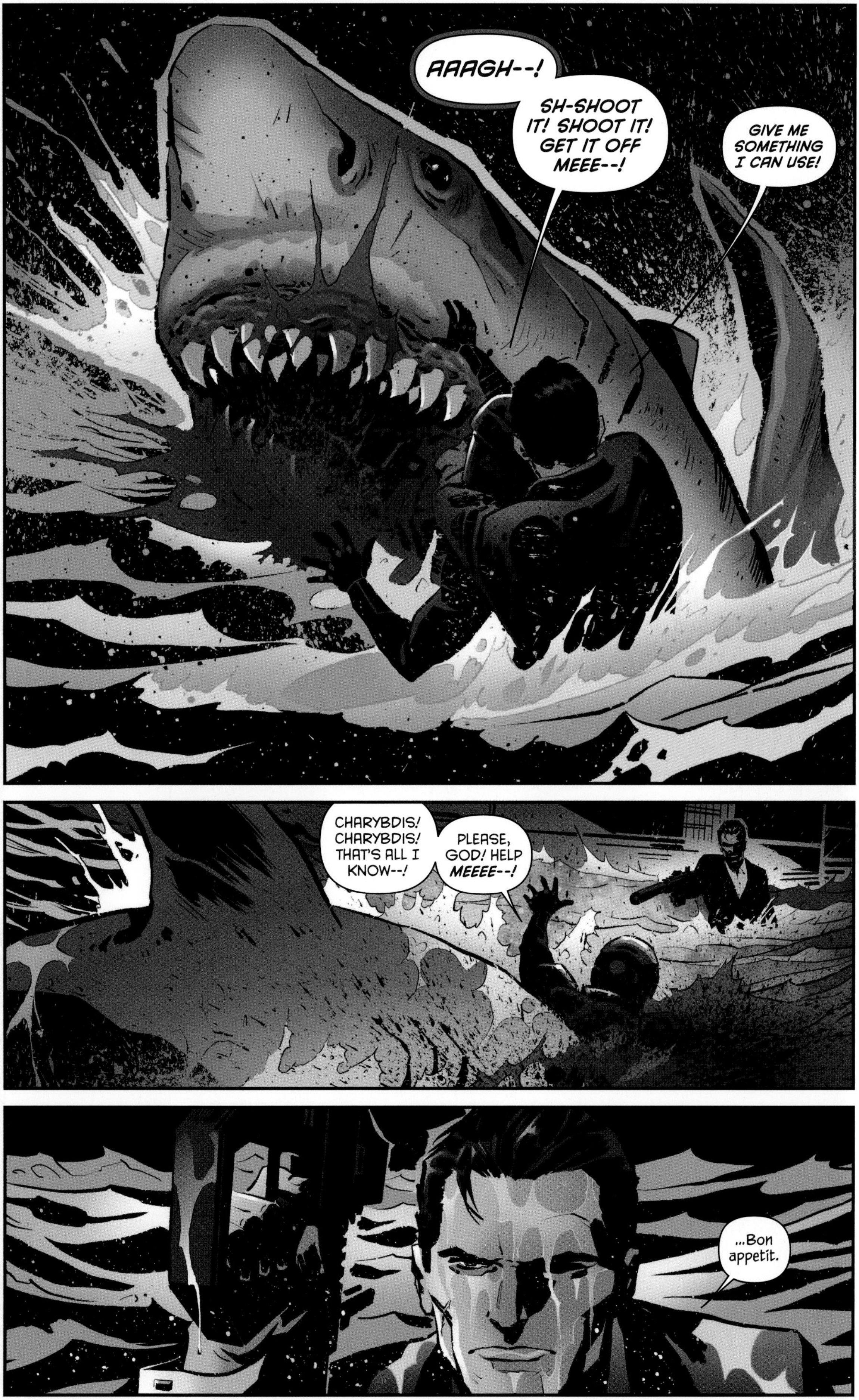
AAAGH--!
SH-SHOOT IT! SHOOT IT! GET IT OFF MEEE--!
GIVE ME SOMETHING I CAN USE!
CHARYBDIS! CHARYBDIS! THAT'S ALL I KNOW--!
PLEASE, GOD! HELP MEEEE--!
...Bon appetit.

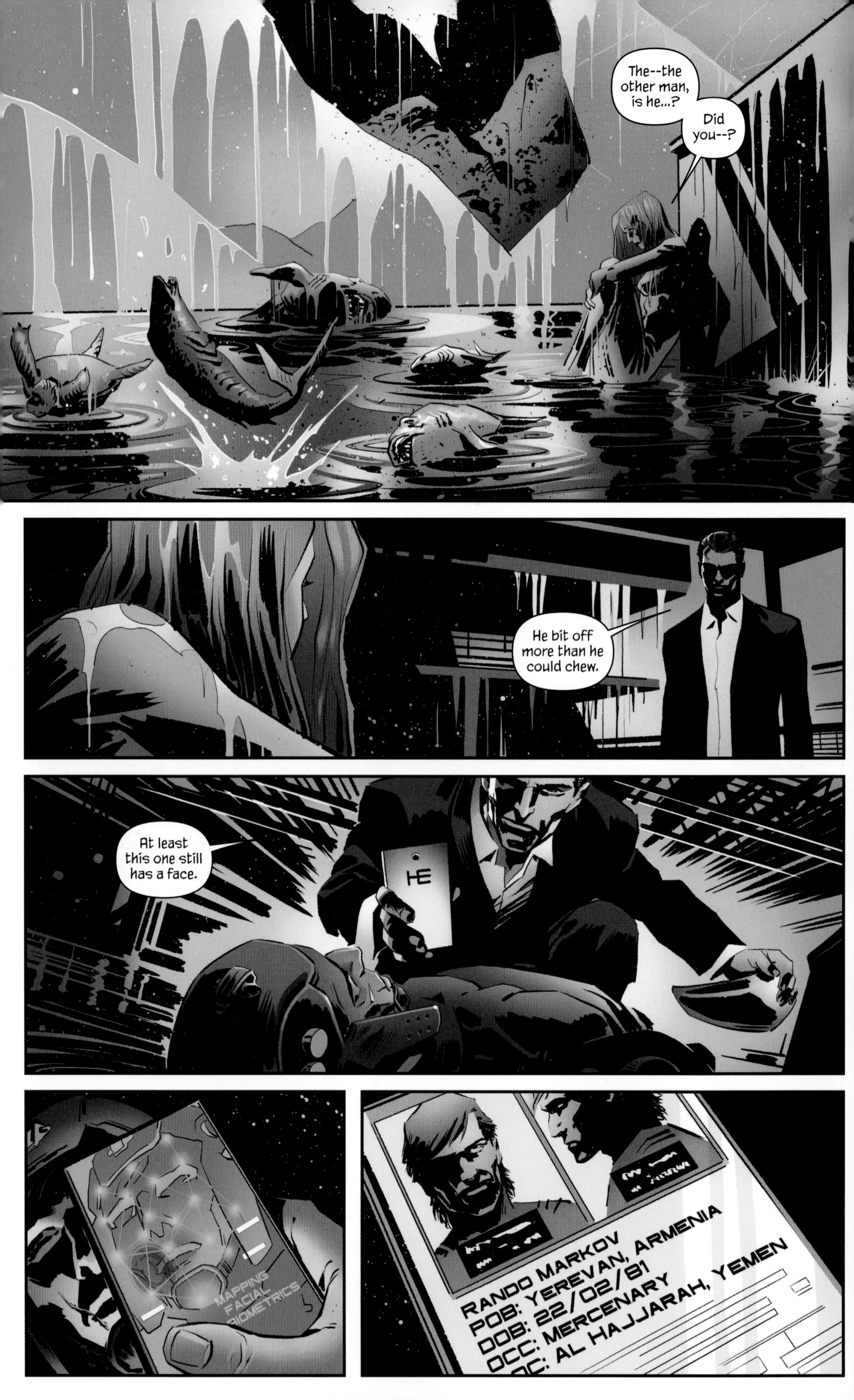
The--the other man, is he...?
Did you--?
He bit off more than he could chew.
At least this one still has a face.
HE
MAPPING FACIAL BIOMETRICS
RANDO MARKOV
POB: YEREVAN, ARMENIA
DOB: 22/02/81
OCC: MERCENARY
OC: AL HAJJARAH, YEMEN

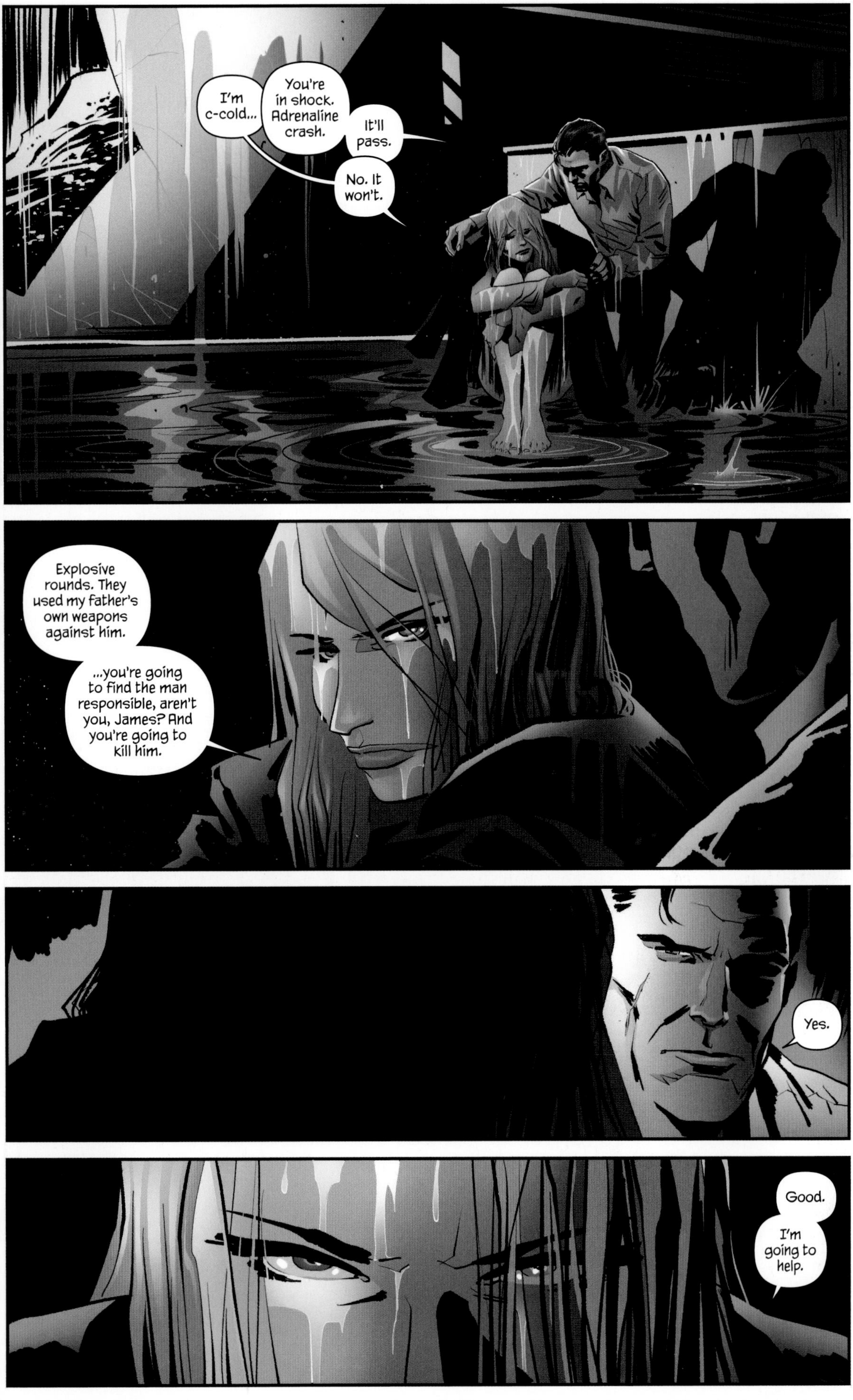
I'm c-cold...
You're in shock. Adrenaline crash.
It'll pass.
No. It won't.
Explosive rounds. They used my father's own weapons against him.
...you're going to find the man responsible, aren't you, James? And you're going to kill him.
Yes.
Good.
I'm going to help.

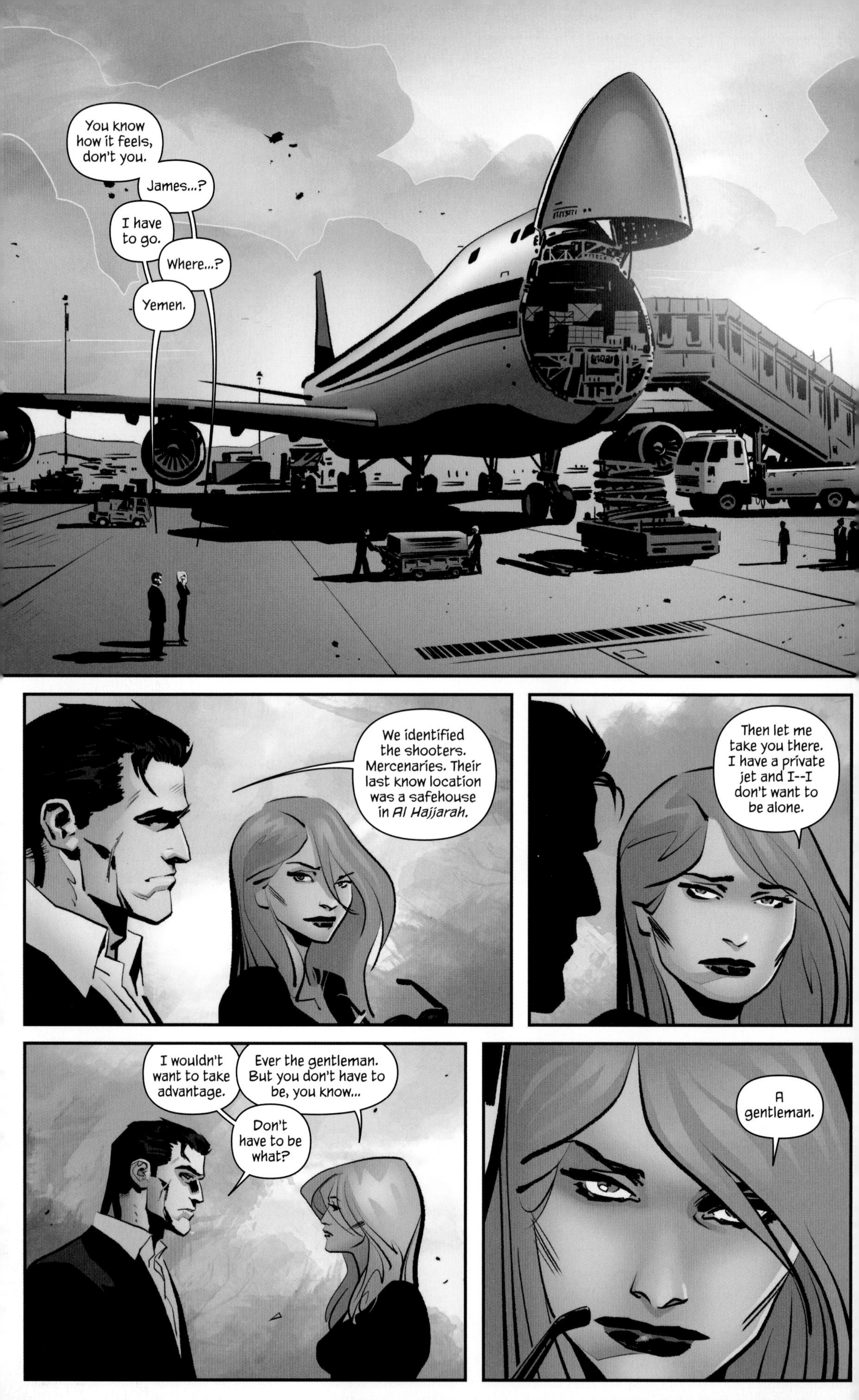
You know how it feels, don't you.
James...?
I have to go.
Where...?
Yemen.
We identified the shooters. Mercenaries. Their last know location was a safehouse in *Al Hajjarah.*
Then let me take you there. I have a private jet and I--I don't want to be alone.
I wouldn't want to take advantage.
Ever the gentleman. But you don't have to be, you know...
Don't have to be what?
A gentleman.

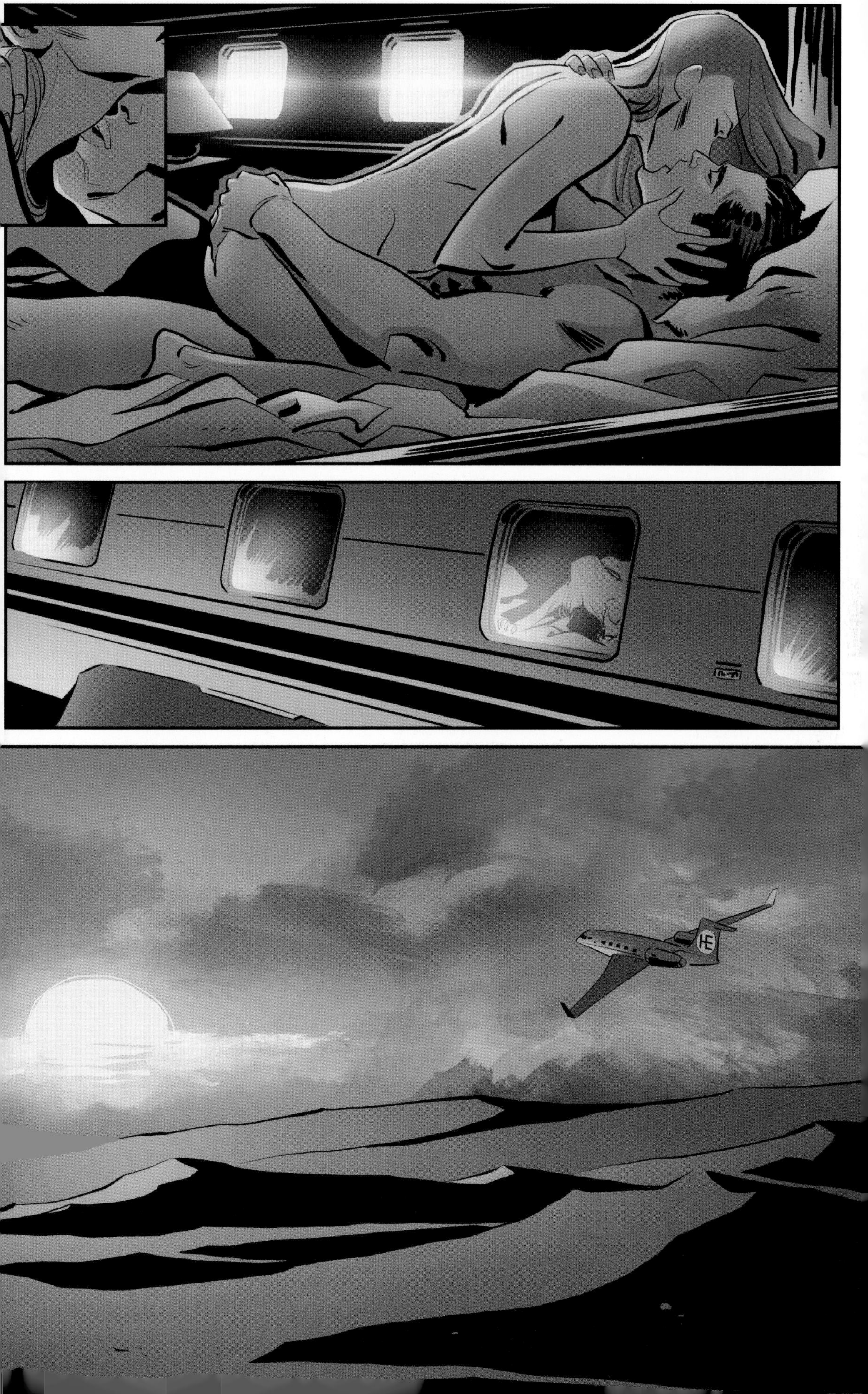

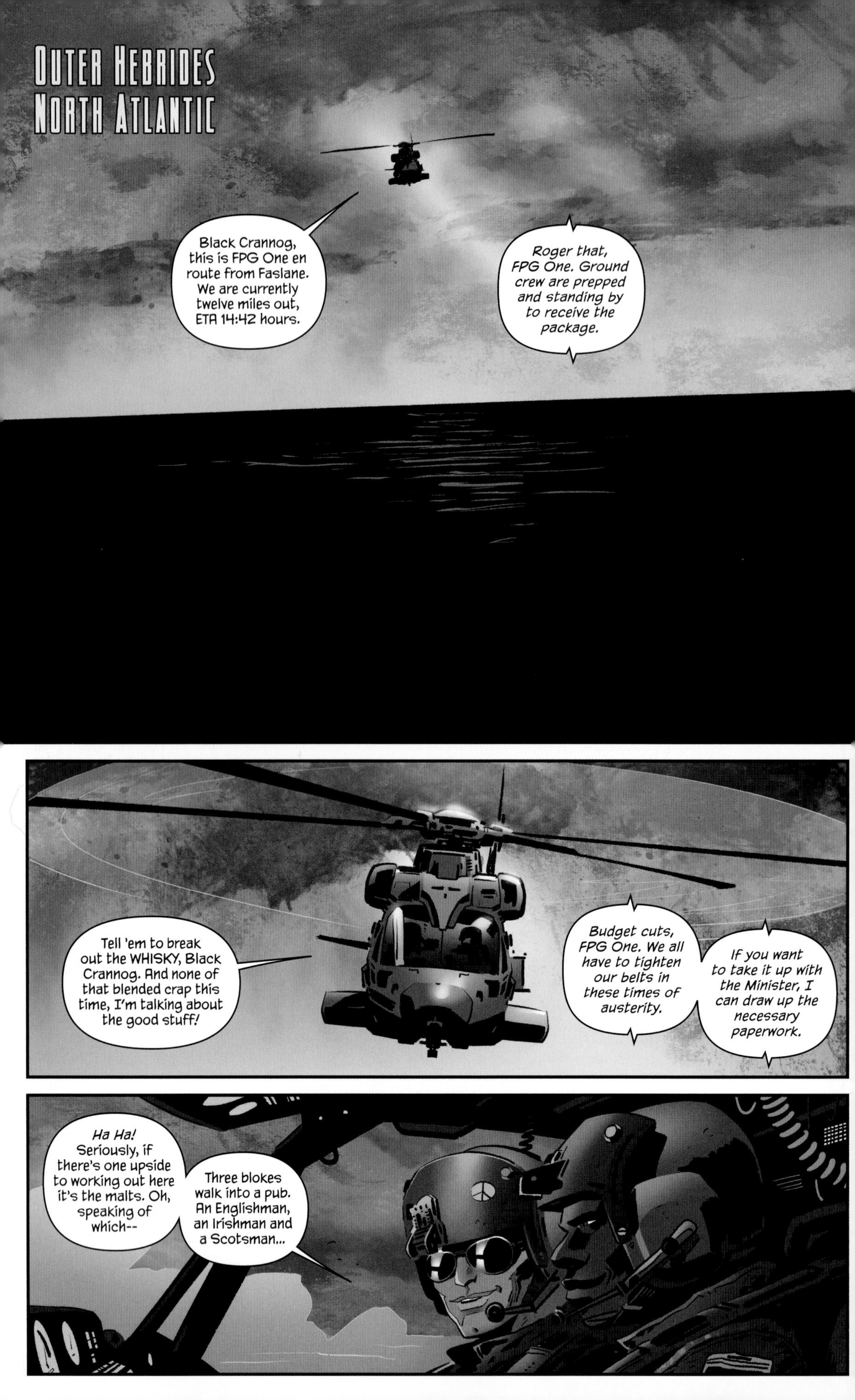
OUTER HEBRIDES NORTH ATLANTIC
Black Crannog, this is FPG One en route from Faslane. We are currently twelve miles out, ETA 14:42 hours.
Roger that, FPG One. Ground crew are prepped and standing by to receive the package.
Tell 'em to break out the WHISKY, Black Crannog. And none of that blended crap this time, I'm talking about the good stuff!
Budget cuts, FPG One. We all have to tighten our belts in these times of austerity.
If you want to take it up with the Minister, I can draw up the necessary paperwork.
Ha Ha! Seriously, if there's one upside to working out here it's the malts. Oh, speaking of which--
Three blokes walk into a pub. An Englishman, an Irishman and a Scotsman...

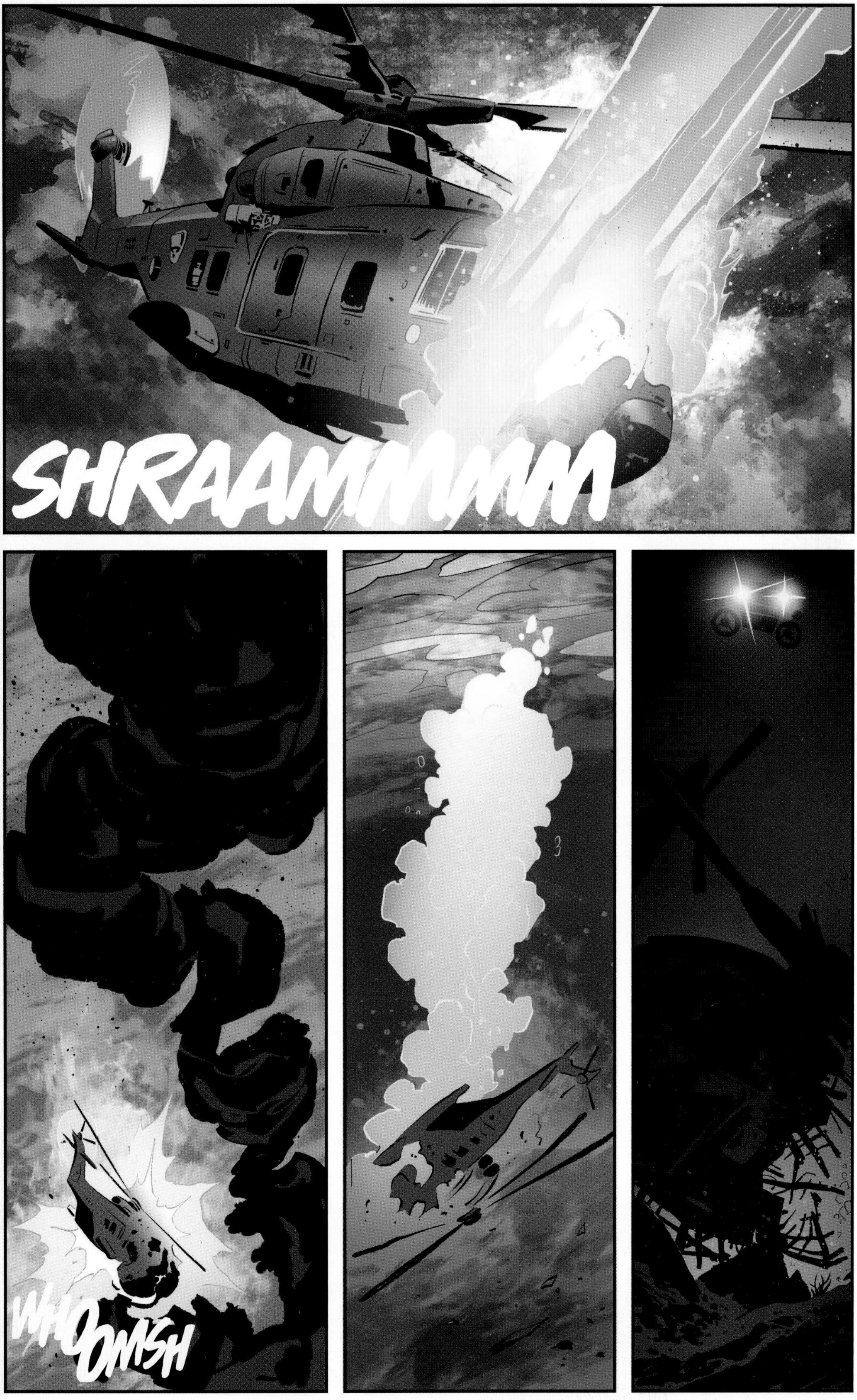
SHRAAMMMM
WHOOMSH

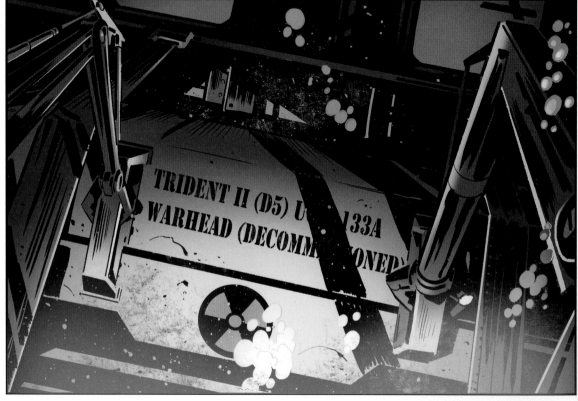

TRIDENT II (D5) U___ __ 33A
WARHEAD (DECOMM___ __ONED)

ISSUE 3

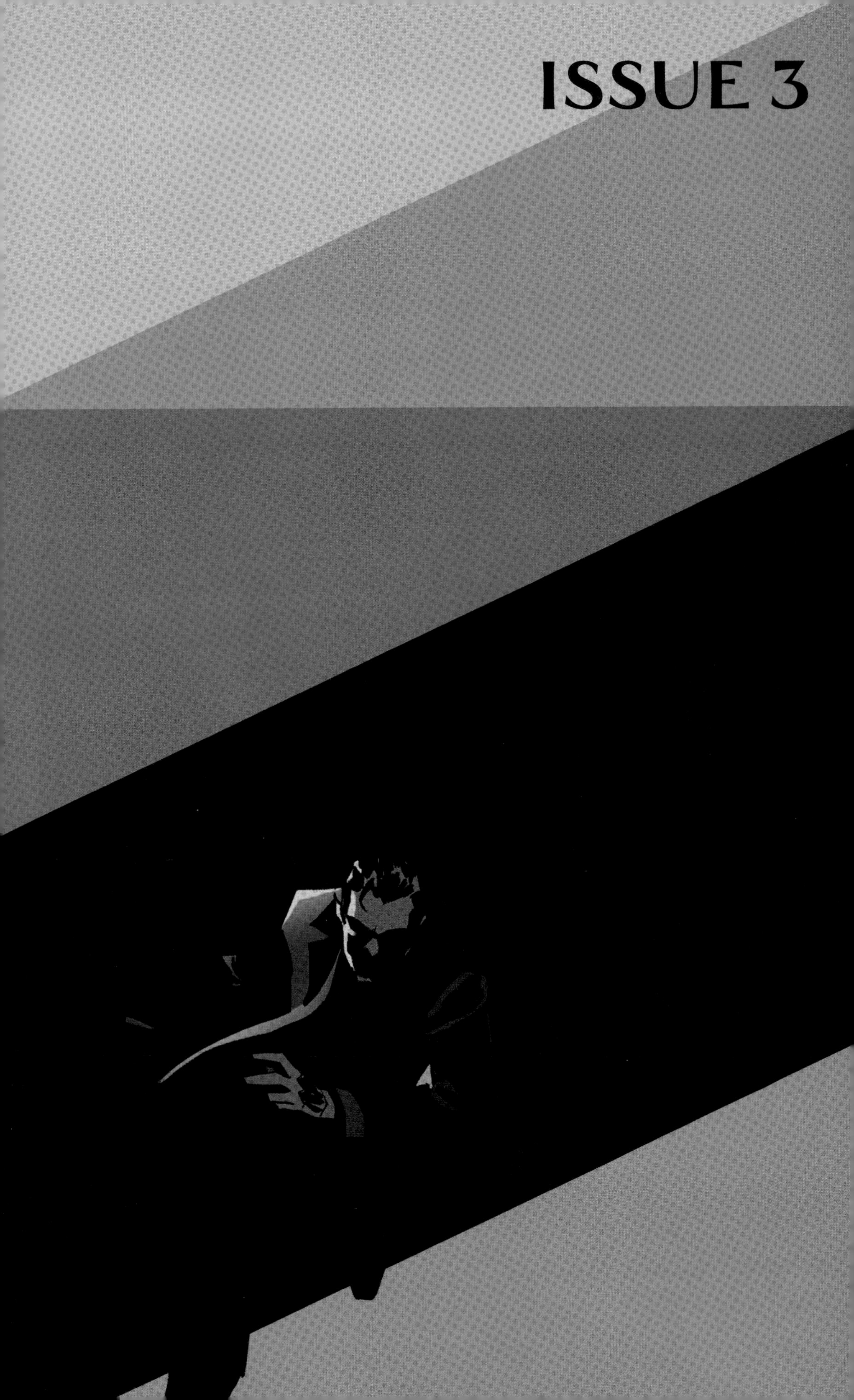

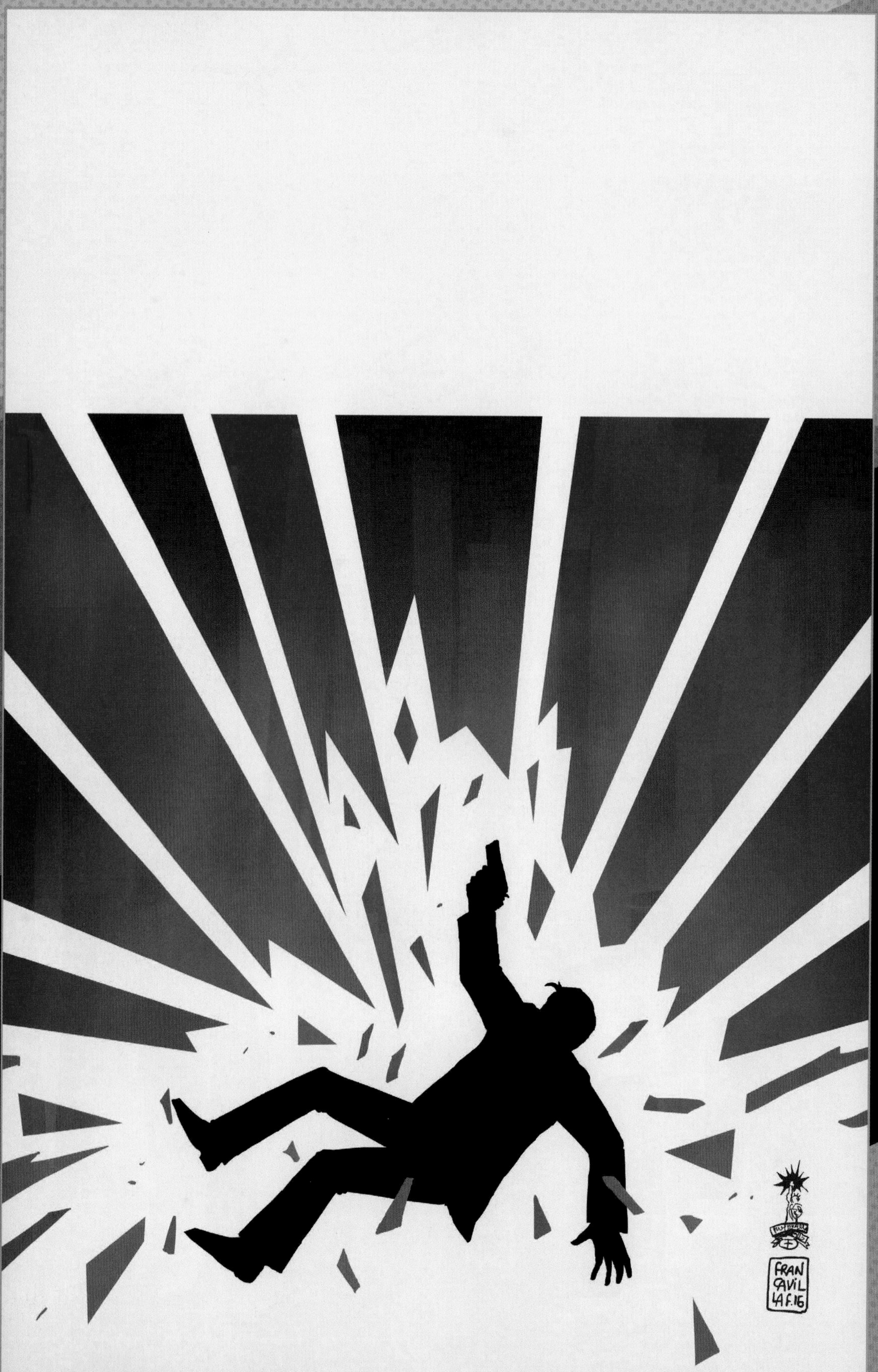

ISSUE 3 COVER
BY FRANCESCO FRANCAVILLA

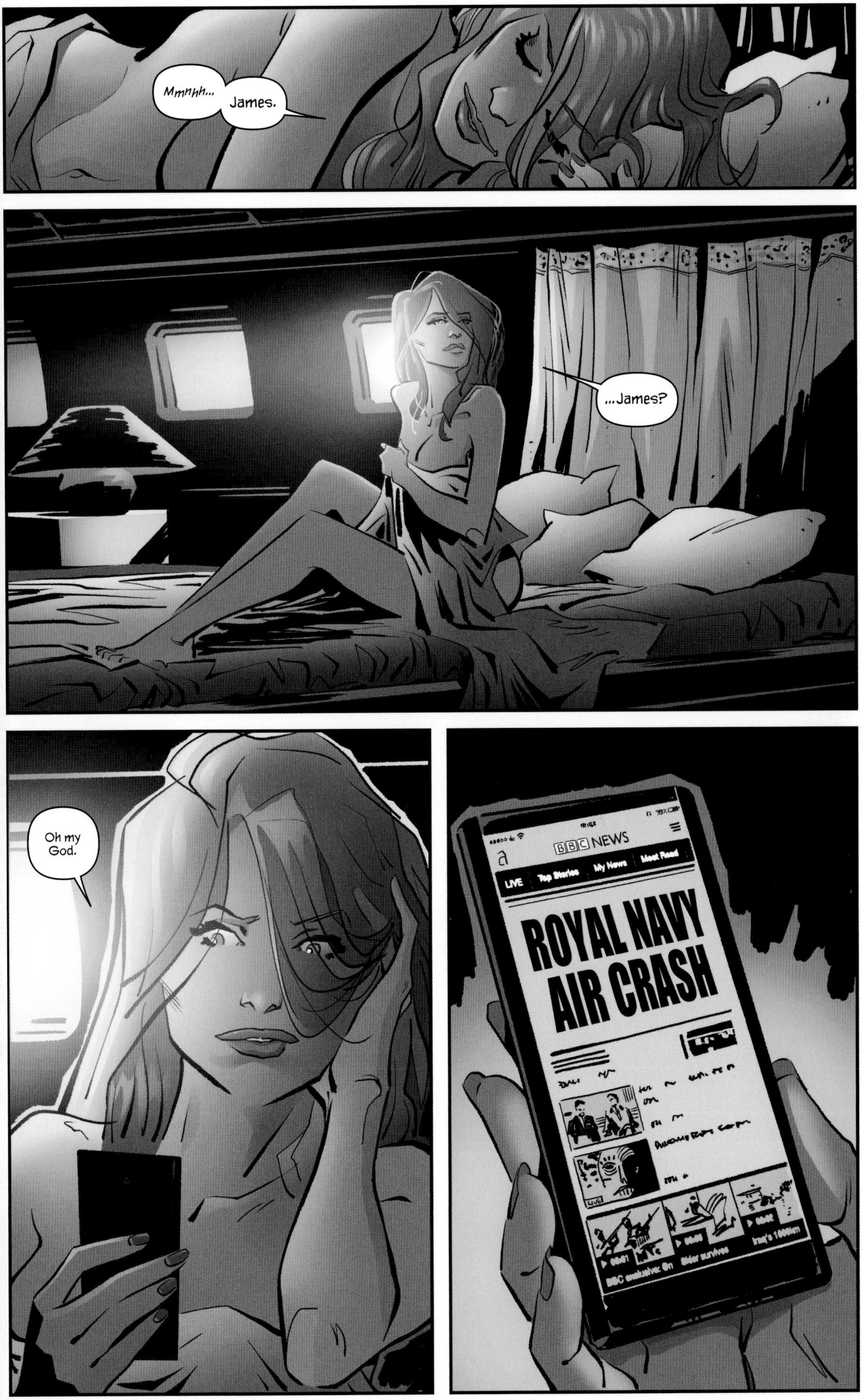
Mmnhh...
James.
...James?
Oh my God.
BBC NEWS
LIVE
Top Stories
My News
Most Read
ROYAL NAVY AIR CRASH

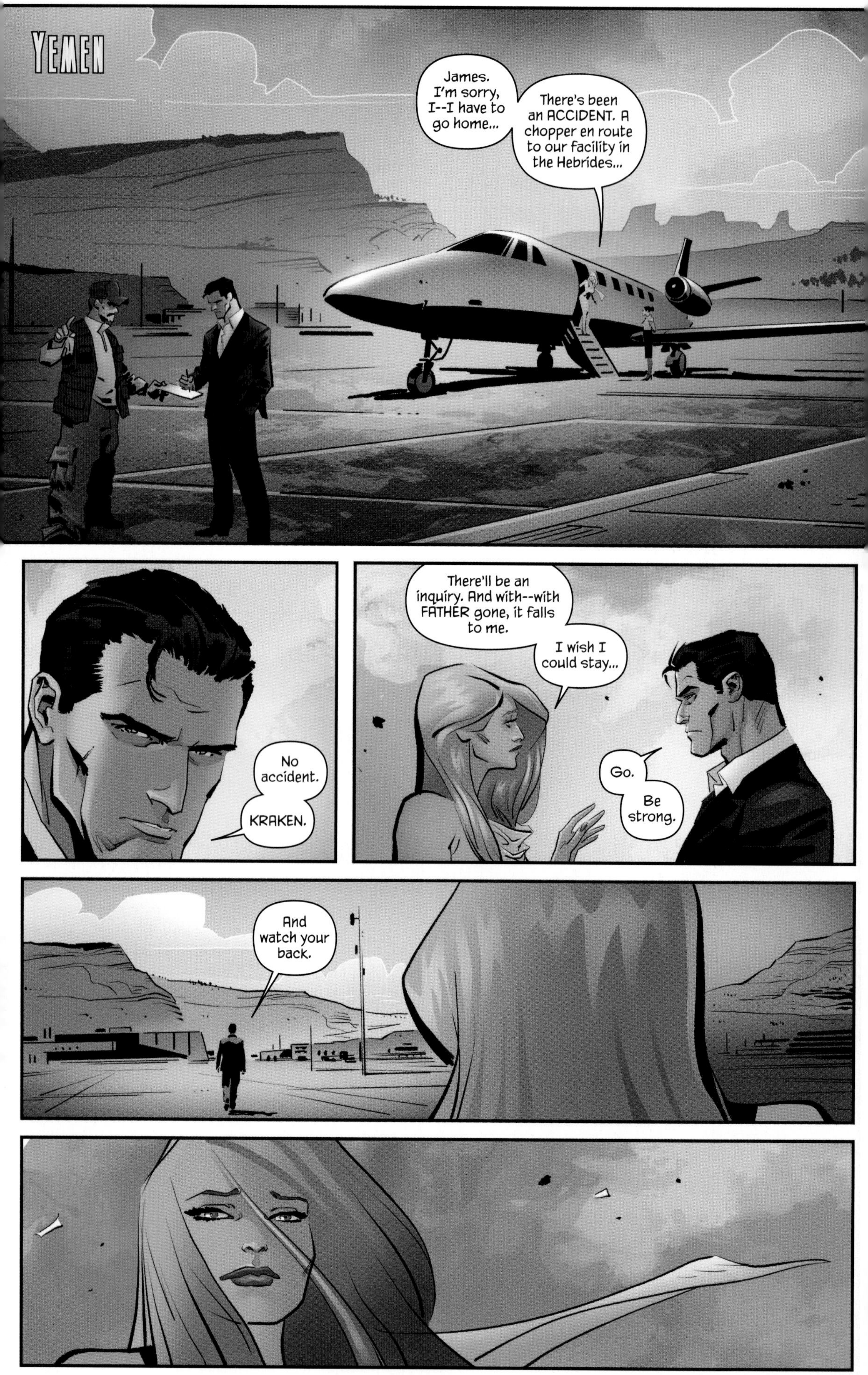
YEMEN
James. I'm sorry, I--I have to go home...
There's been an ACCIDENT. A chopper en route to our facility in the Hebrides...
No accident.
KRAKEN.
There'll be an inquiry. And with--with FATHER gone, it falls to me.
I wish I could stay...
Go.
Be strong.
And watch your back.

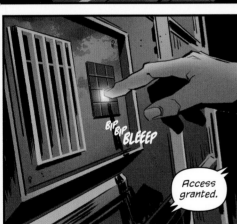

BIP BIP BLEEP

Access granted.

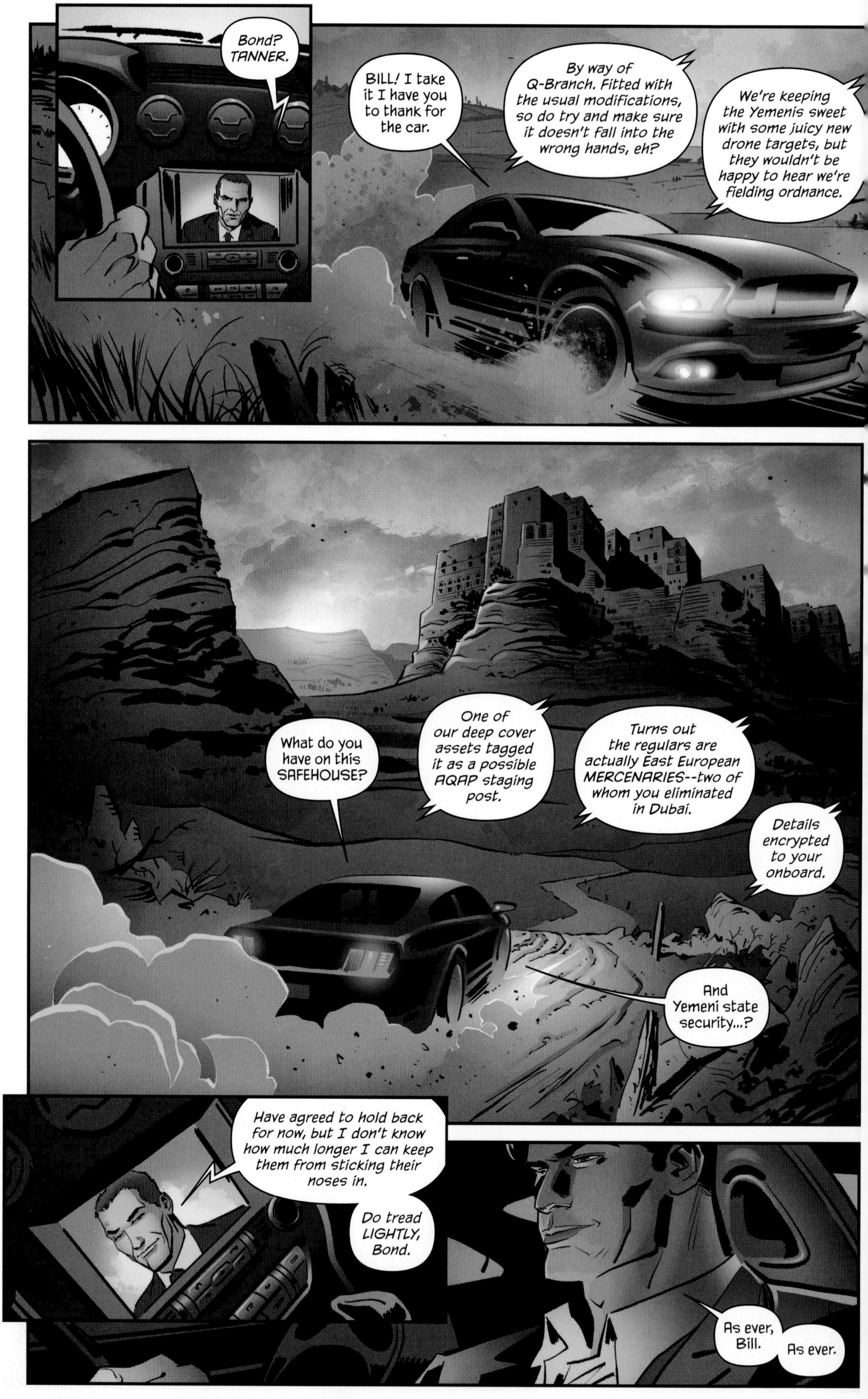
Bond? TANNER.
BILL! I take it I have you to thank for the car.
By way of Q-Branch. Fitted with the usual modifications, so do try and make sure it doesn't fall into the wrong hands, eh?
We're keeping the Yemenis sweet with some juicy new drone targets, but they wouldn't be happy to hear we're fielding ordnance.
What do you have on this SAFEHOUSE?
One of our deep cover assets tagged it as a possible AQAP staging post.
Turns out the regulars are actually East European MERCENARIES--two of whom you eliminated in Dubai.
Details encrypted to your onboard.
And Yemeni state security...?
Have agreed to hold back for now, but I don't know how much longer I can keep them from sticking their noses in.
Do tread LIGHTLY, Bond.
As ever, Bill.
As ever.

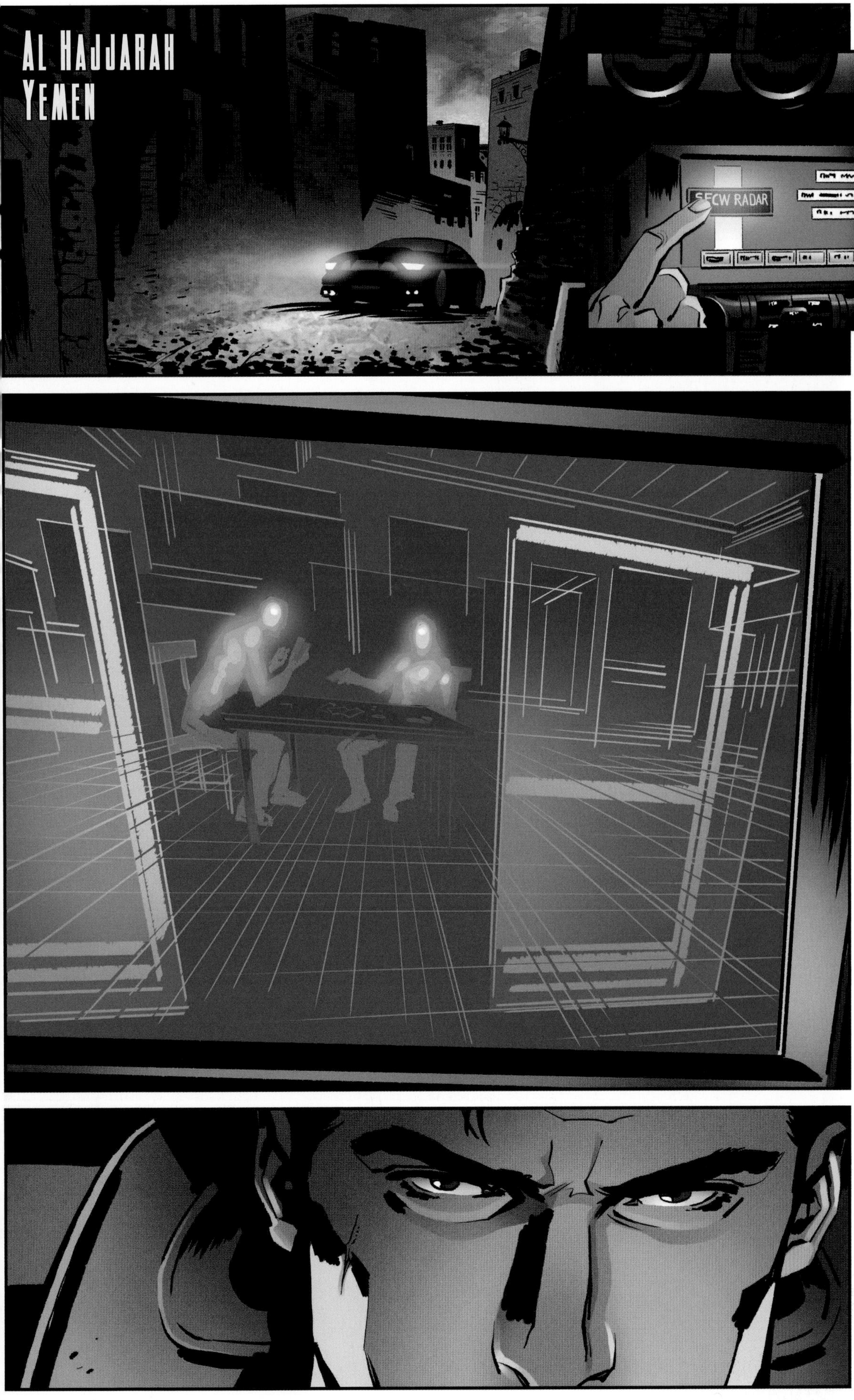
AL HAJJARAH
YEMEN
SECW RADAR

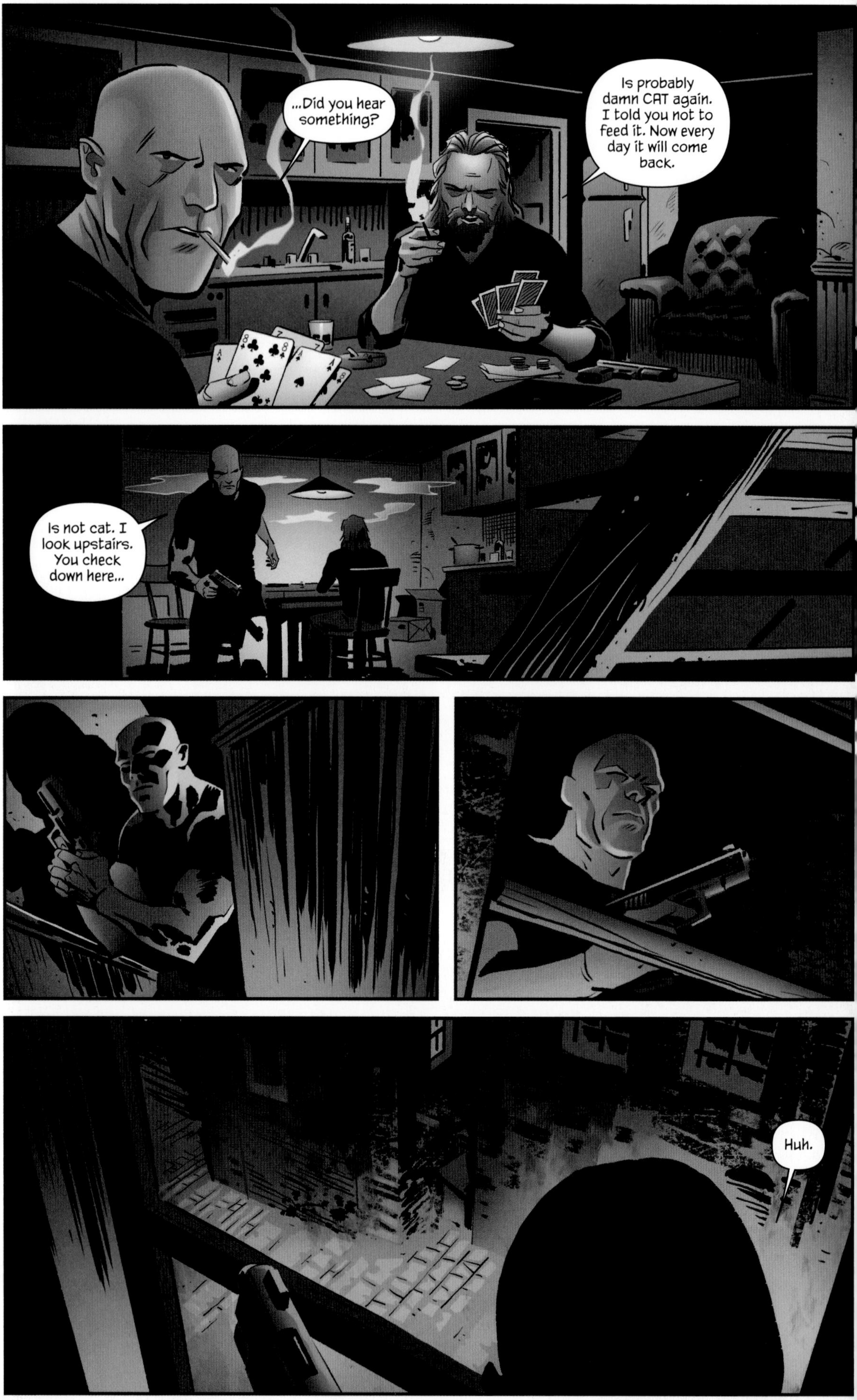
...Did you hear something?
Is probably damn CAT again. I told you not to feed it. Now every day it will come back.
Is not cat. I look upstairs. You check down here...
Huh.

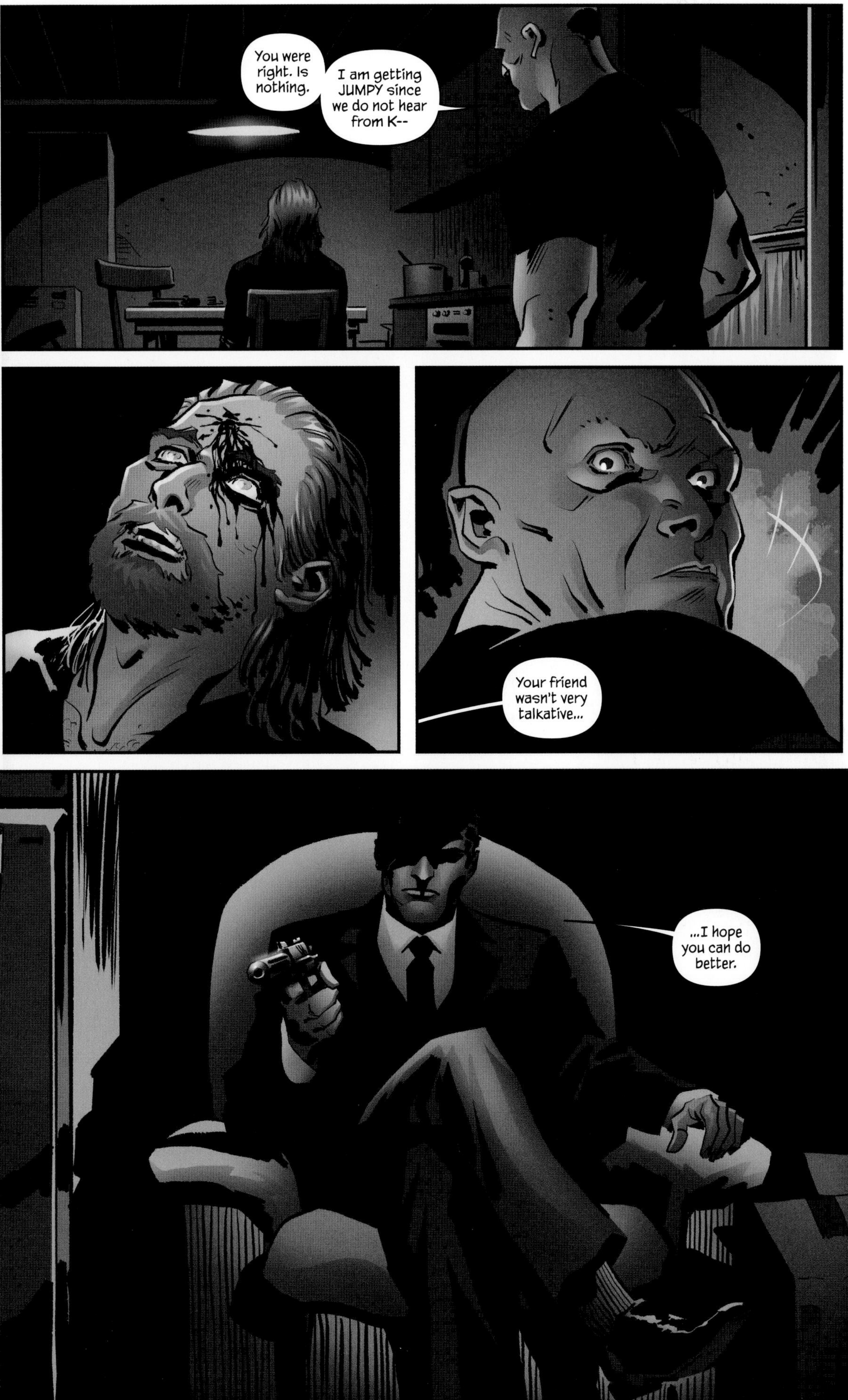

You were right. Is nothing.
I am getting JUMPY since we do not hear from K--
Your friend wasn't very talkative...
...I hope you can do better.

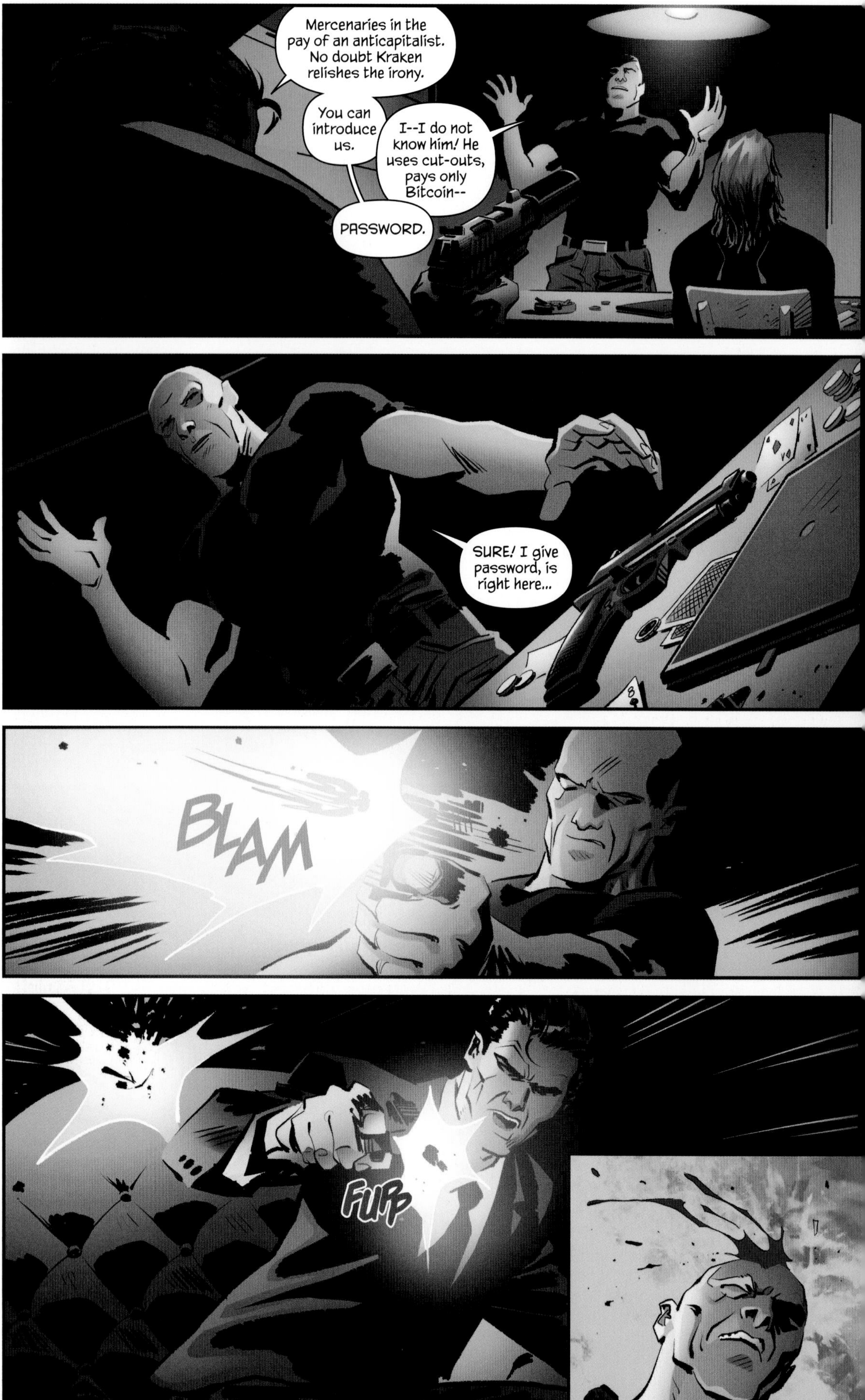
Mercenaries in the pay of an anticapitalist. No doubt Kraken relishes the irony.
You can introduce us.
I--I do not know him! He uses cut-outs, pays only Bitcoin--
PASSWORD.
SURE! I give password, is right here...
BLAM
FUPP

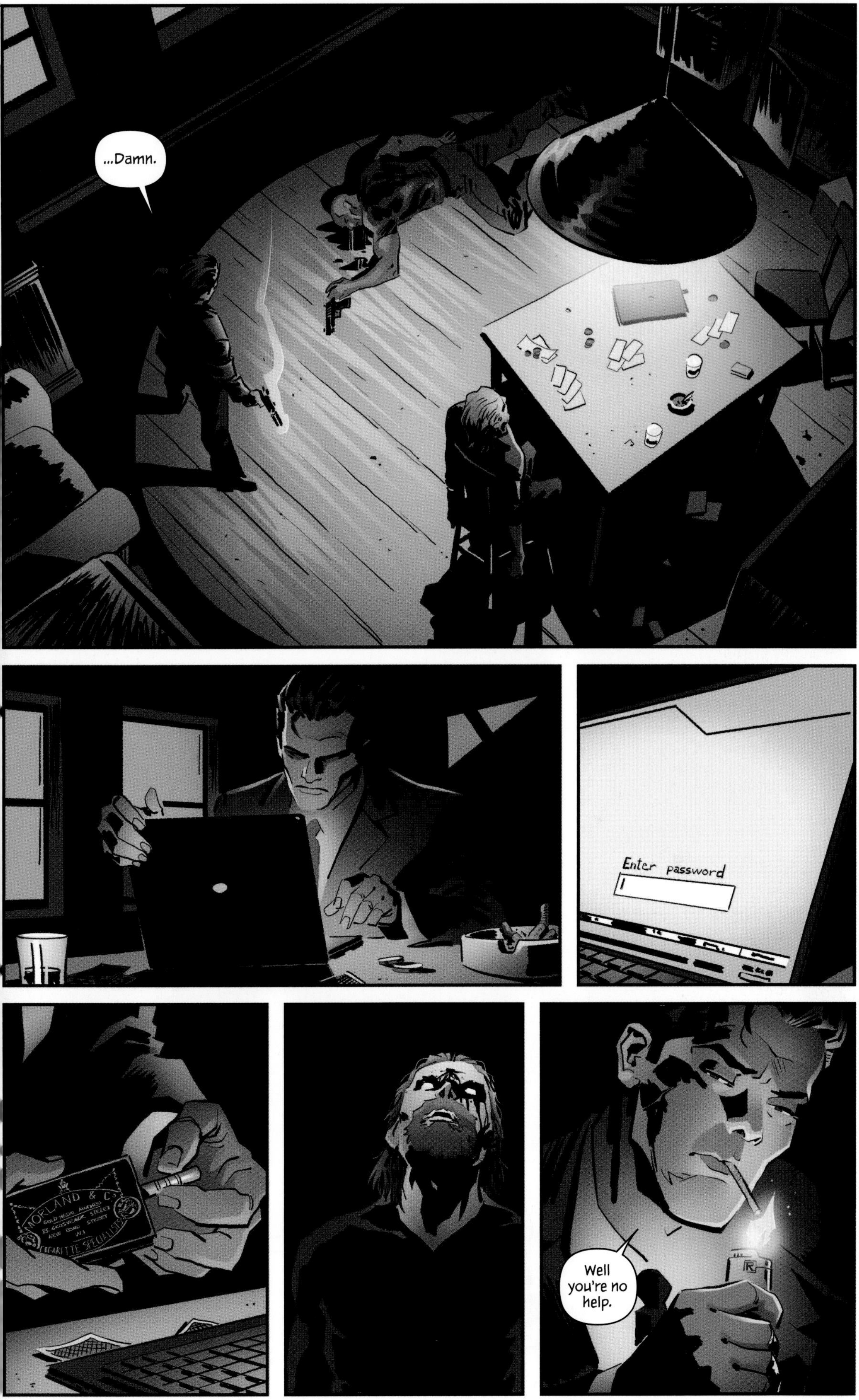
...Damn.
Enter password
MORLAND & Co
GOLD MEDAL AWARDED
NEW BOND STREET
CIGARETTE SPECIALISTS
Well you're no help.

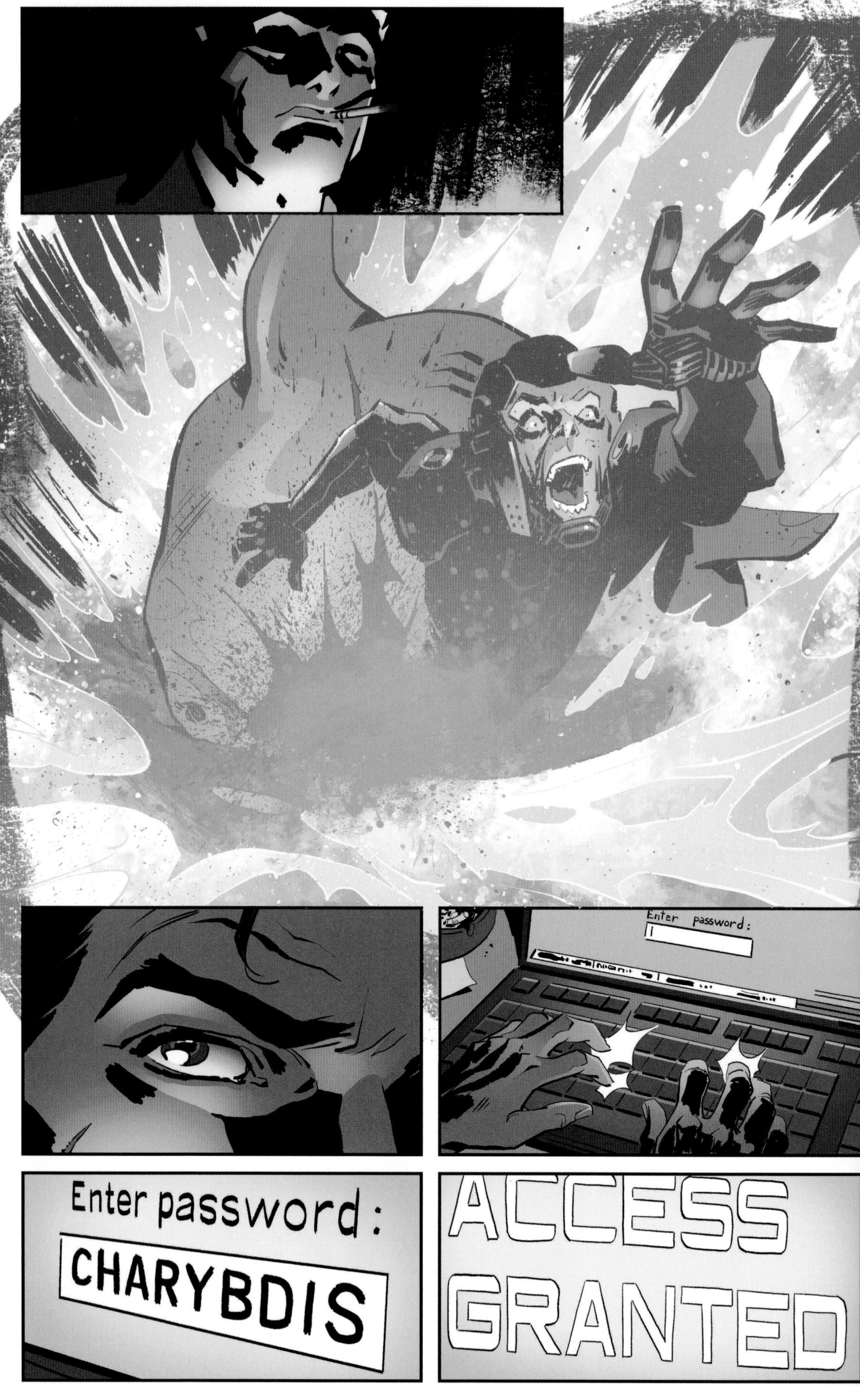
Enter password:
Enter password :
CHARYBDIS
ACCESS GRANTED

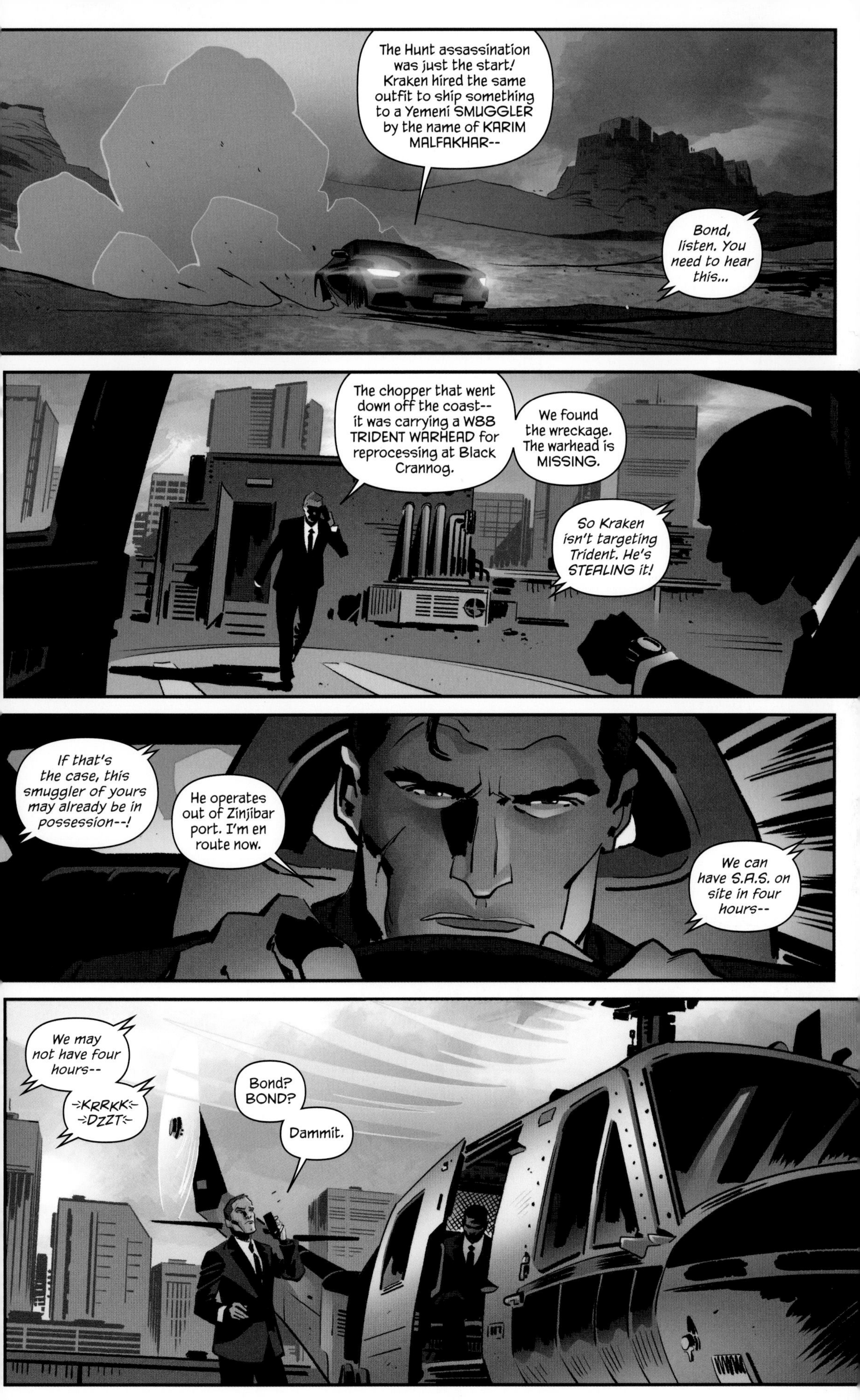
The Hunt assassination was just the start! Kraken hired the same outfit to ship something to a Yemeni SMUGGLER by the name of KARIM MALFAKHAR--
Bond, listen. You need to hear this...
The chopper that went down off the coast-- it was carrying a W88 TRIDENT WARHEAD for reprocessing at Black Crannog.
We found the wreckage. The warhead is MISSING.
So Kraken isn't targeting Trident. He's STEALING it!
If that's the case, this smuggler of yours may already be in possession--!
He operates out of Zinjibar port. I'm en route now.
We can have S.A.S. on site in four hours--
We may not have four hours--
KRRKK DZZT
Bond? BOND?
Dammit.

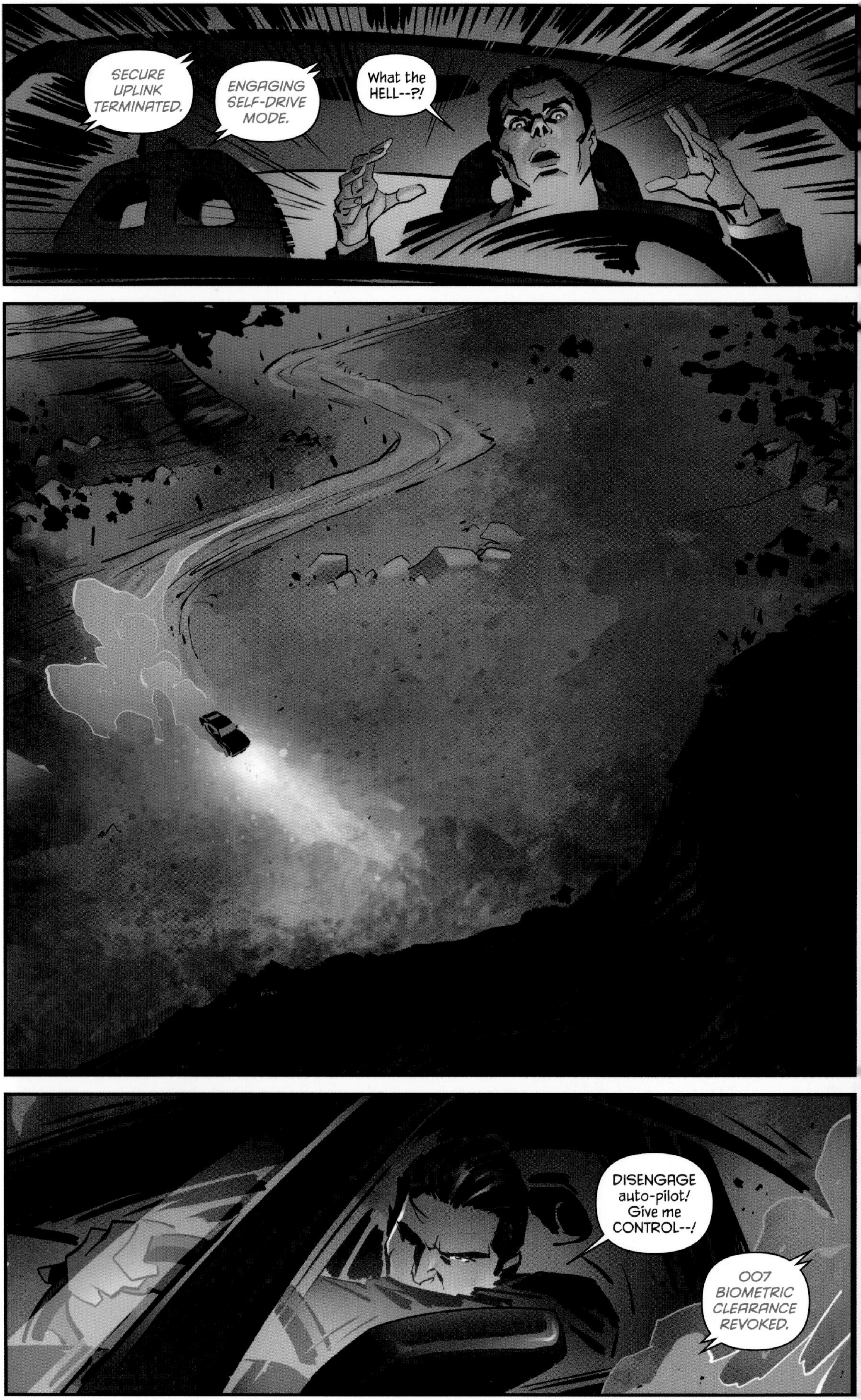
SECURE UPLINK TERMINATED.
ENGAGING SELF-DRIVE MODE.
What the HELL--?!
DISENGAGE auto-pilot! Give me CONTROL--!
007 BIOMETRIC CLEARANCE REVOKED.

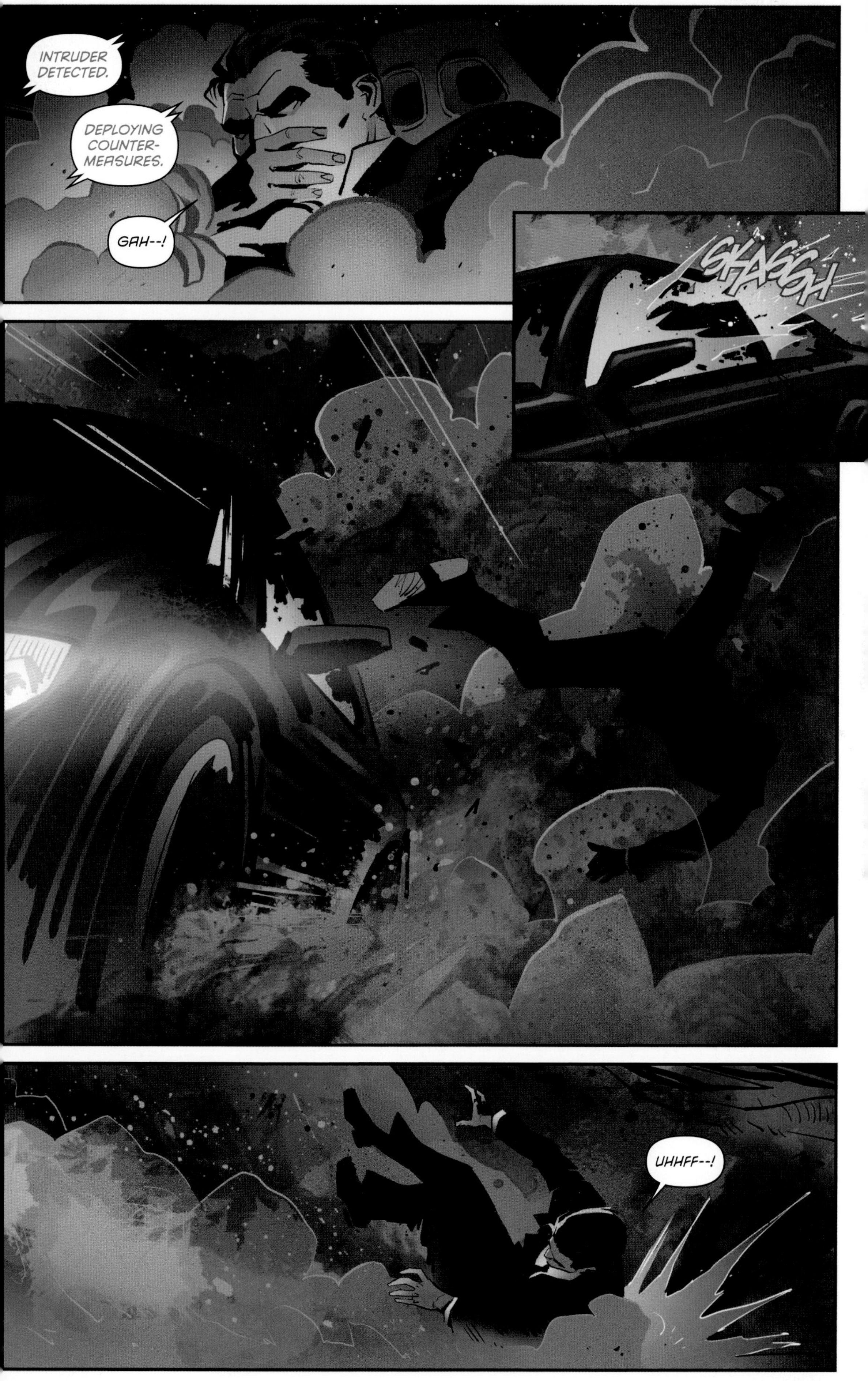
INTRUDER DETECTED.
DEPLOYING COUNTER-MEASURES.
GAH--!
SKASSGH
UHHFF--!

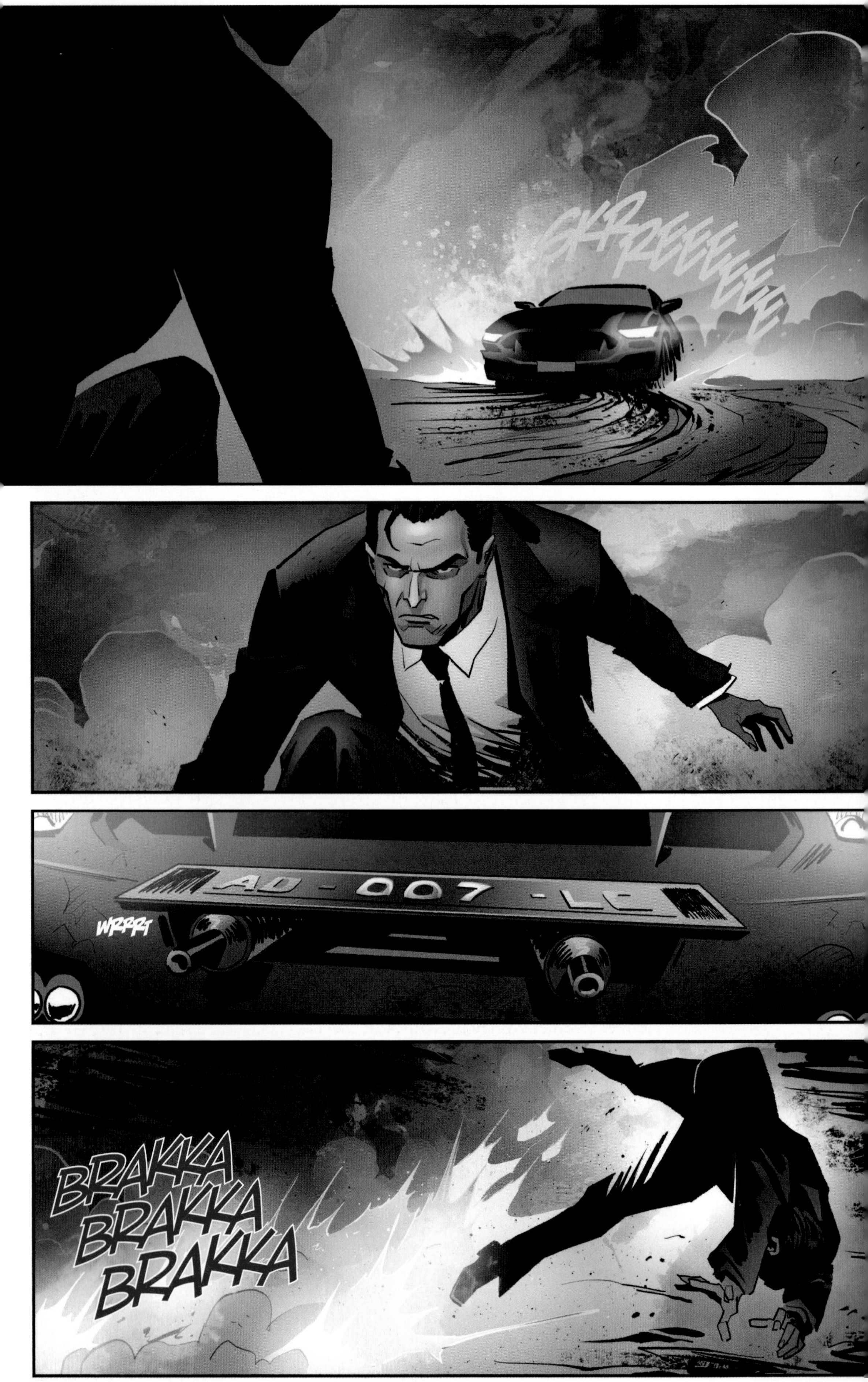
SKREEEEEEE
AD - 007 - LC
WRRRT
BRAKKA
BRAKKA
BRAKKA

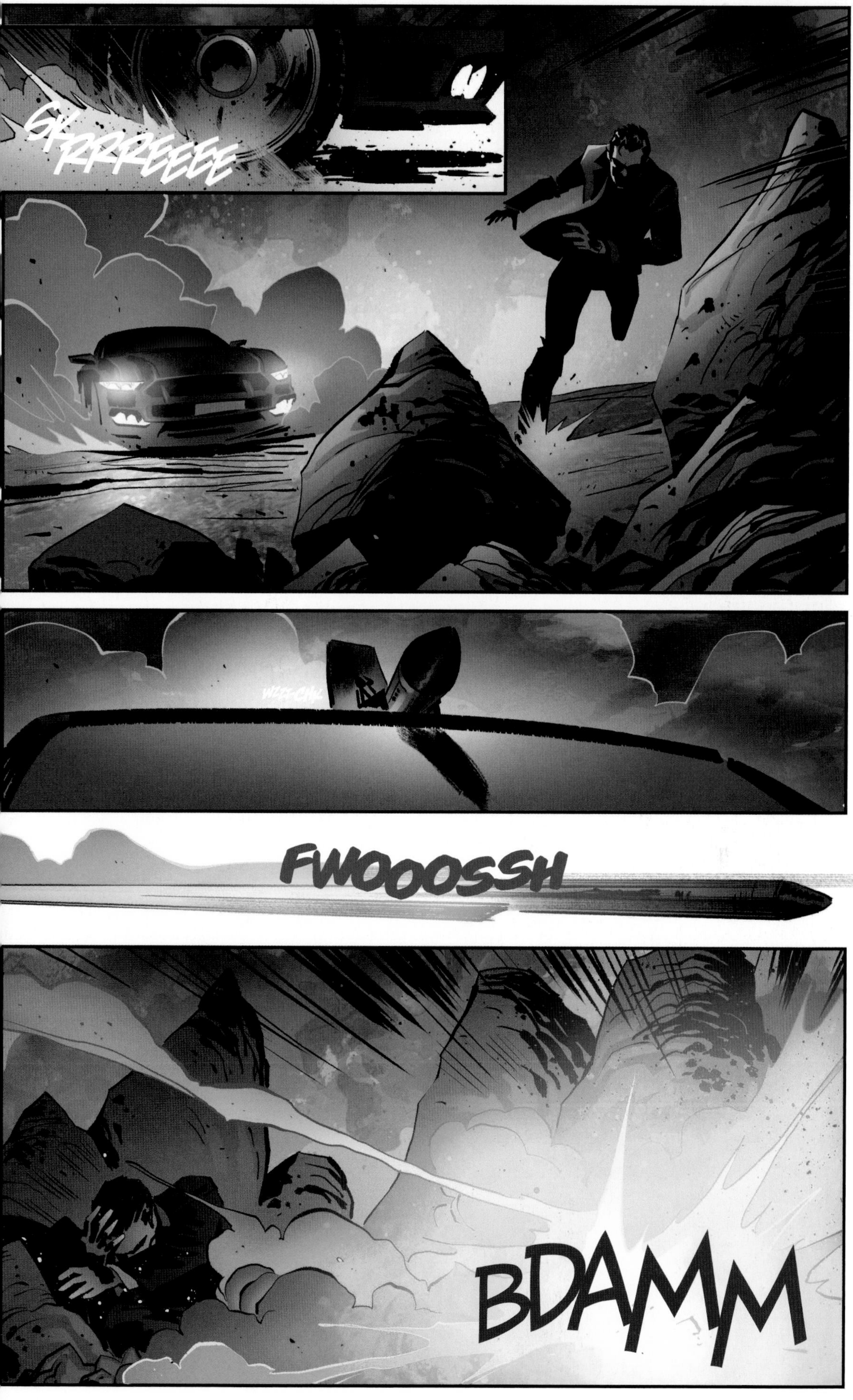
SKRRREEEEE
FWOOOSSH
BDAMM

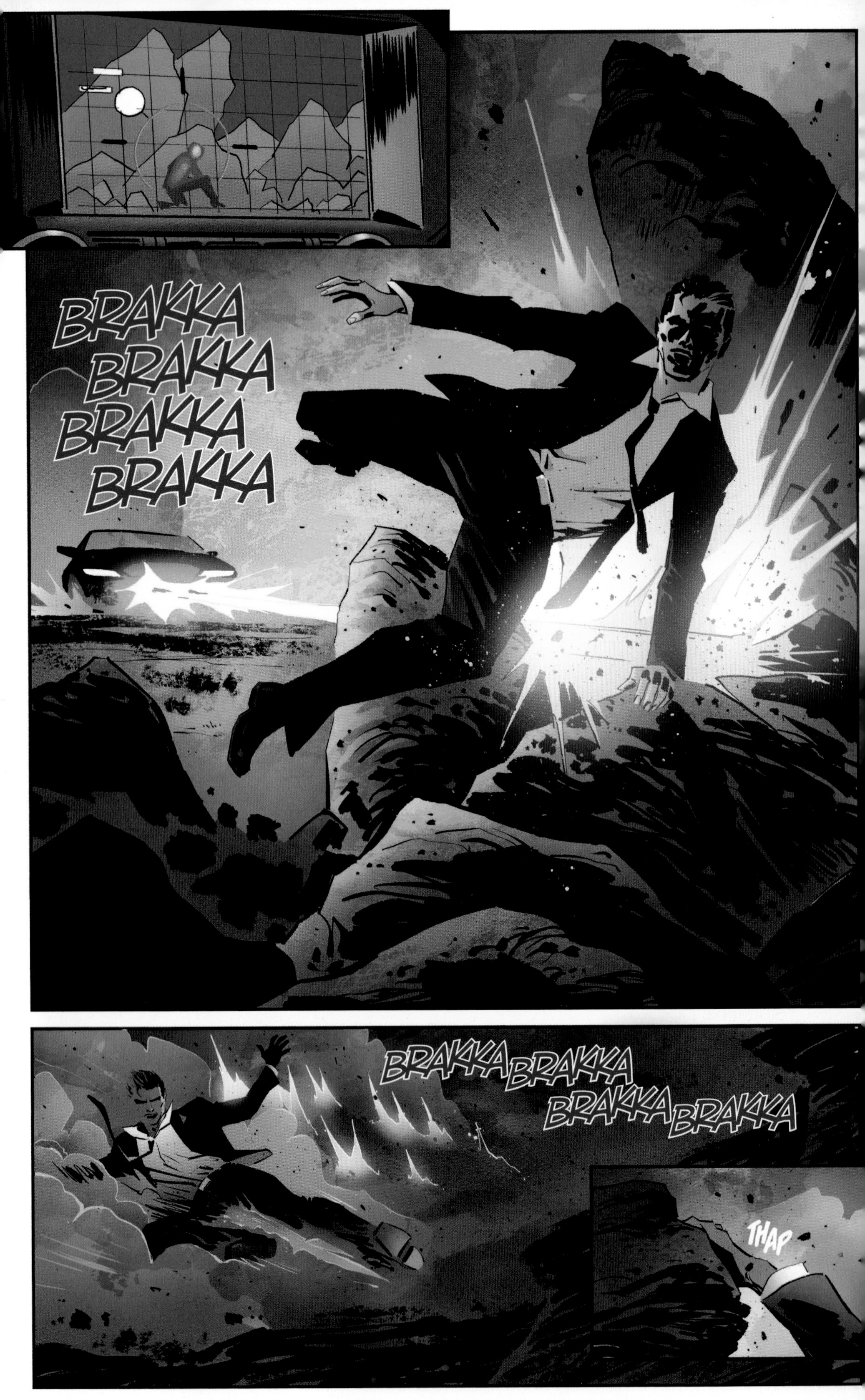
BRAKKA
BRAKKA
BRAKKA
BRAKKA
BRAKKA BRAKKA
BRAKKA BRAKKA
THAP

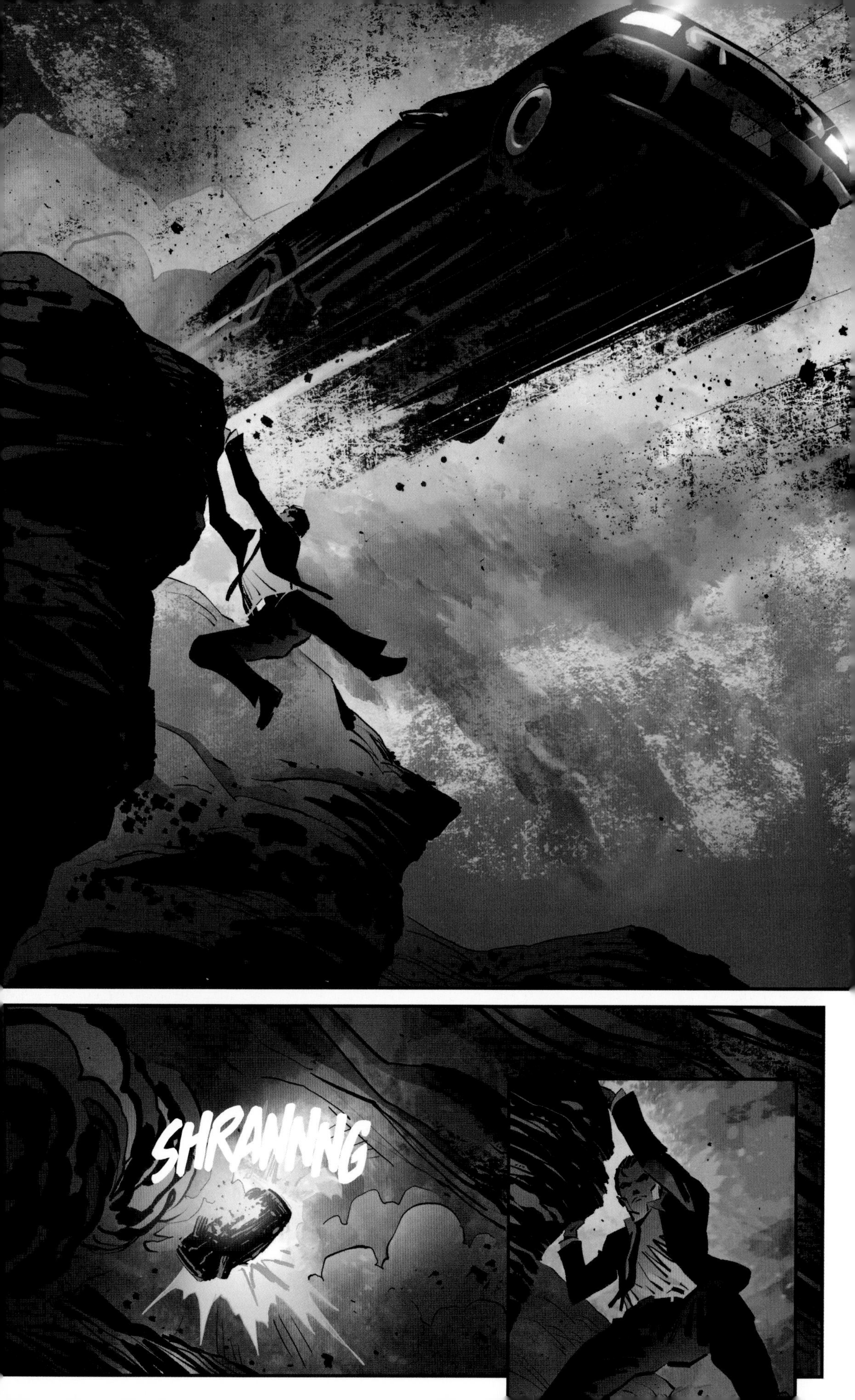
SHRANNNG

ZZZP-KT

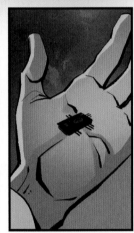

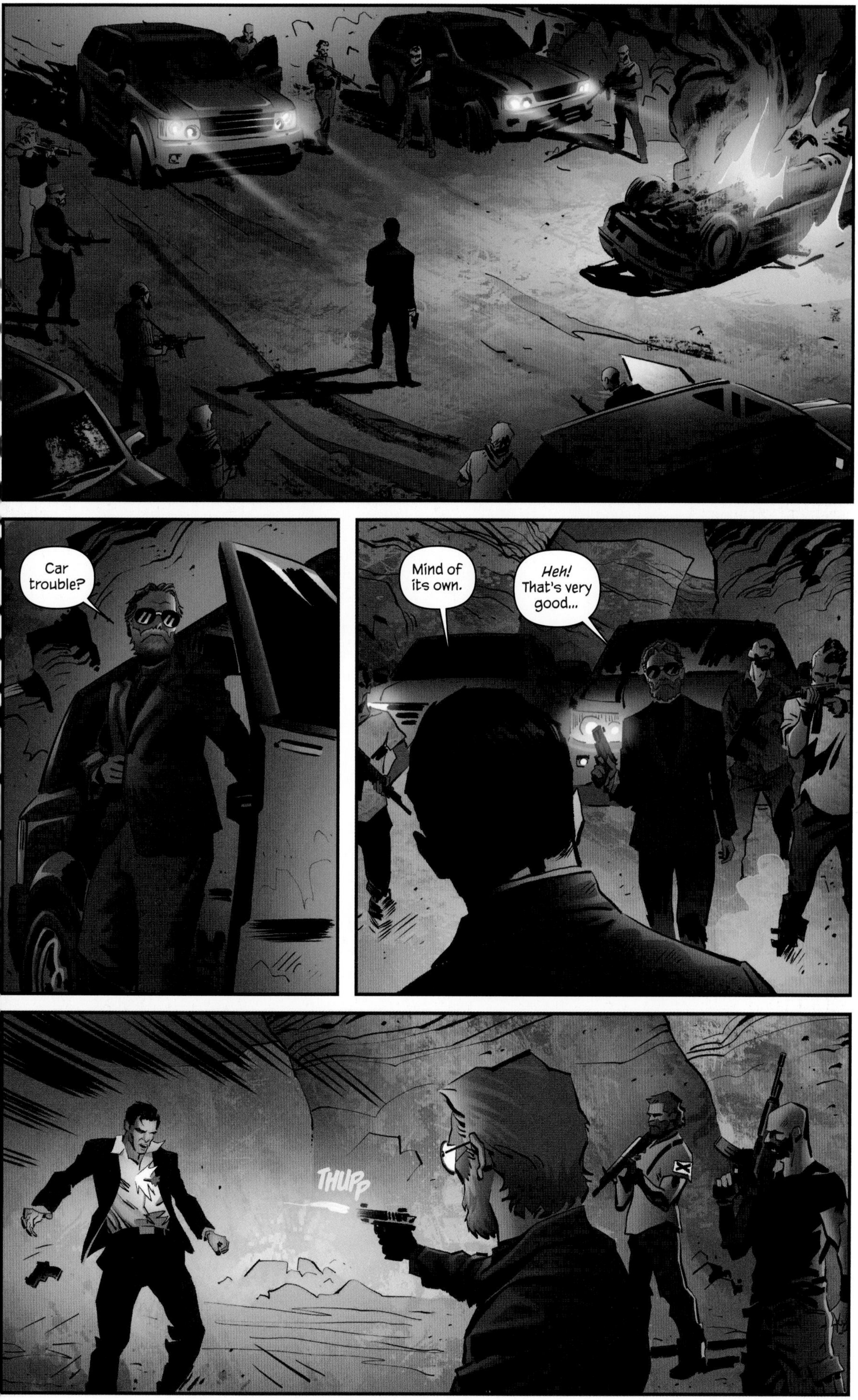
Car trouble?
Mind of its own.
Heh! That's very good...
THUPP

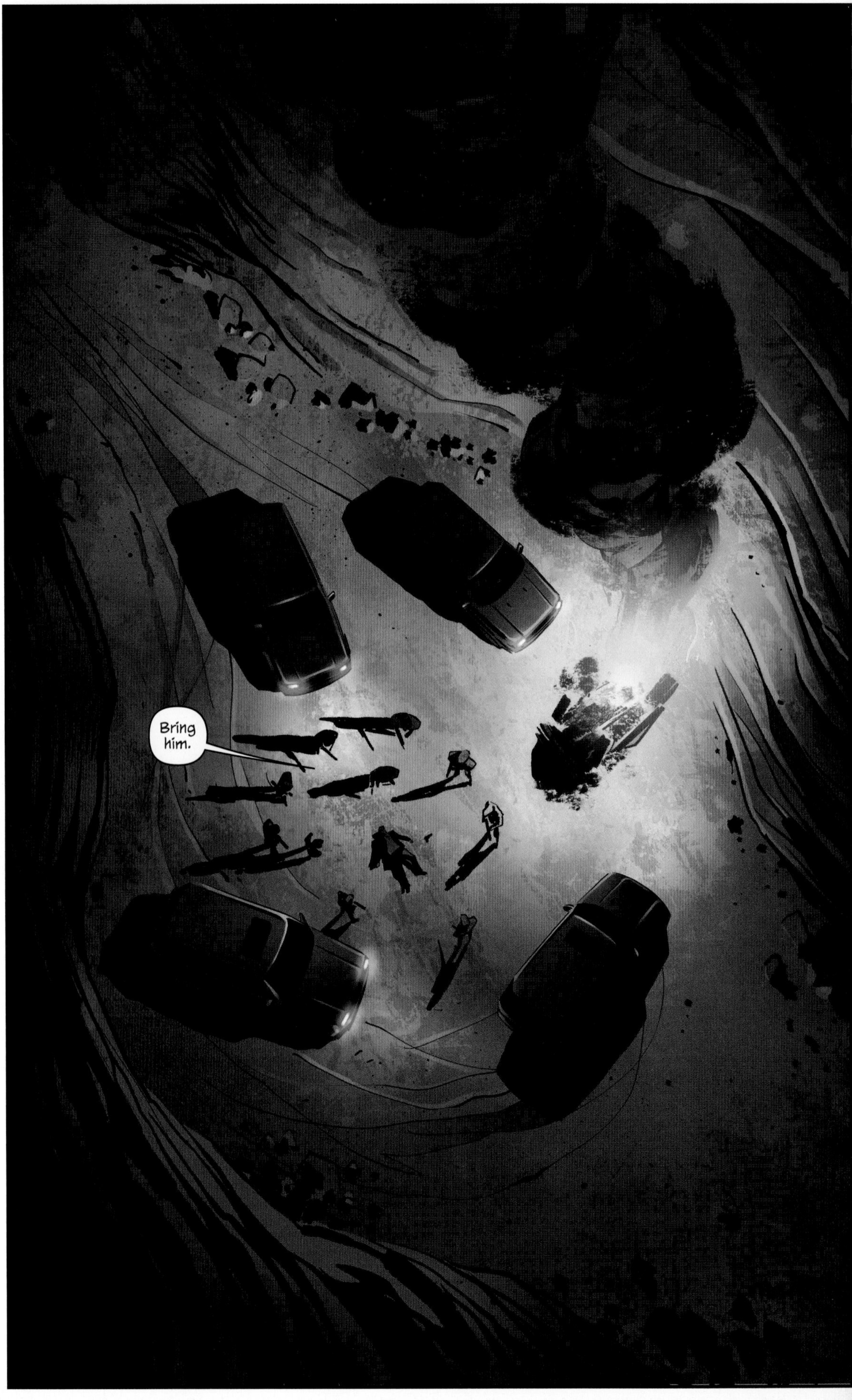
Bring him.

ISSUE 4

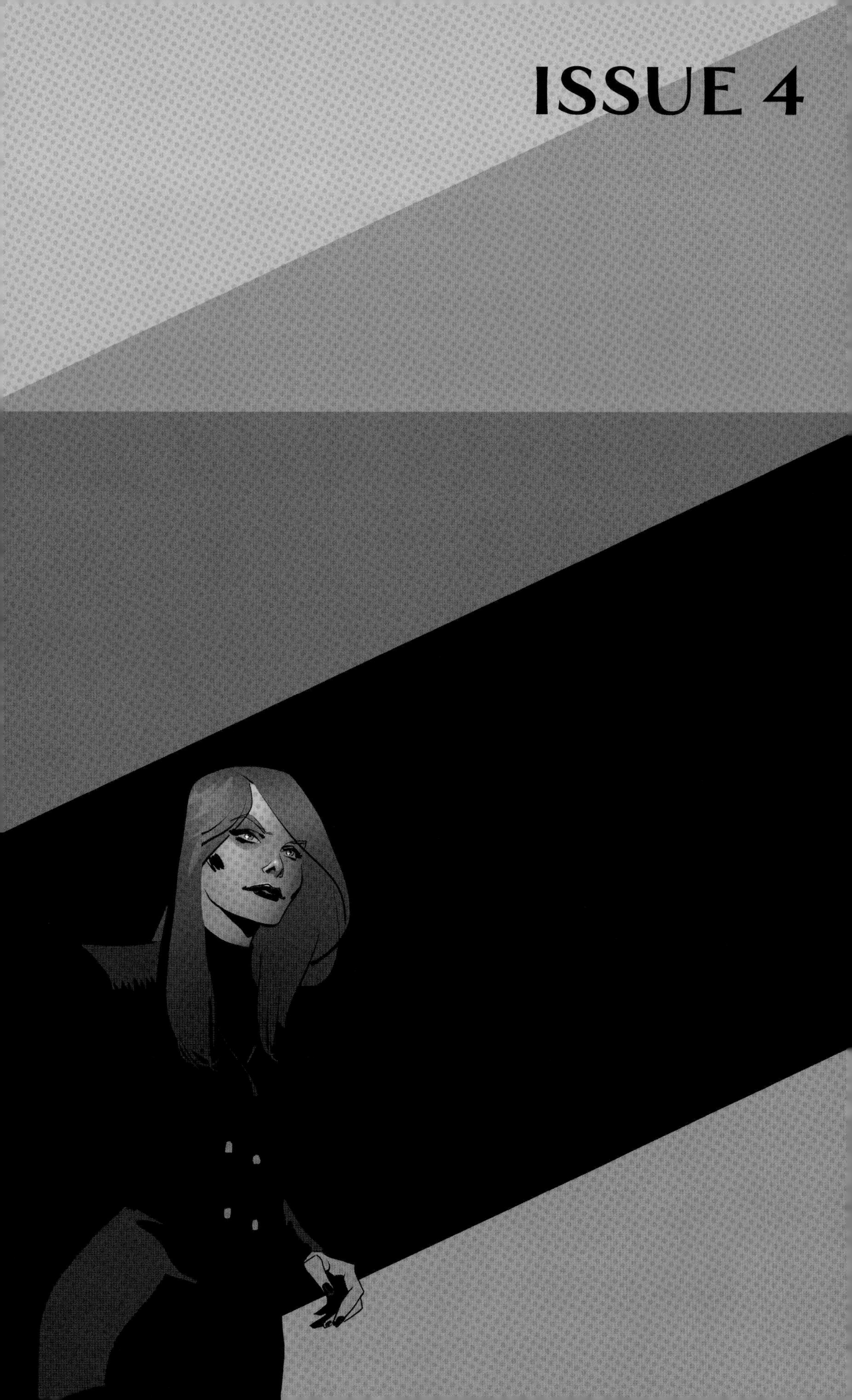

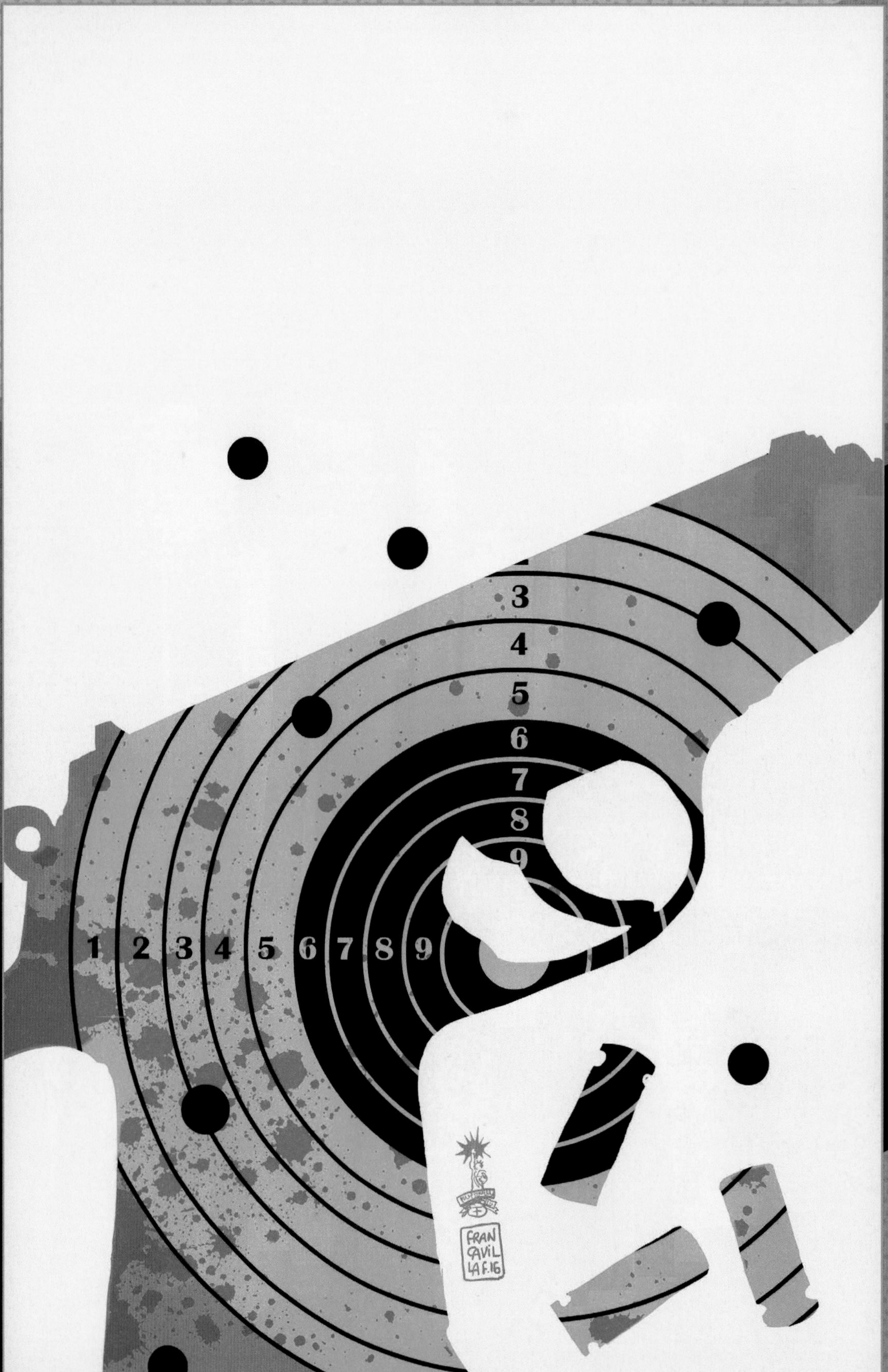
3
4
5
6
7
8
9
1 2 3 4 5 6 7 8 9
FRAN CAVIL LA F.16

ISSUE 4 COVER
BY FRANCESCO FRANCAVILLA

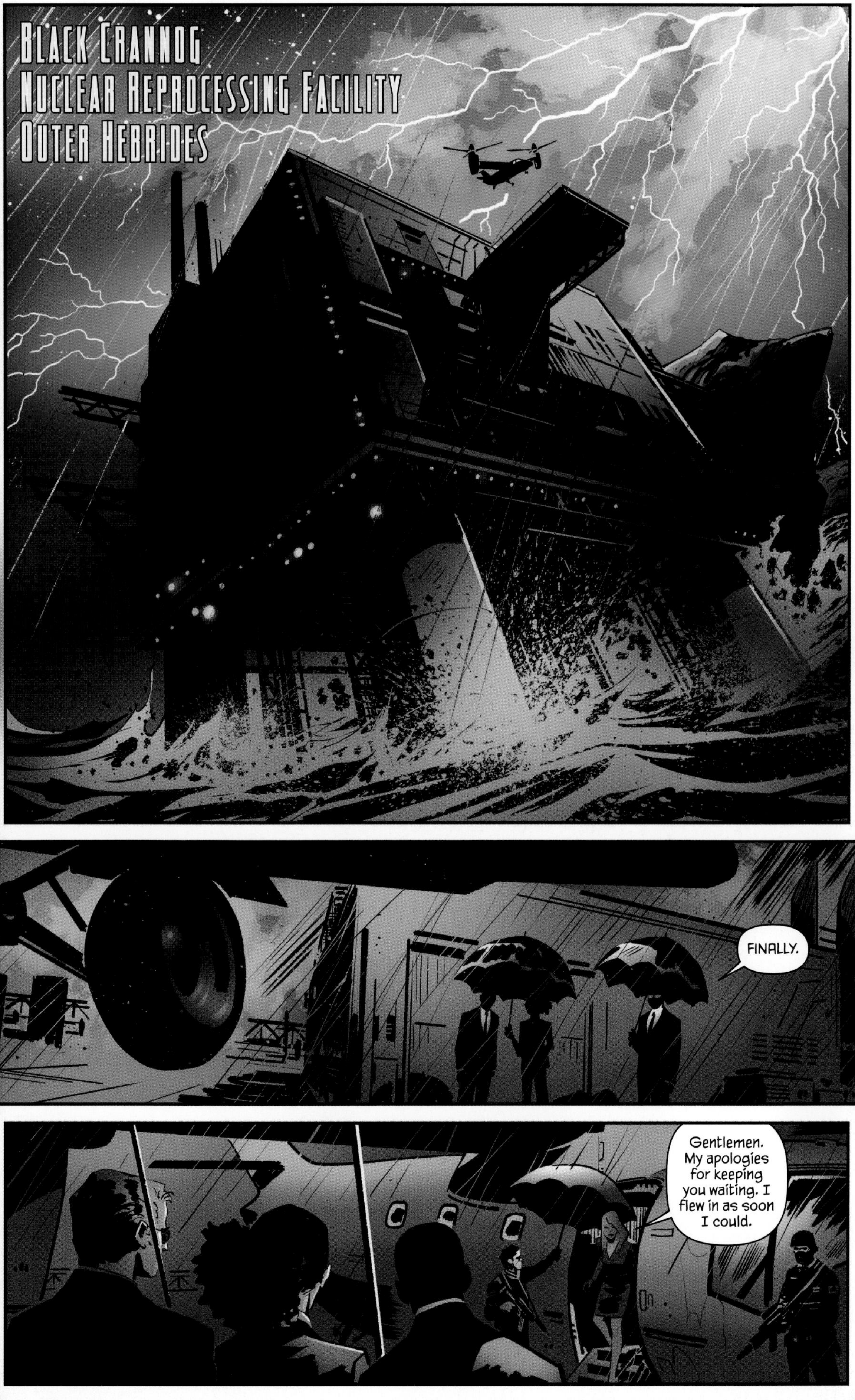
BLACK CRANNOG
NUCLEAR REPROCESSING FACILITY
OUTER HEBRIDES
FINALLY.
Gentlemen. My apologies for keeping you waiting. I flew in as soon I could.

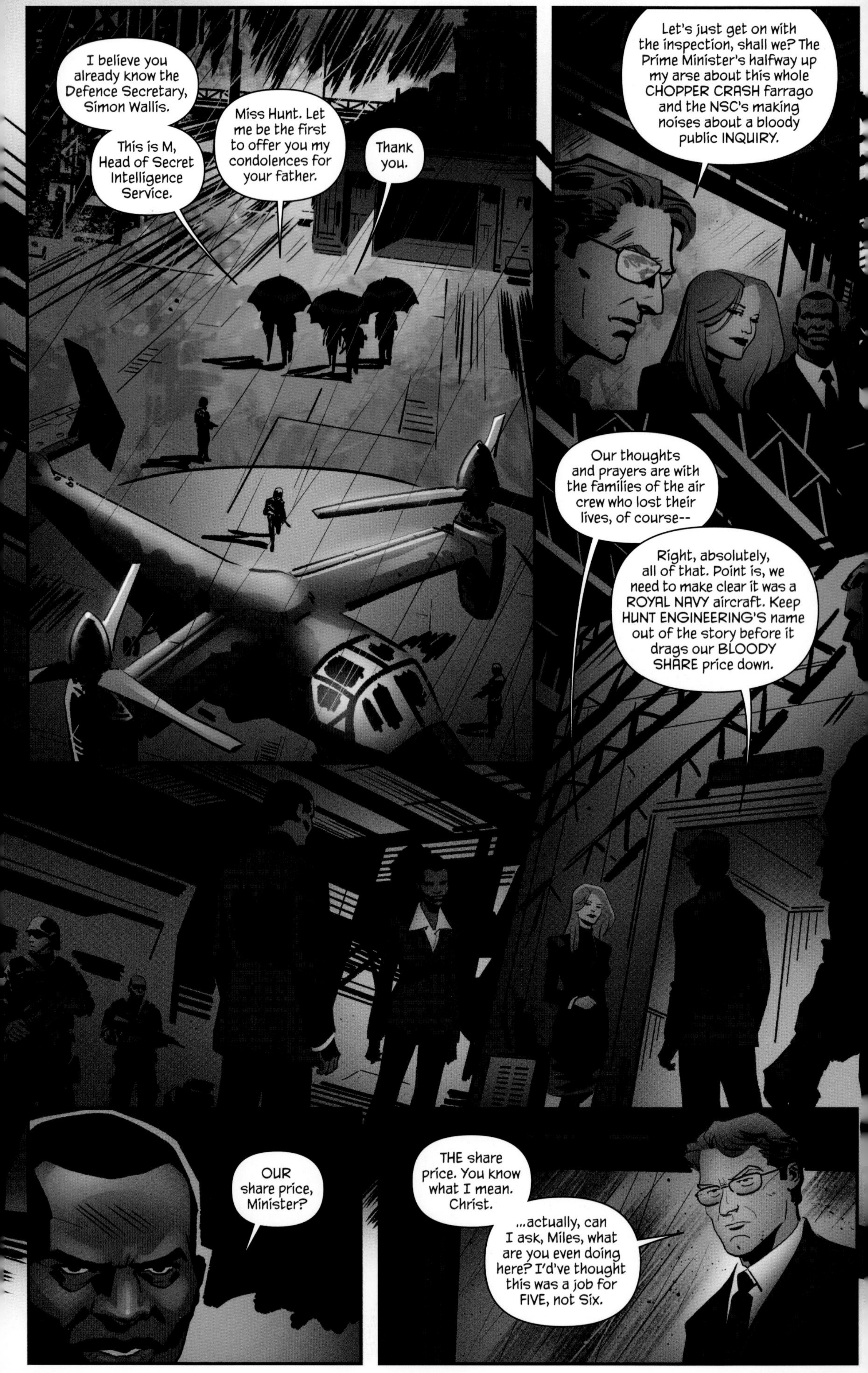
I believe you already know the Defence Secretary, Simon Wallis.
This is M, Head of Secret Intelligence Service.
Miss Hunt. Let me be the first to offer you my condolences for your father.
Thank you.
Let's just get on with the inspection, shall we? The Prime Minister's halfway up my arse about this whole CHOPPER CRASH farrago and the NSC's making noises about a bloody public INQUIRY.
Our thoughts and prayers are with the families of the air crew who lost their lives, of course--
Right, absolutely, all of that. Point is, we need to make clear it was a ROYAL NAVY aircraft. Keep HUNT ENGINEERING'S name out of the story before it drags our BLOODY SHARE price down.
OUR share price, Minister?
THE share price. You know what I mean. Christ.
...actually, can I ask, Miles, what are you even doing here? I'd've thought this was a job for FIVE, not Six.

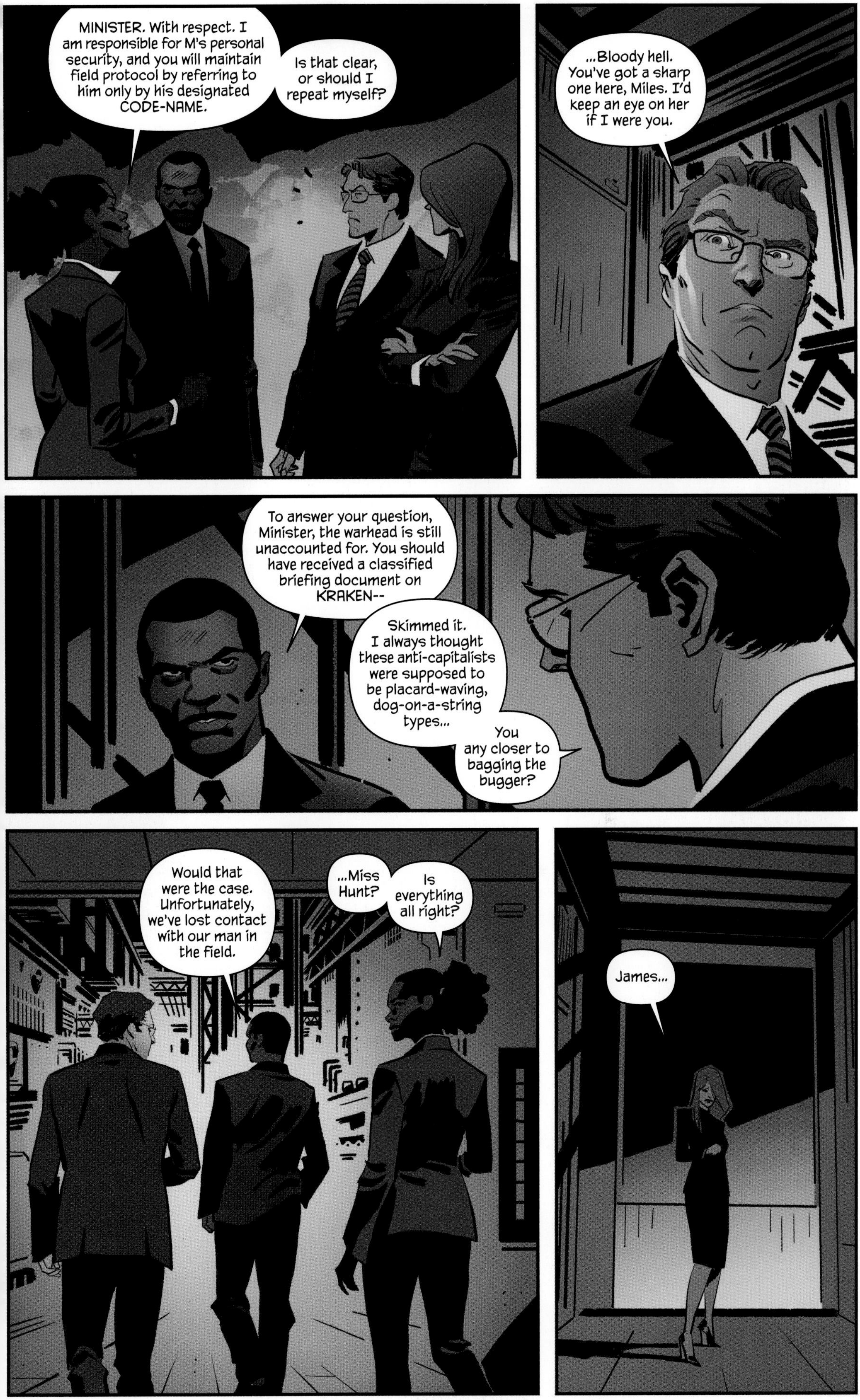
MINISTER. With respect. I am responsible for M's personal security, and you will maintain field protocol by referring to him only by his designated CODE-NAME.
Is that clear, or should I repeat myself?
...Bloody hell. You've got a sharp one here, Miles. I'd keep an eye on her if I were you.
To answer your question, Minister, the warhead is still unaccounted for. You should have received a classified briefing document on KRAKEN--
Skimmed it. I always thought these anti-capitalists were supposed to be placard-waving, dog-on-a-string types...
You any closer to bagging the bugger?
Would that were the case. Unfortunately, we've lost contact with our man in the field.
...Miss Hunt?
Is everything all right?
James...

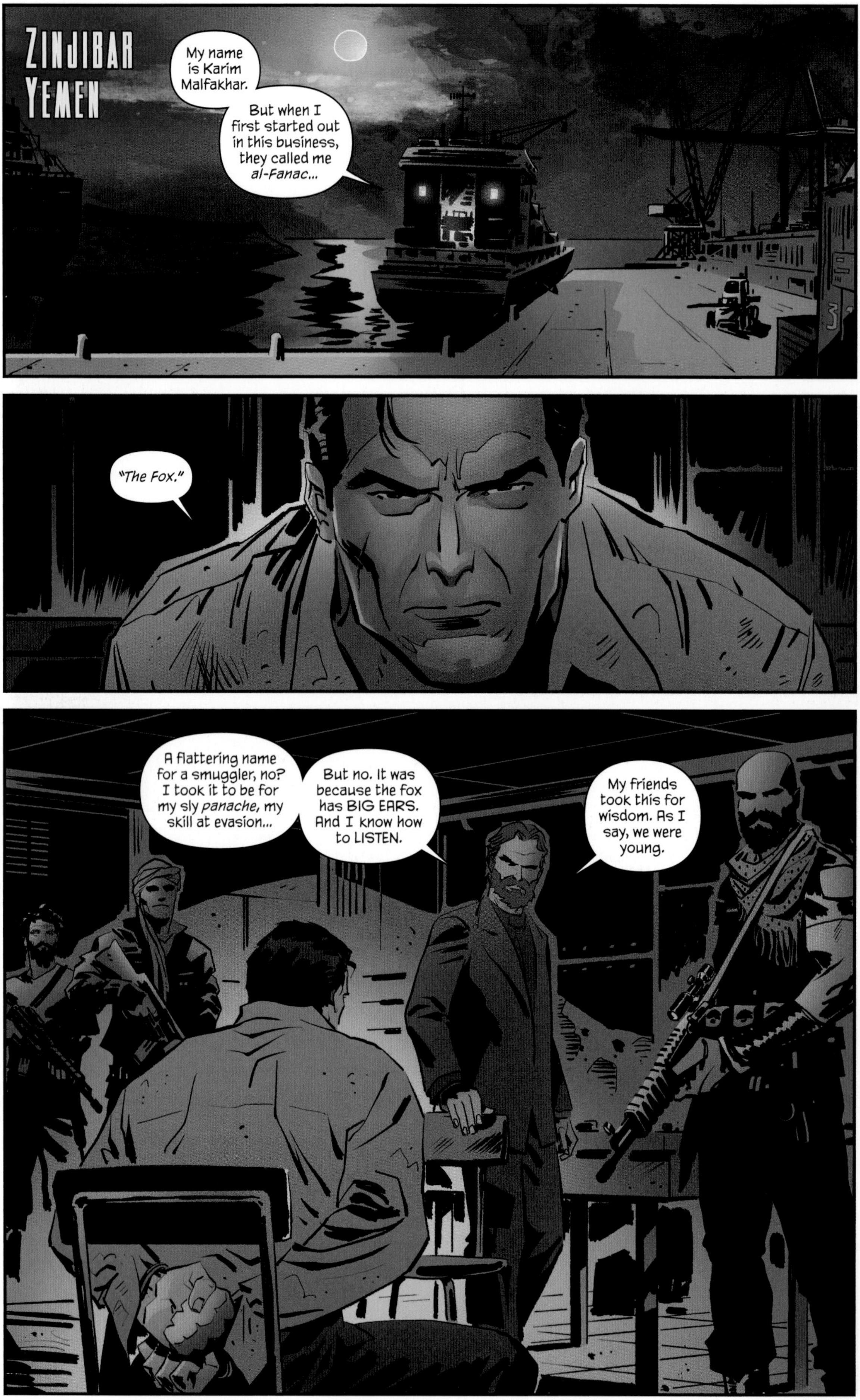
Zinjibar Yemen
My name is Karim Malfakhar.
But when I first started out in this business, they called me *al-Fanac*...
"The Fox."
A flattering name for a smuggler, no? I took it to be for my sly *panache*, my skill at evasion...
But no. It was because the fox has BIG EARS. And I know how to LISTEN.
My friends took this for wisdom. As I say, we were young.

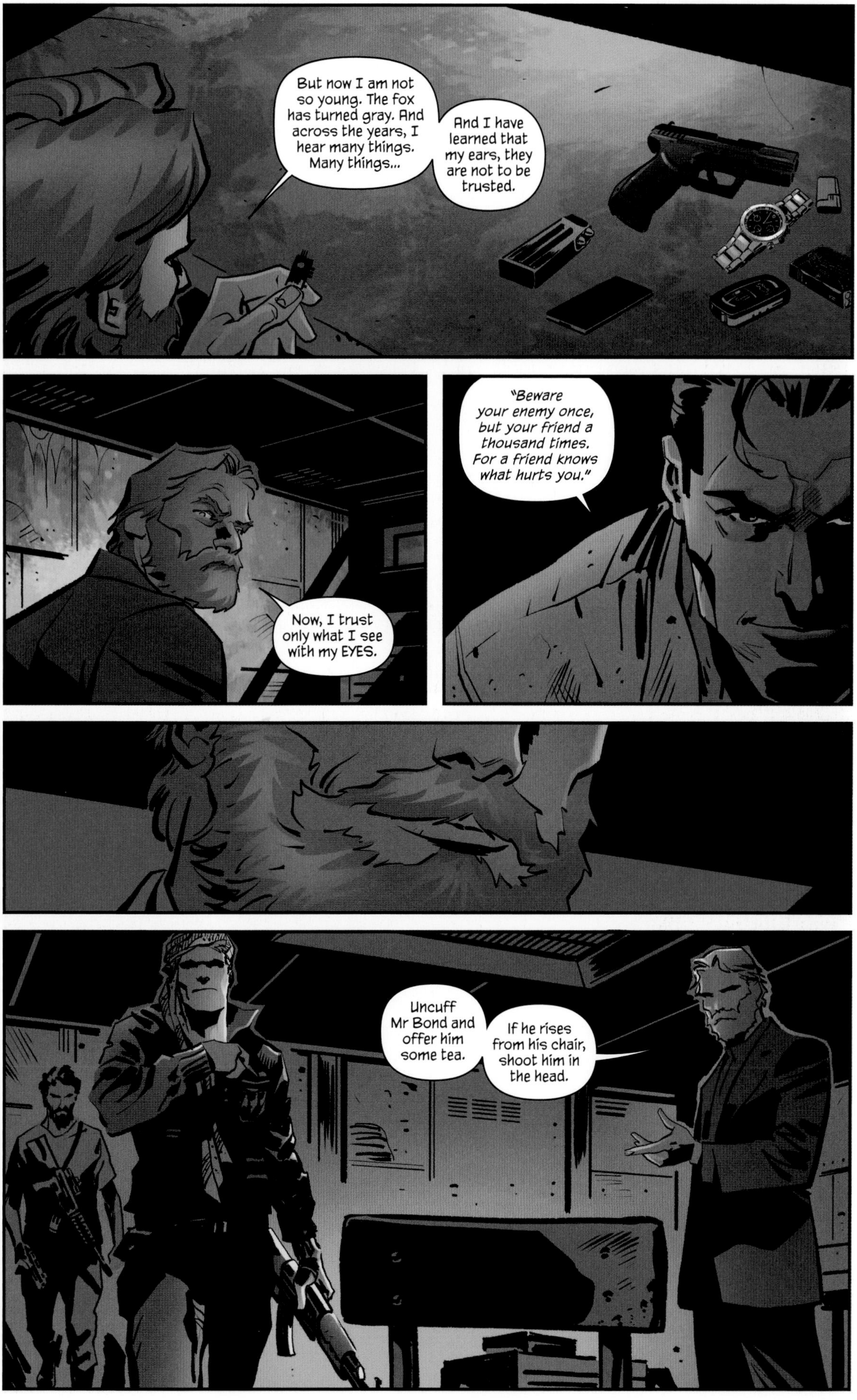
But now I am not so young. The fox has turned gray. And across the years, I hear many things. Many things...
And I have learned that my ears, they are not to be trusted.
Now, I trust only what I see with my EYES.
"Beware your enemy once, but your friend a thousand times. For a friend knows what hurts you."
Uncuff Mr Bond and offer him some tea.
If he rises from his chair, shoot him in the head.

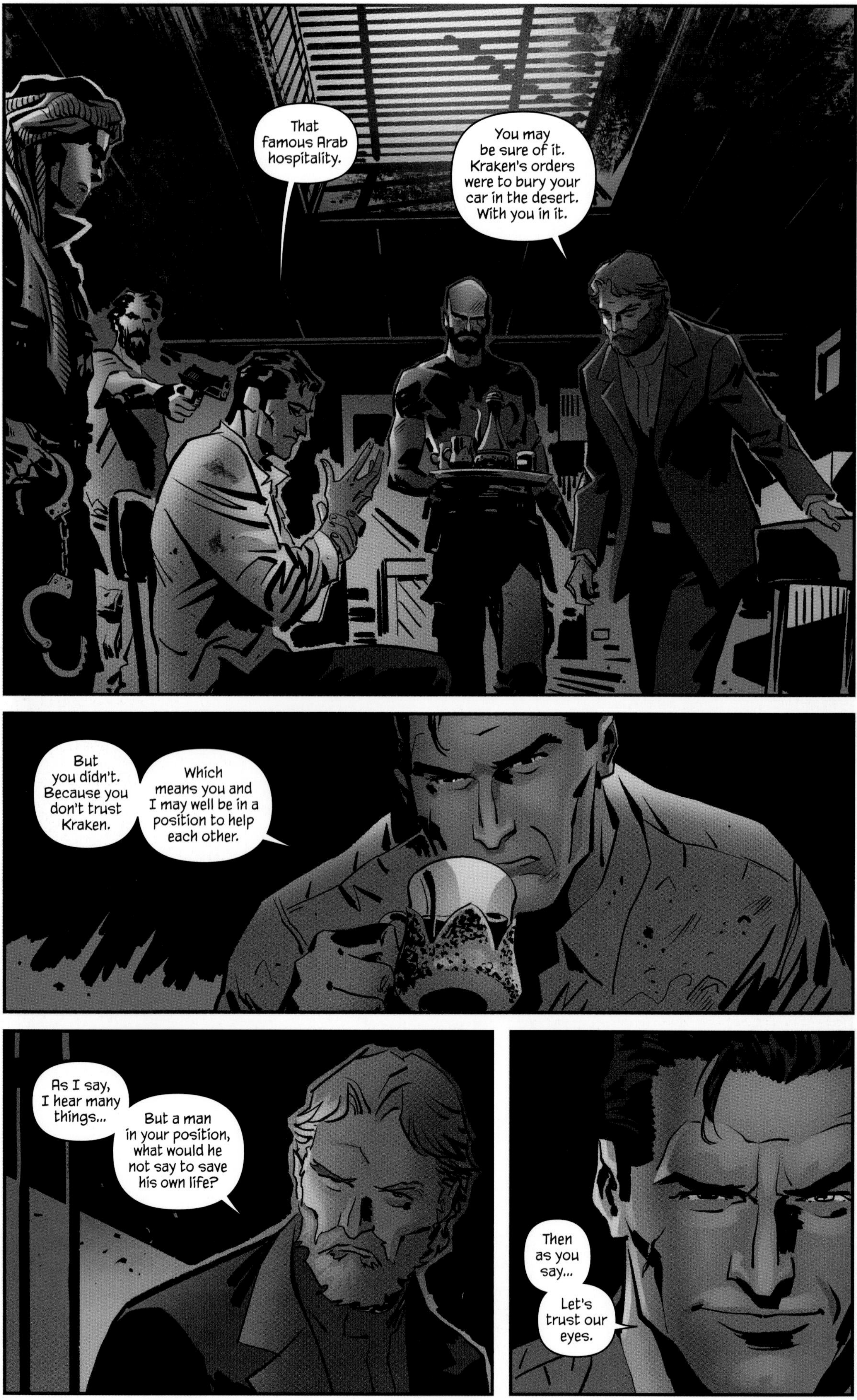
That famous Arab hospitality.
You may be sure of it. Kraken's orders were to bury your car in the desert. With you in it.
But you didn't. Because you don't trust Kraken.
Which means you and I may well be in a position to help each other.
As I say, I hear many things...
But a man in your position, what would he not say to save his own life?
Then as you say...
Let's trust our eyes.

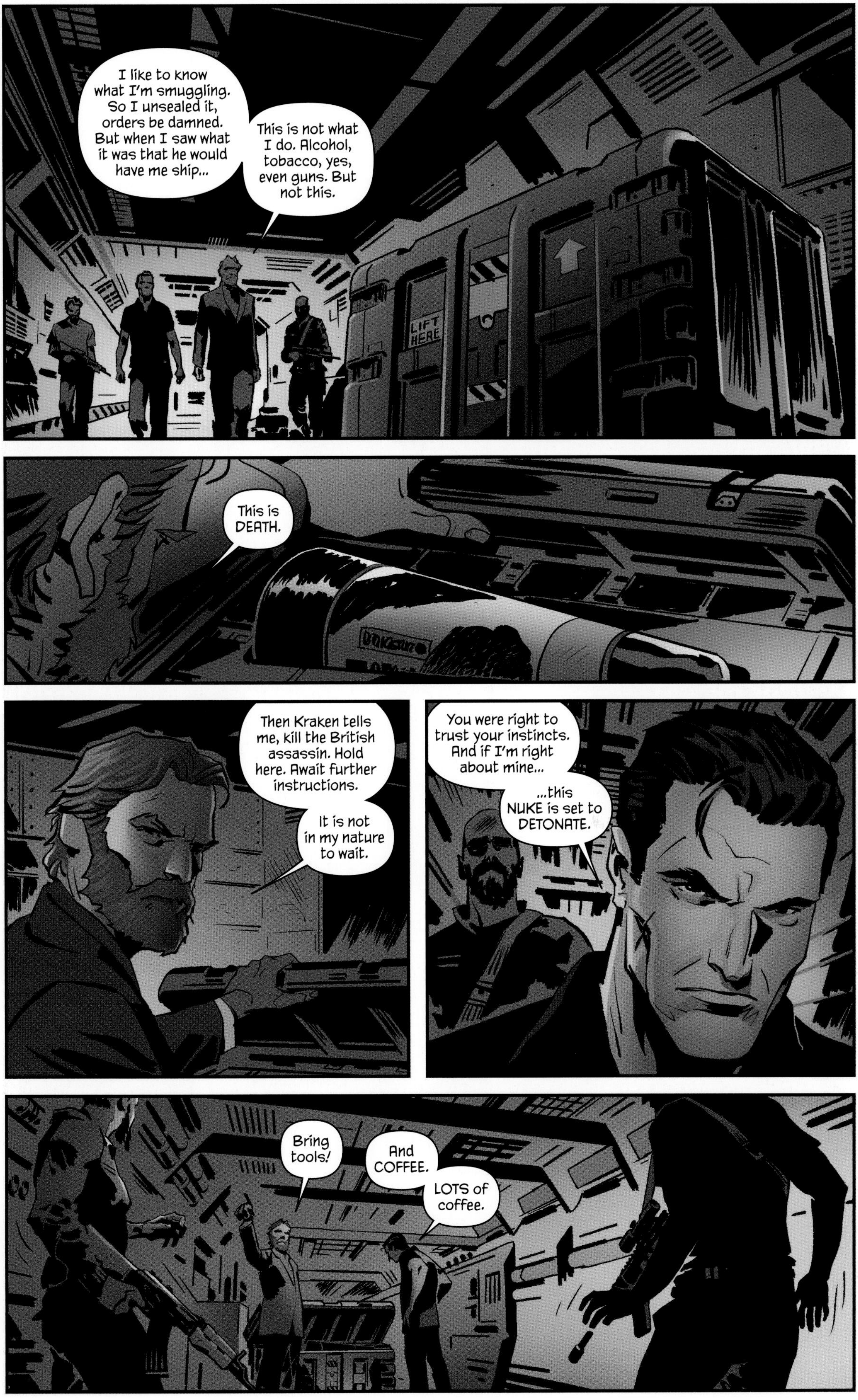
I like to know what I'm smuggling. So I unsealed it, orders be damned. But when I saw what it was that he would have me ship...
This is not what I do. Alcohol, tobacco, yes, even guns. But not this.
LIFT HERE
This is DEATH.
Then Kraken tells me, kill the British assassin. Hold here. Await further instructions.
It is not in my nature to wait.
You were right to trust your instincts. And if I'm right about mine...
...this NUKE is set to DETONATE.
Bring tools!
And COFFEE.
LOTS of coffee.

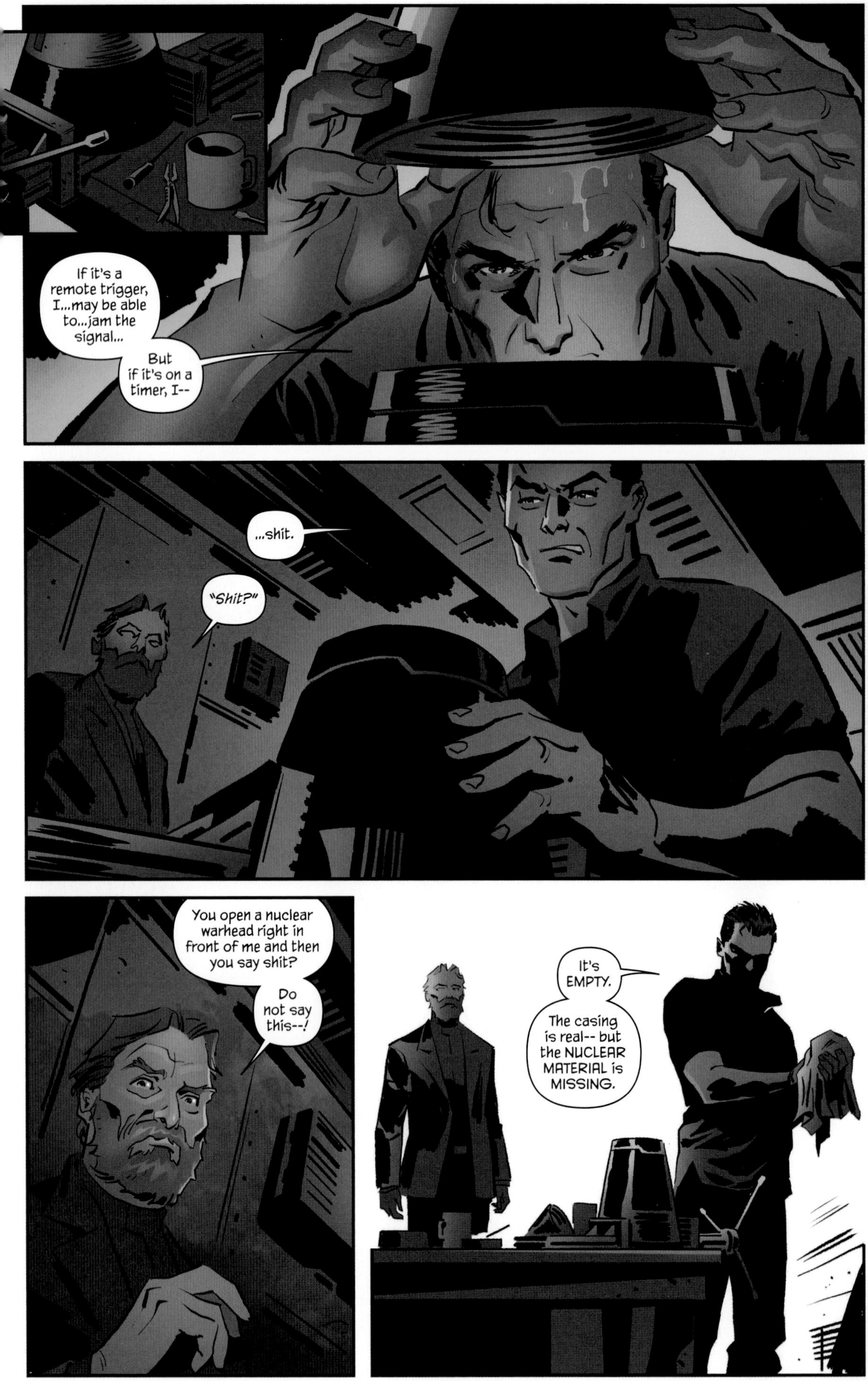
If it's a remote trigger, I...may be able to...jam the signal...
But if it's on a timer, I--
...shit.
"Shit?"
You open a nuclear warhead right in front of me and then you say shit?
Do not say this--!
It's EMPTY.
The casing is real-- but the NUCLEAR MATERIAL is MISSING.

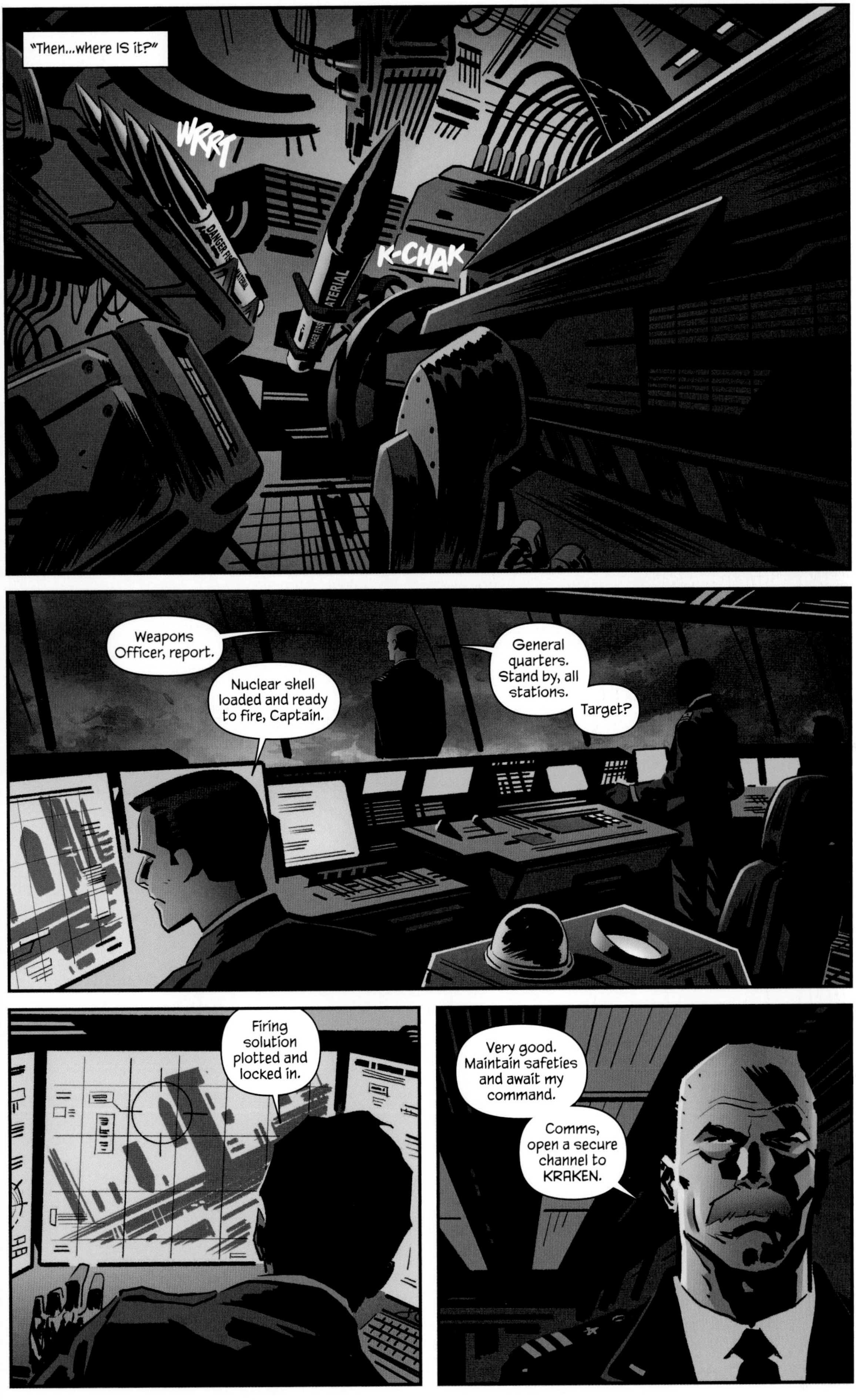
"Then...where IS it?"
WRRT
K-CHAK
Weapons Officer, report.
Nuclear shell loaded and ready to fire, Captain.
General quarters. Stand by, all stations.
Target?
Firing solution plotted and locked in.
Very good. Maintain safeties and await my command.
Comms, open a secure channel to KRAKEN.

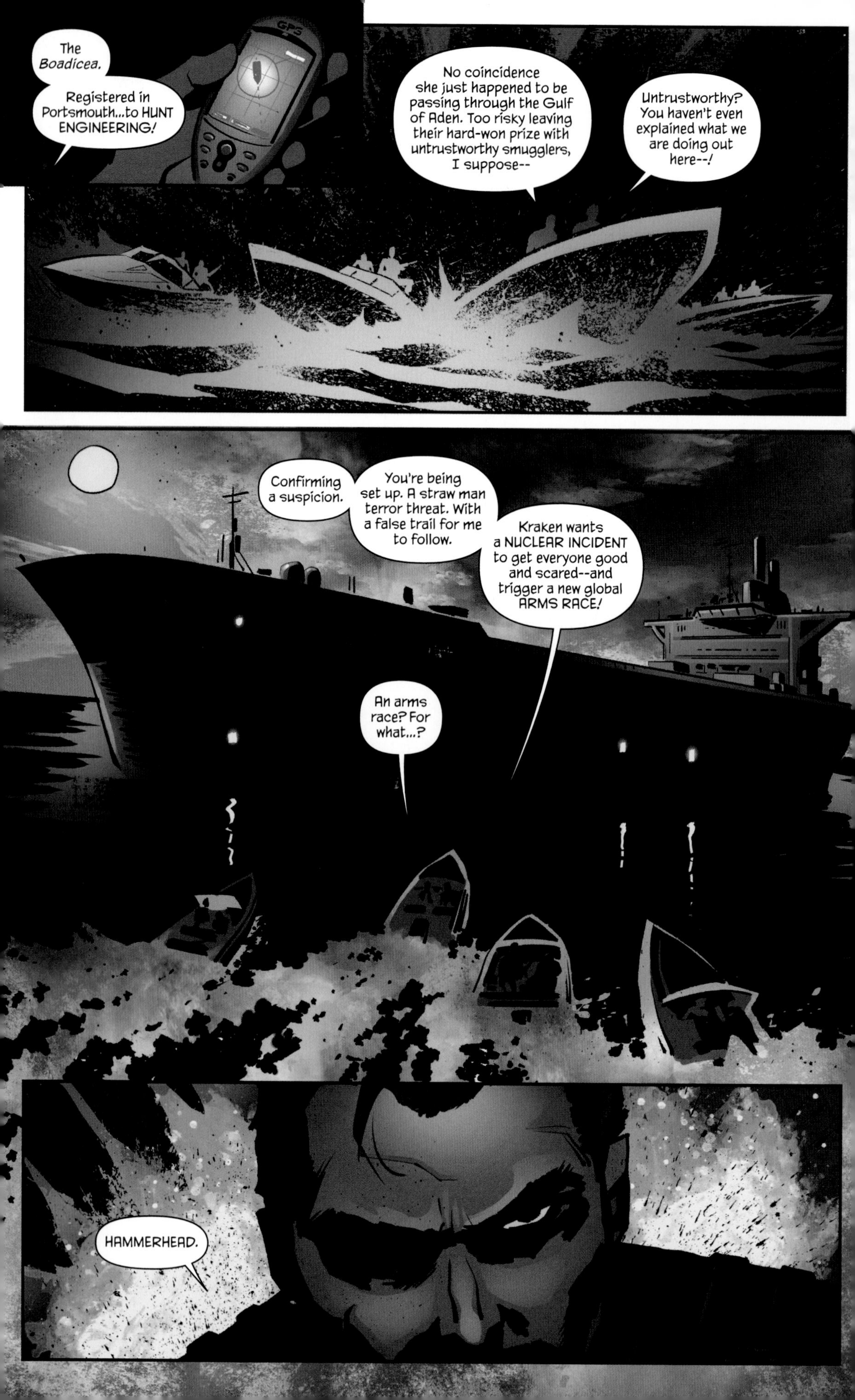

The *Boadicea.*
Registered in Portsmouth...to HUNT ENGINEERING!
No coincidence she just happened to be passing through the Gulf of Aden. Too risky leaving their hard-won prize with untrustworthy smugglers, I suppose--
Untrustworthy? You haven't even explained what we are doing out here--!
Confirming a suspicion.
You're being set up. A straw man terror threat. With a false trail for me to follow.
Kraken wants a NUCLEAR INCIDENT to get everyone good and scared--and trigger a new global ARMS RACE!
An arms race? For what...?
HAMMERHEAD.

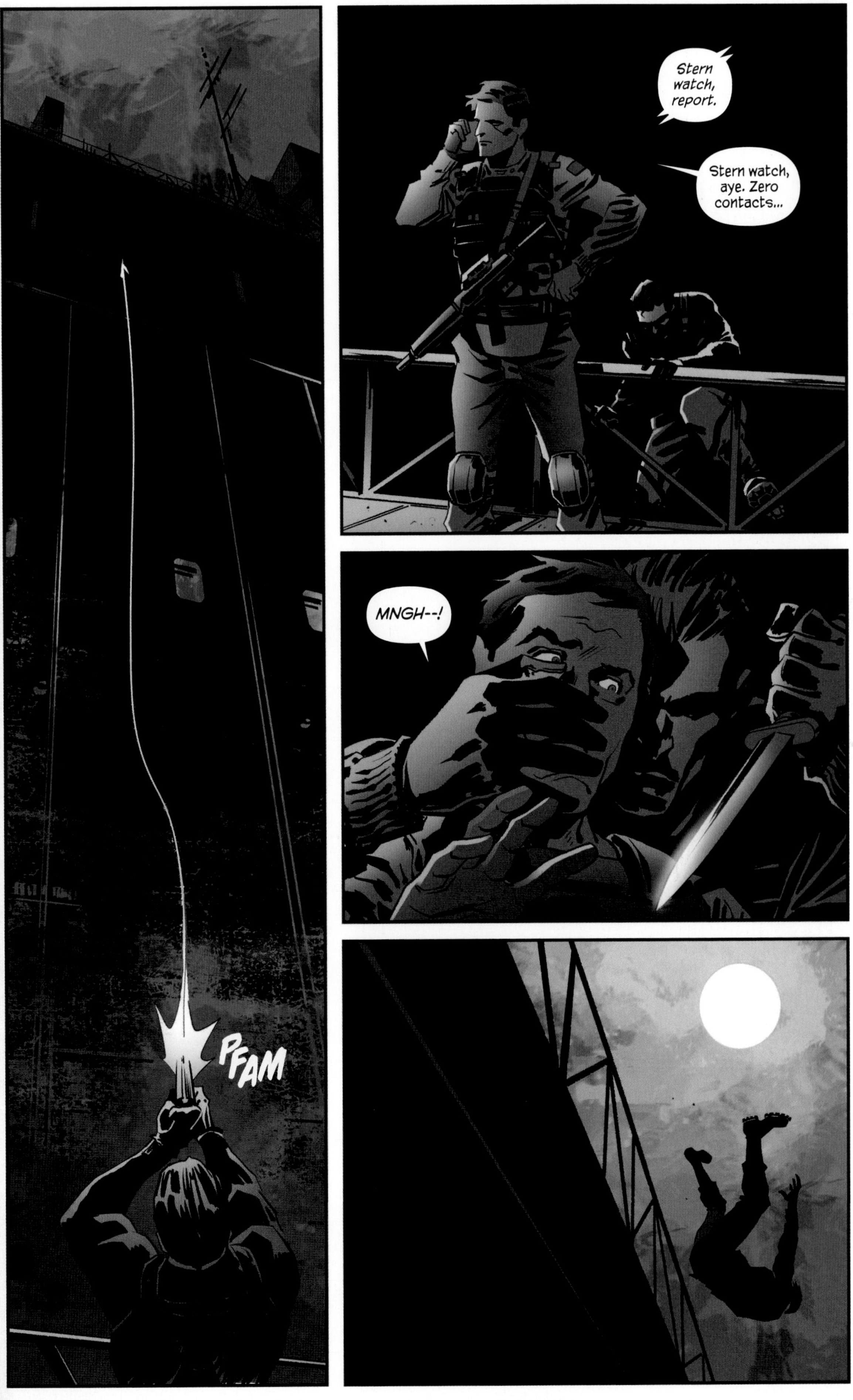
PFAM
Stern watch, report.
Stern watch, aye. Zero contacts...
MNGH--!

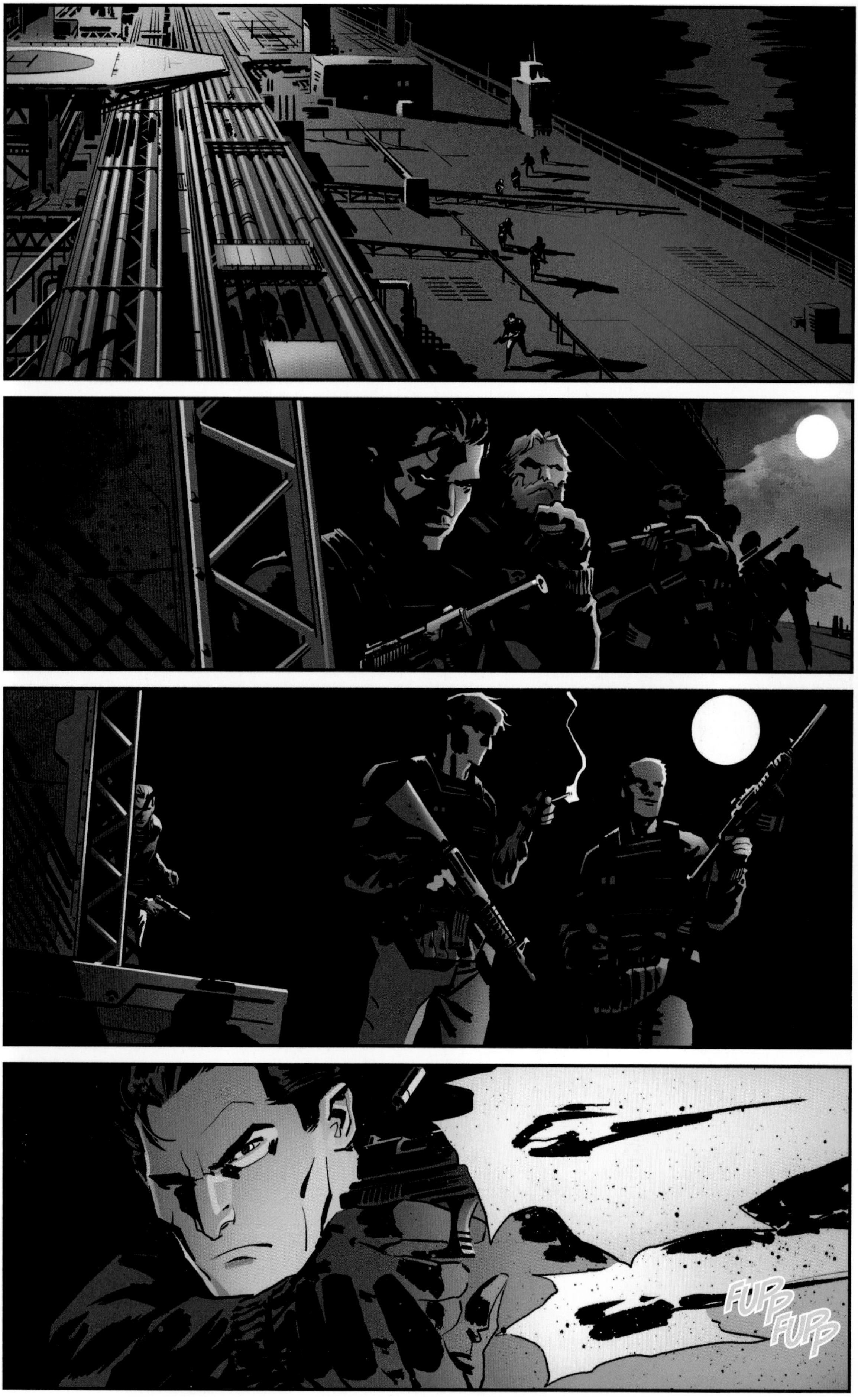
FUPP
FUPP

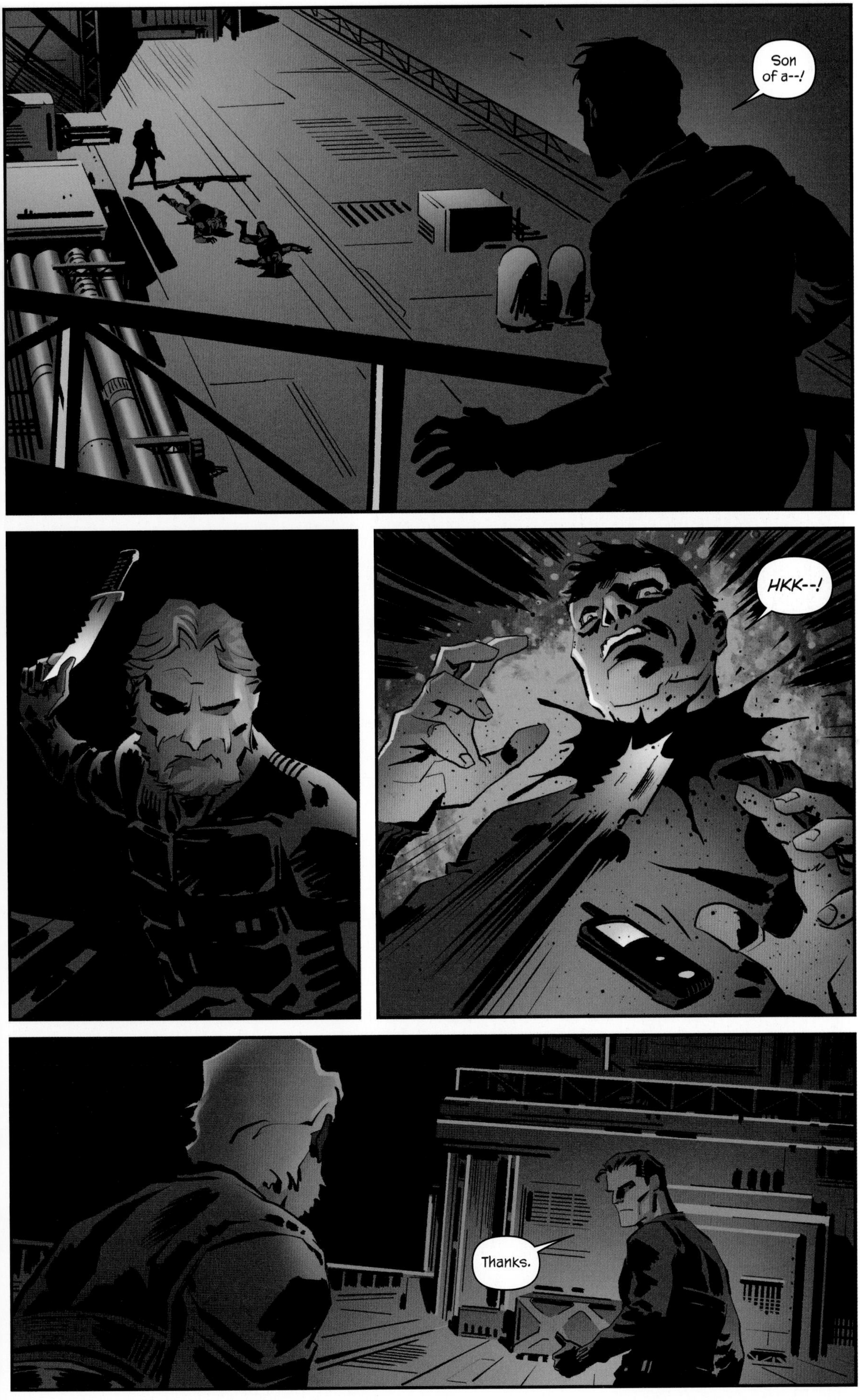
Son of a--!
HKK--!
Thanks.

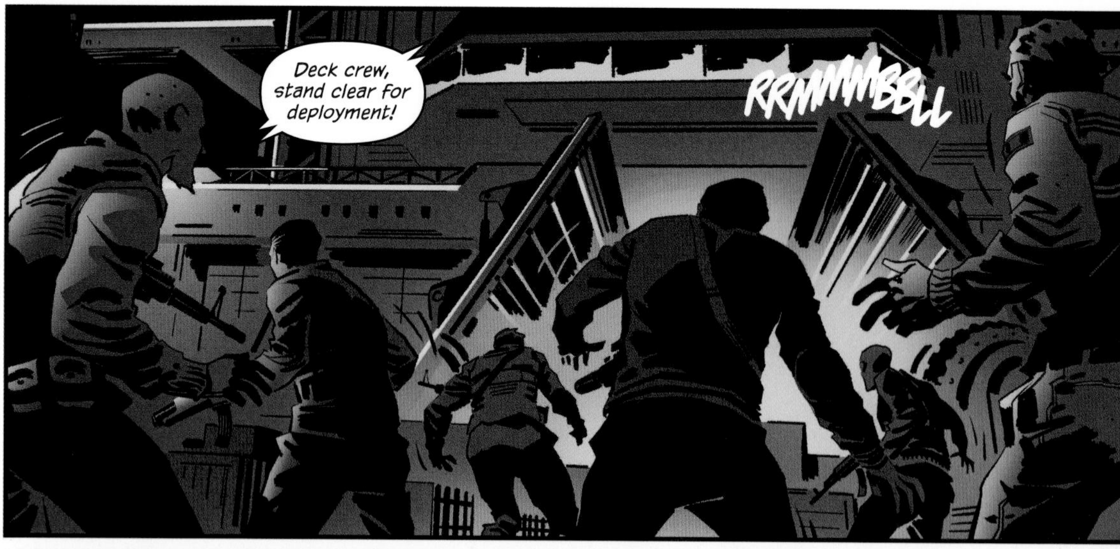
Deck crew, stand clear for deployment!
RRMMMBBLL

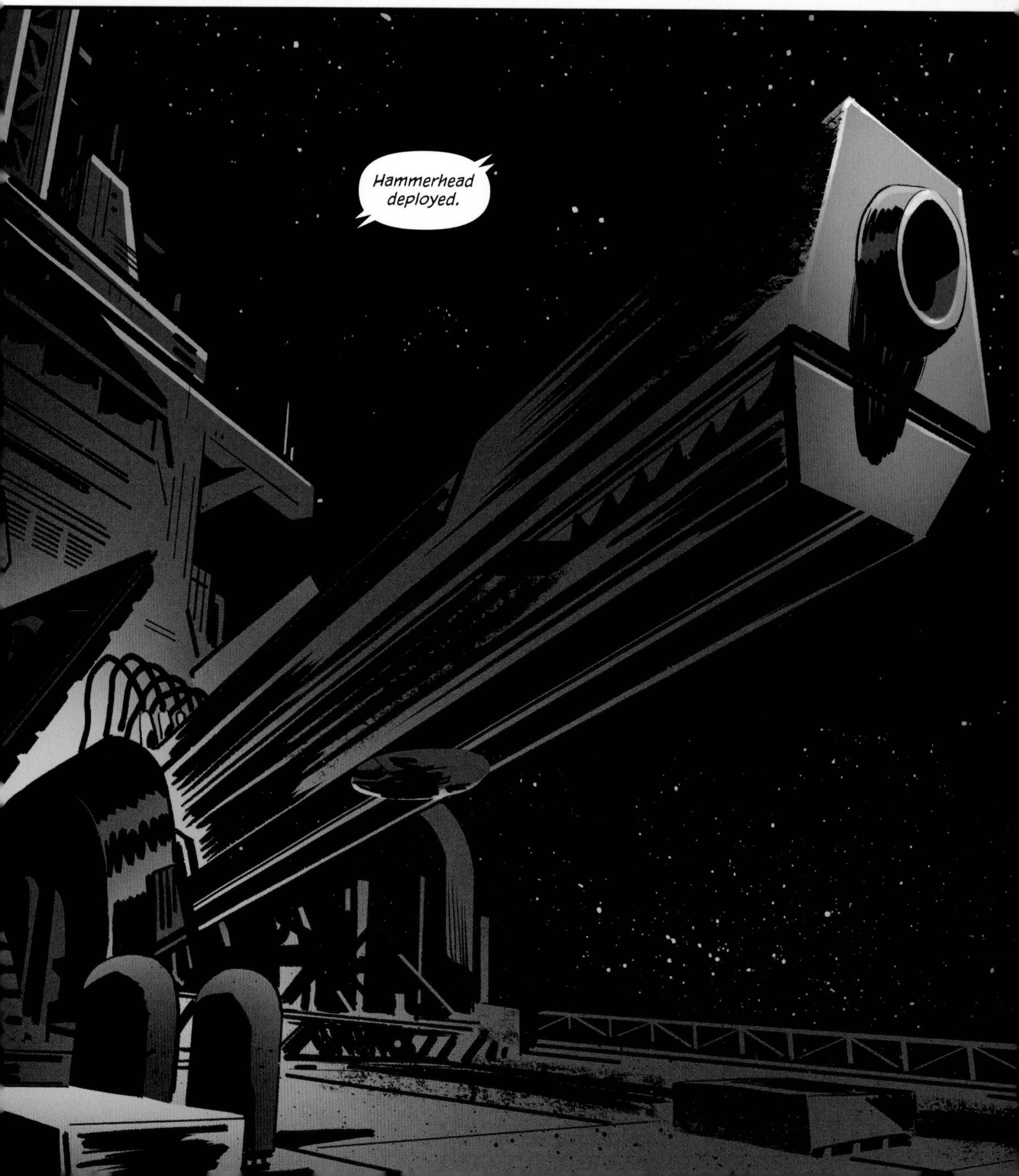
Hammerhead deployed.

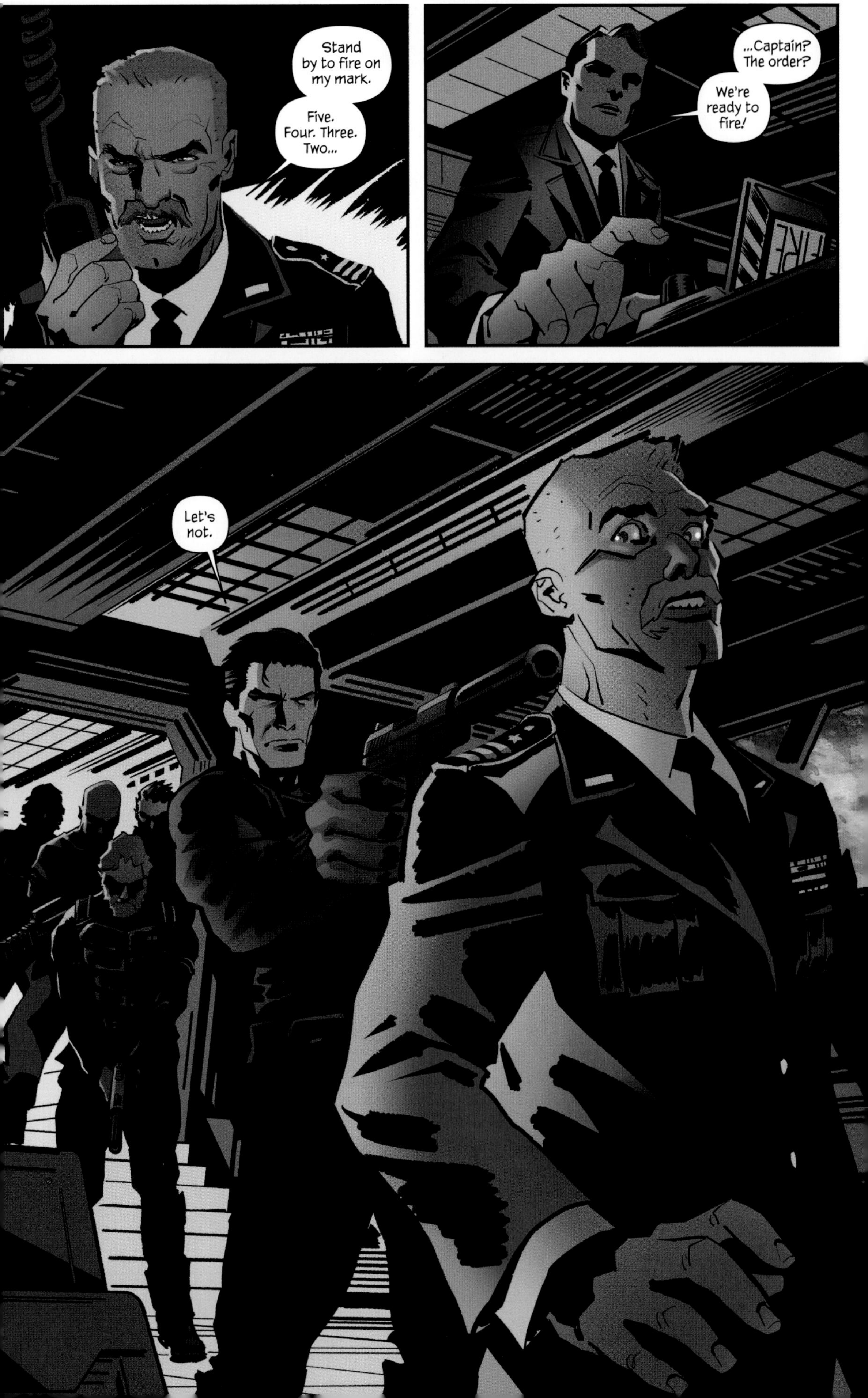
Stand by to fire on my mark.
Five. Four. Three. Two...
...Captain? The order?
We're ready to fire!
Let's not.

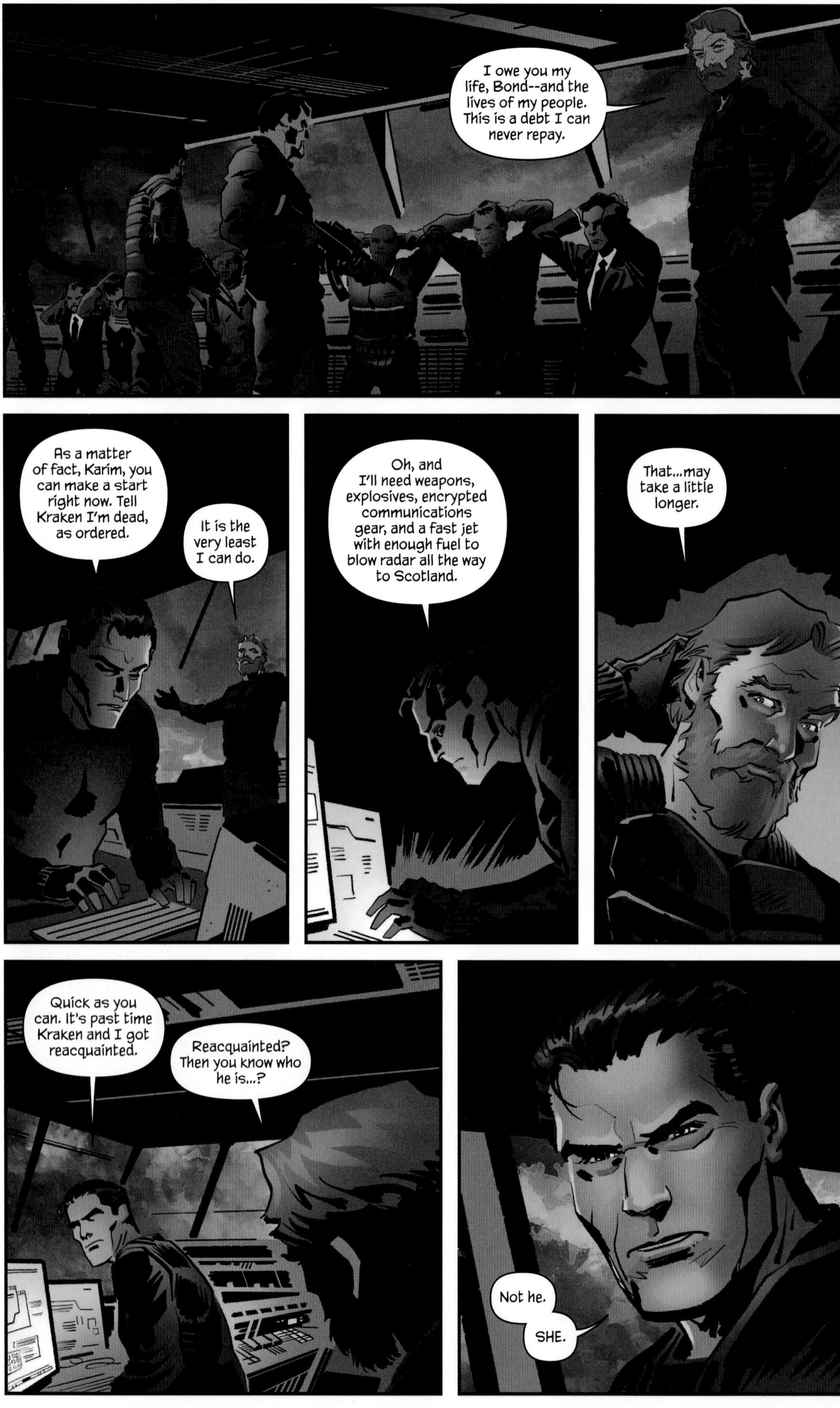
I owe you my life, Bond--and the lives of my people. This is a debt I can never repay.
As a matter of fact, Karim, you can make a start right now. Tell Kraken I'm dead, as ordered.
It is the very least I can do.
Oh, and I'll need weapons, explosives, encrypted communications gear, and a fast jet with enough fuel to blow radar all the way to Scotland.
That...may take a little longer.
Quick as you can. It's past time Kraken and I got reacquainted.
Reacquainted? Then you know who he is...?
Not he.
SHE.

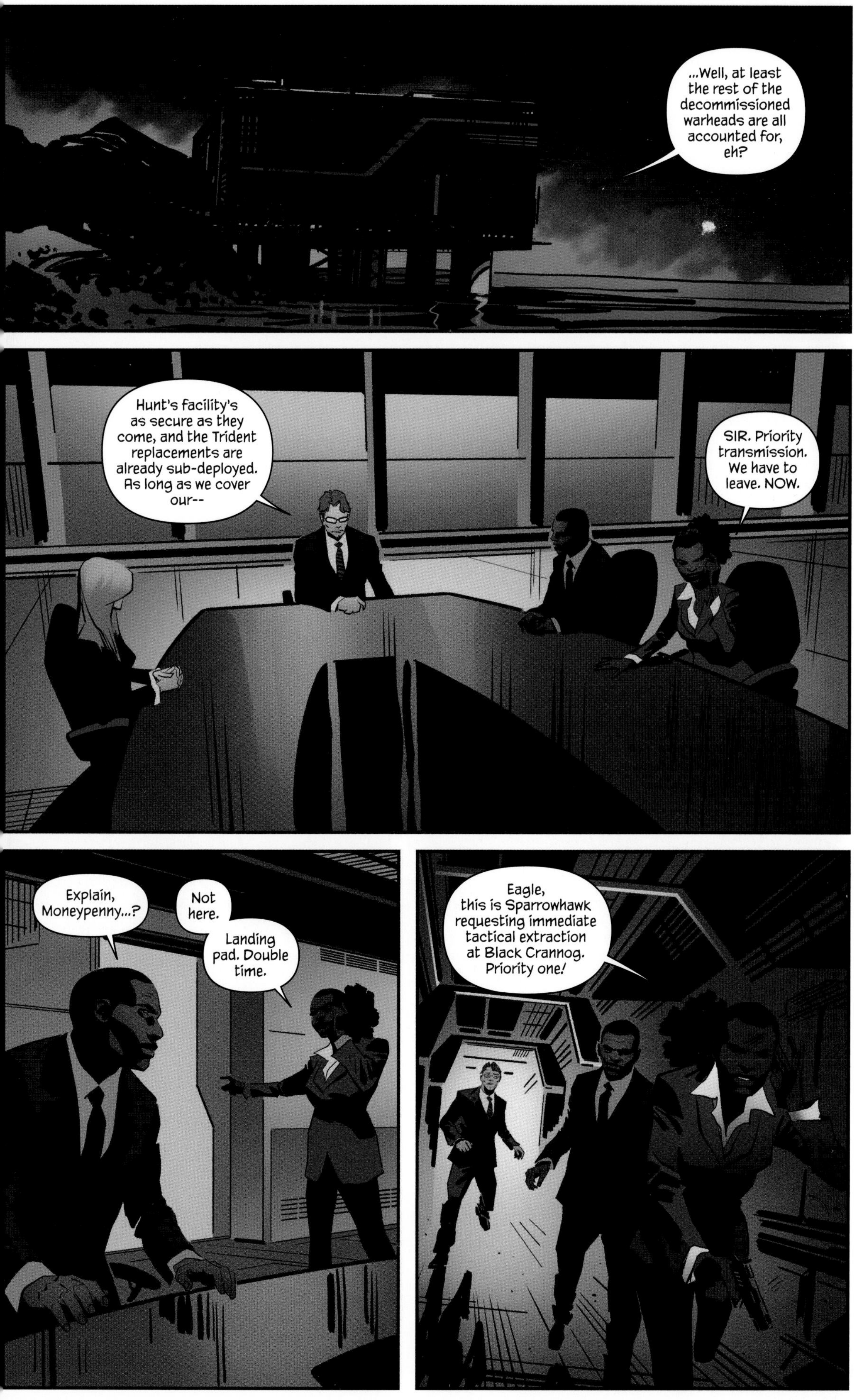
...Well, at least the rest of the decommissioned warheads are all accounted for, eh?
Hunt's facility's as secure as they come, and the Trident replacements are already sub-deployed. As long as we cover our--
SIR. Priority transmission. We have to leave. NOW.
Explain, Moneypenny...?
Not here.
Landing pad. Double time.
Eagle, this is Sparrowhawk requesting immediate tactical extraction at Black Crannog. Priority one!

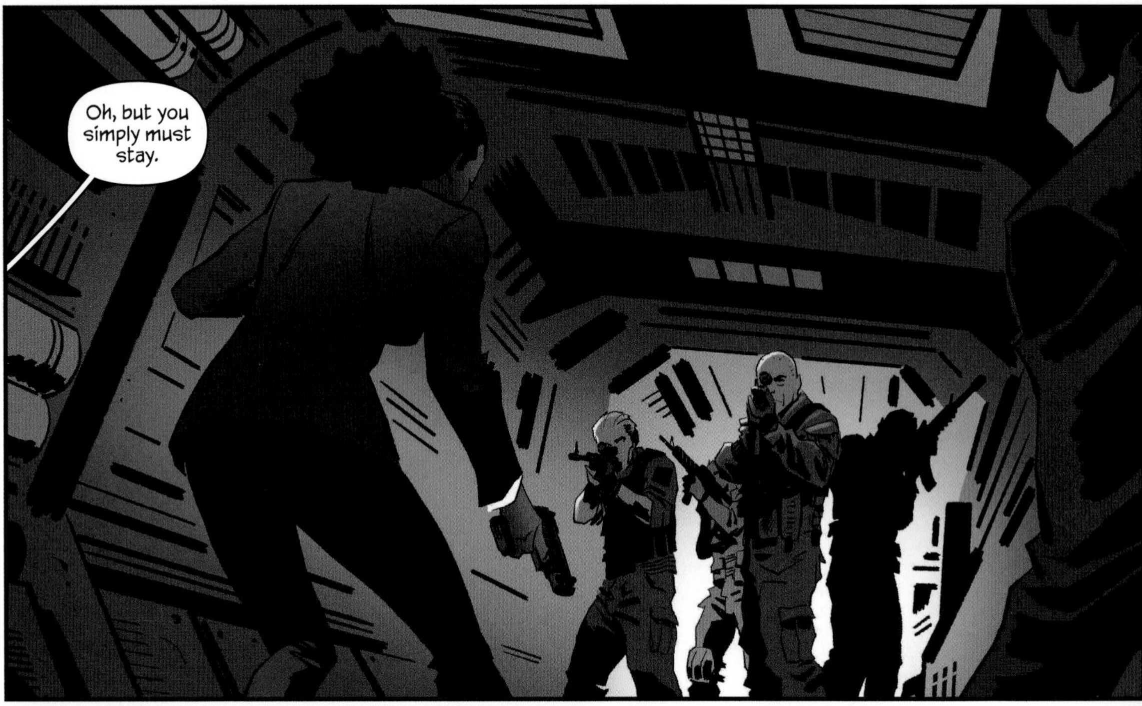
Oh, but you simply must stay.

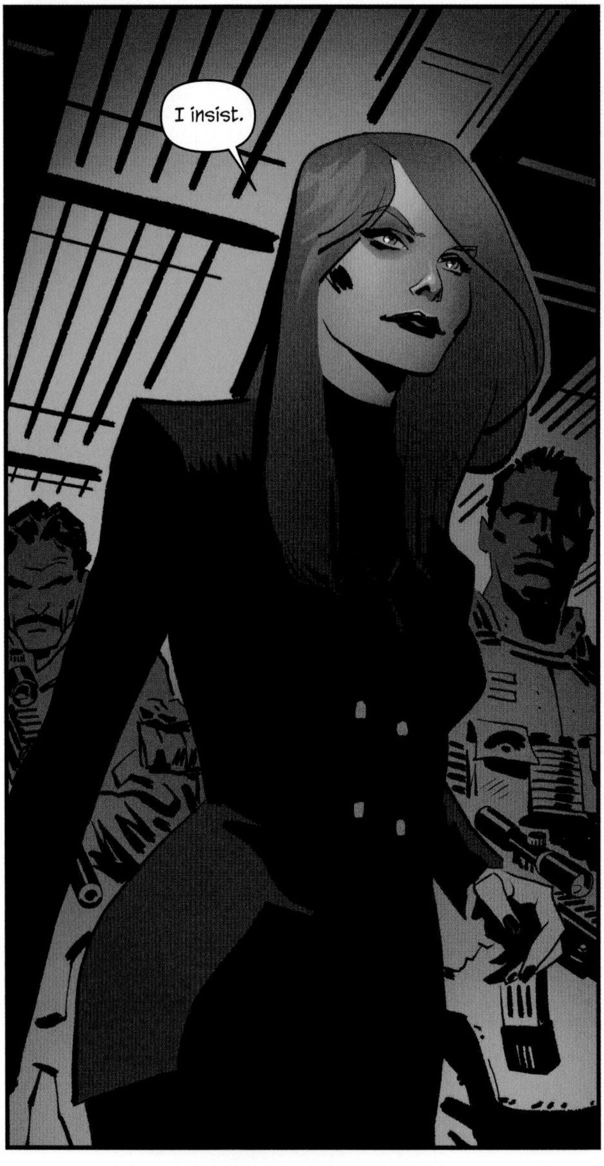
I insist.

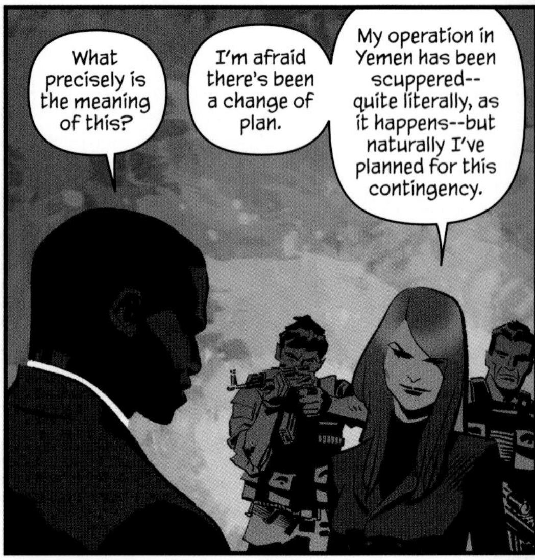
What precisely is the meaning of this?
I'm afraid there's been a change of plan.
My operation in Yemen has been scuppered--quite literally, as it happens--but naturally I've planned for this contingency.

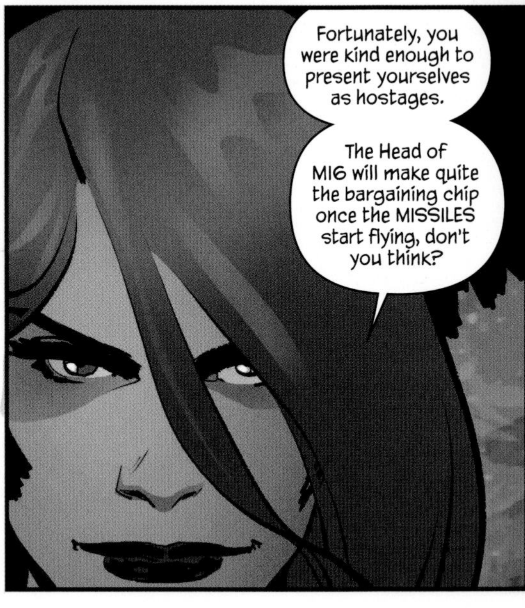
Fortunately, you were kind enough to present yourselves as hostages.
The Head of MI6 will make quite the bargaining chip once the MISSILES start flying, don't you think?

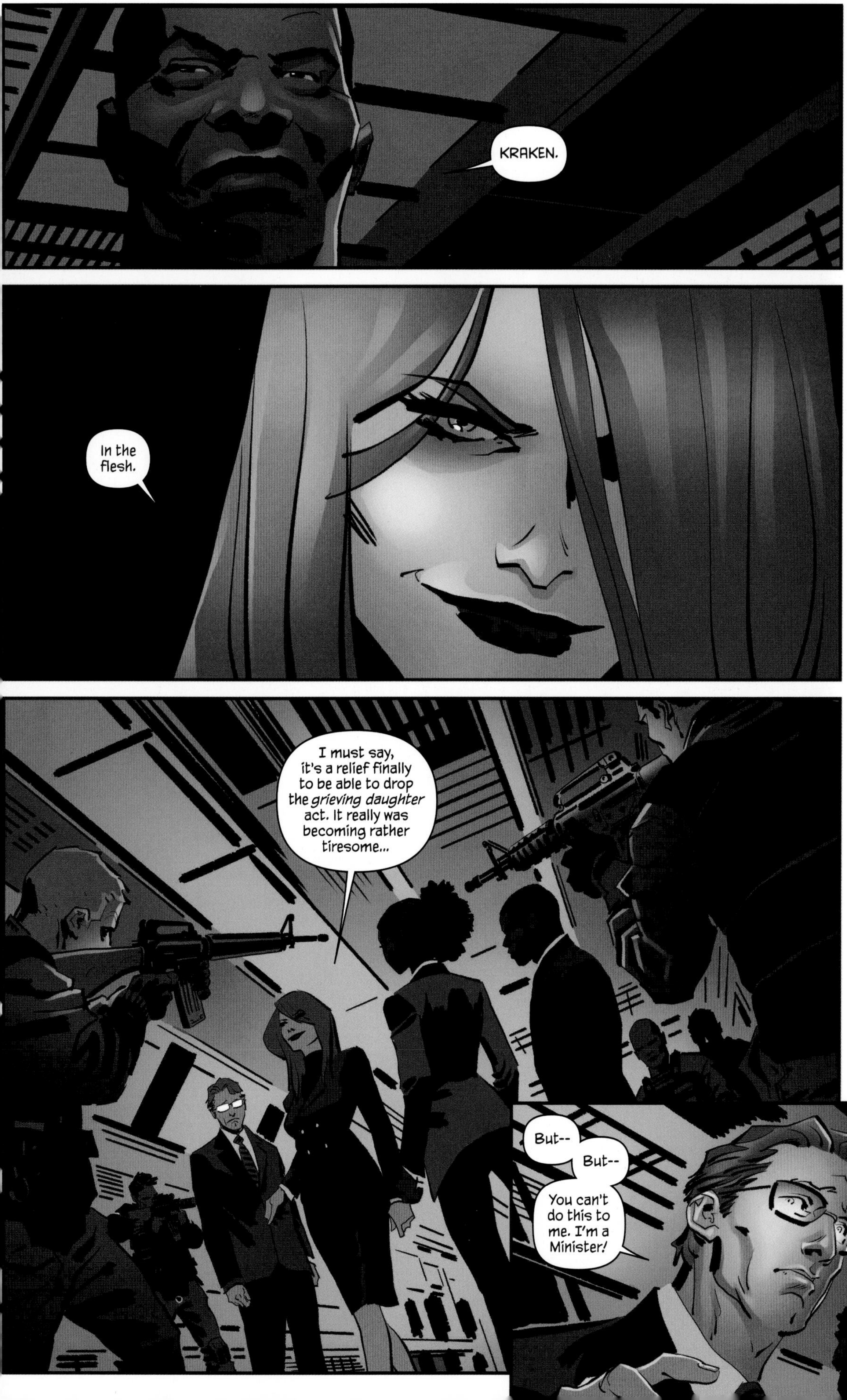
KRAKEN.
In the flesh.
I must say, it's a relief finally to be able to drop the *grieving daughter* act. It really was becoming rather tiresome...
But--
But--
You can't do this to me. I'm a Minister!

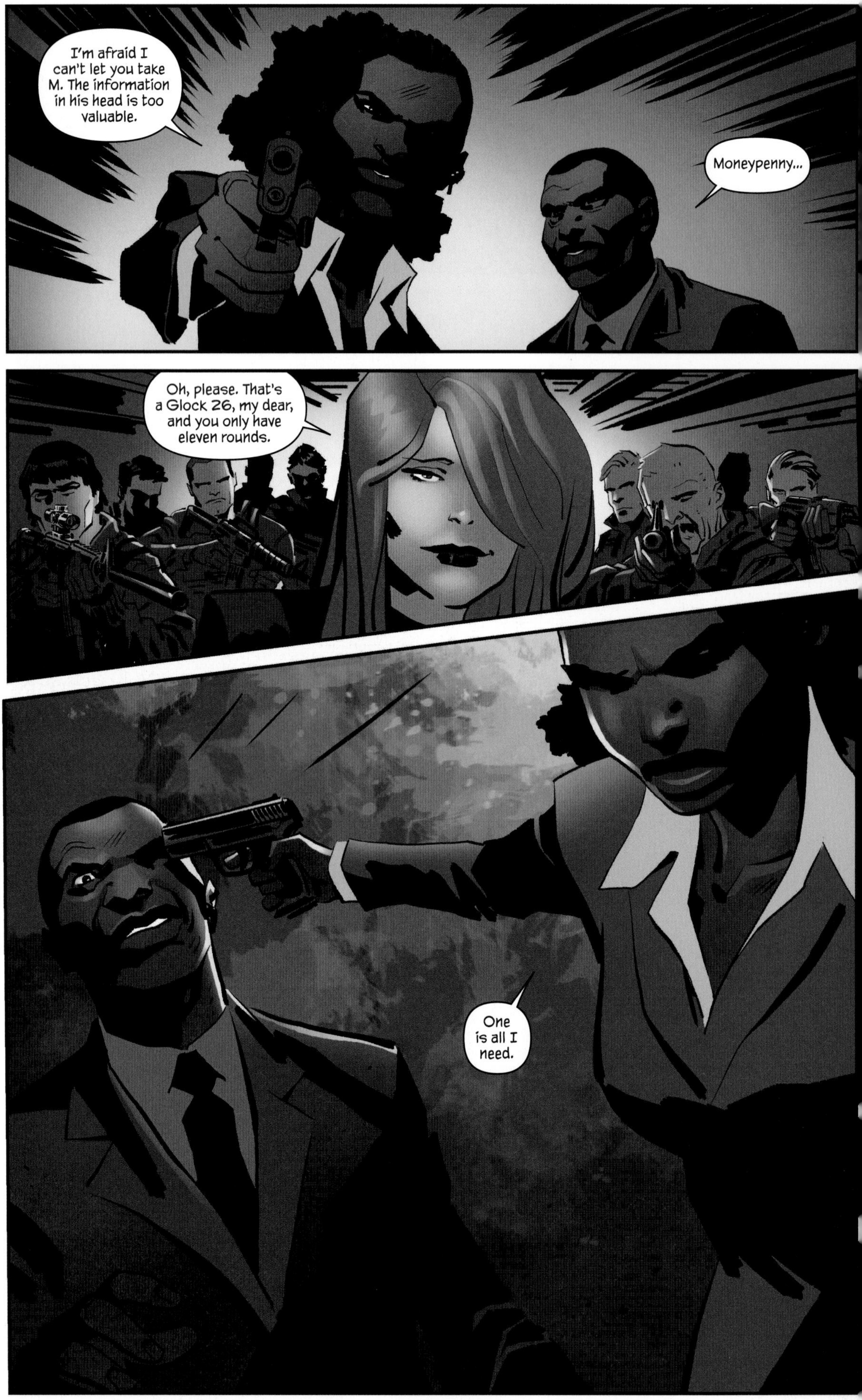
I'm afraid I can't let you take M. The information in his head is too valuable.
Moneypenny...
Oh, please. That's a Glock 26, my dear, and you only have eleven rounds.
One is all I need.

ISSUE 5

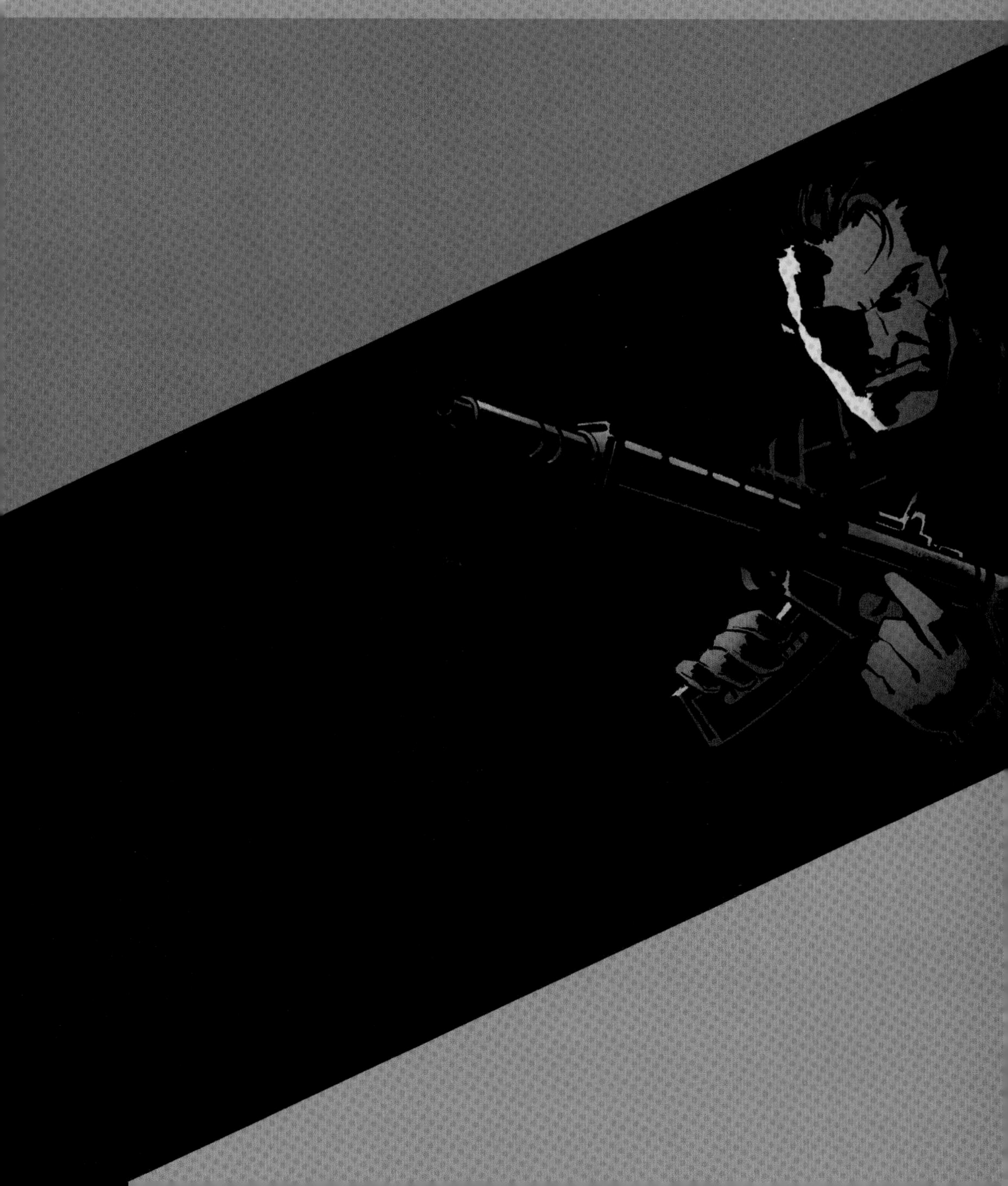

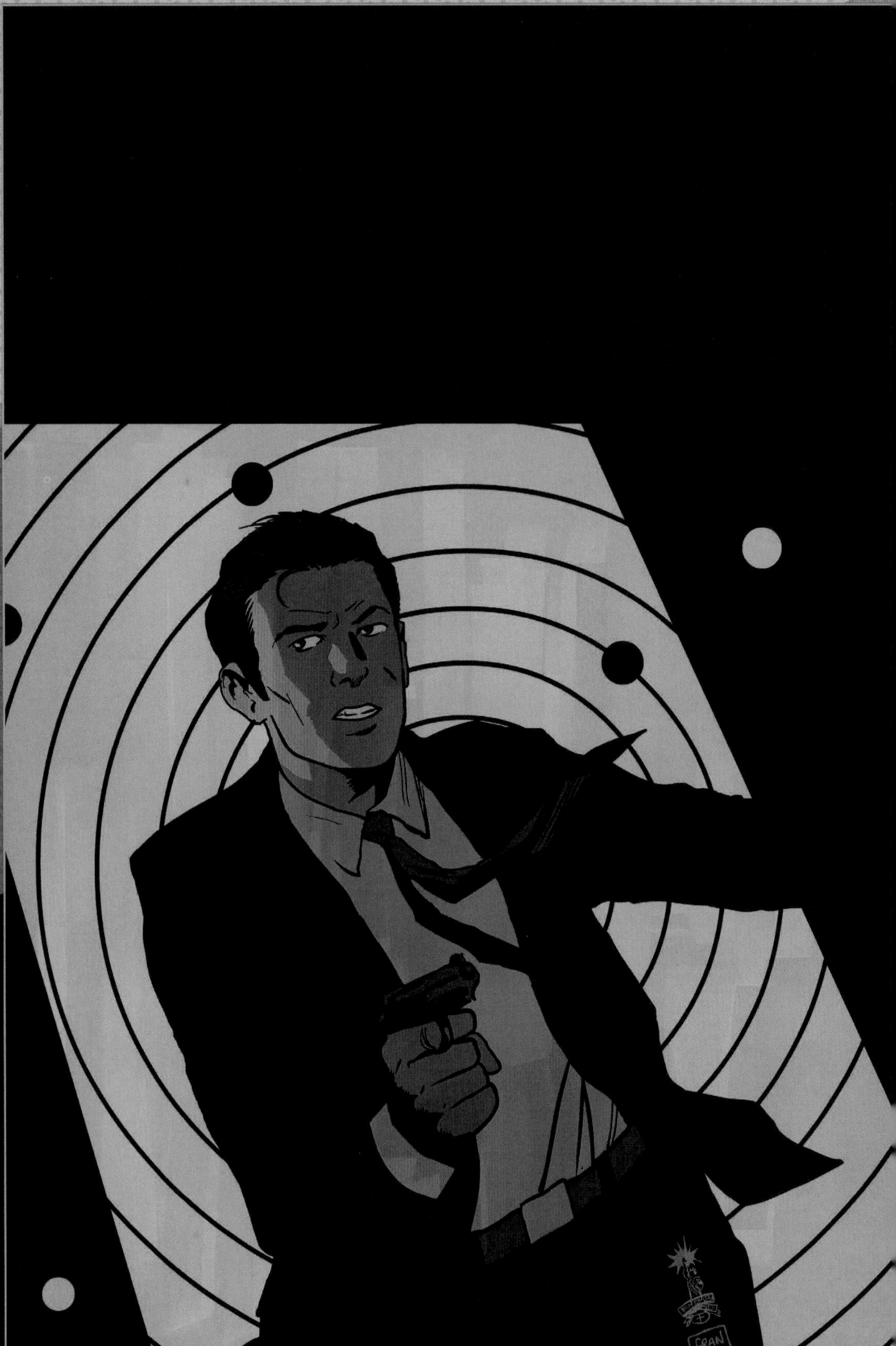

ISSUE 5 COVER
BY FRANCESCO FRANCAVILLA

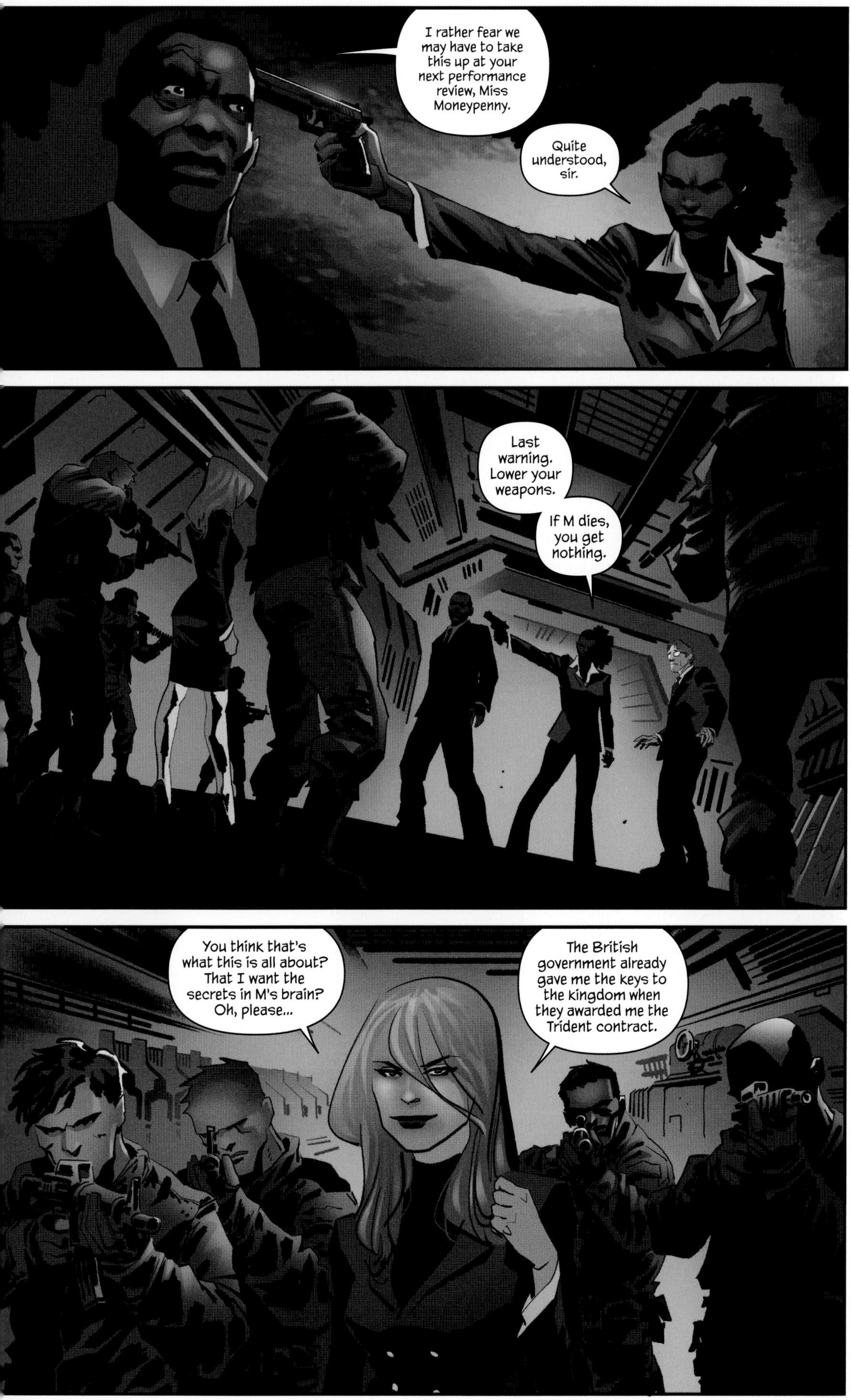
I rather fear we may have to take this up at your next performance review, Miss Moneypenny.
Quite understood, sir.
Last warning. Lower your weapons.
If M dies, you get nothing.
You think that's what this is all about? That I want the secrets in M's brain? Oh, please...
The British government already gave me the keys to the kingdom when they awarded me the Trident contract.

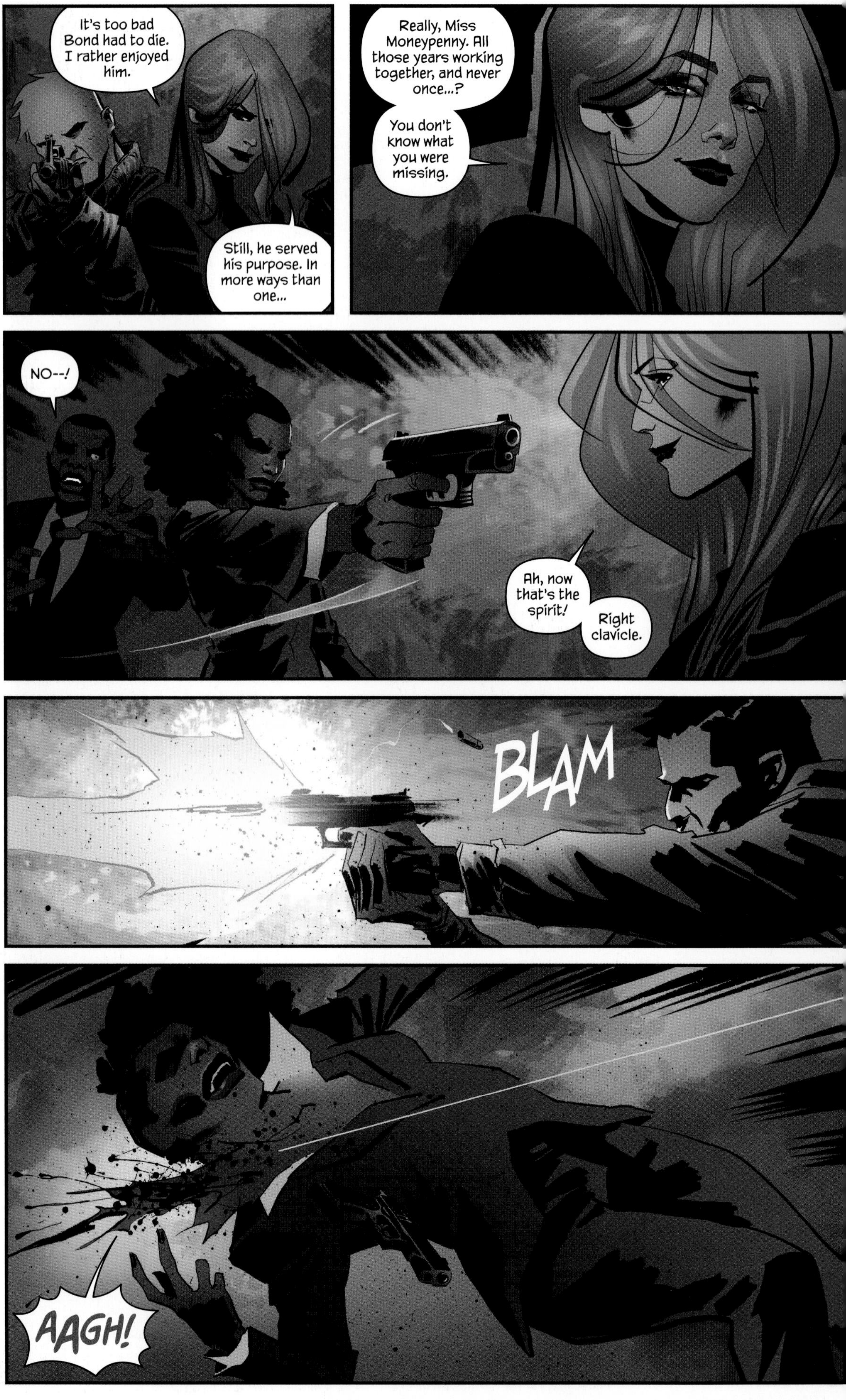
It's too bad Bond had to die. I rather enjoyed him.
Still, he served his purpose. In more ways than one...
Really, Miss Moneypenny. All those years working together, and never once...?
You don't know what you were missing.
NO--!
Ah, now that's the spirit!
Right clavicle.
BLAM
AAGH!

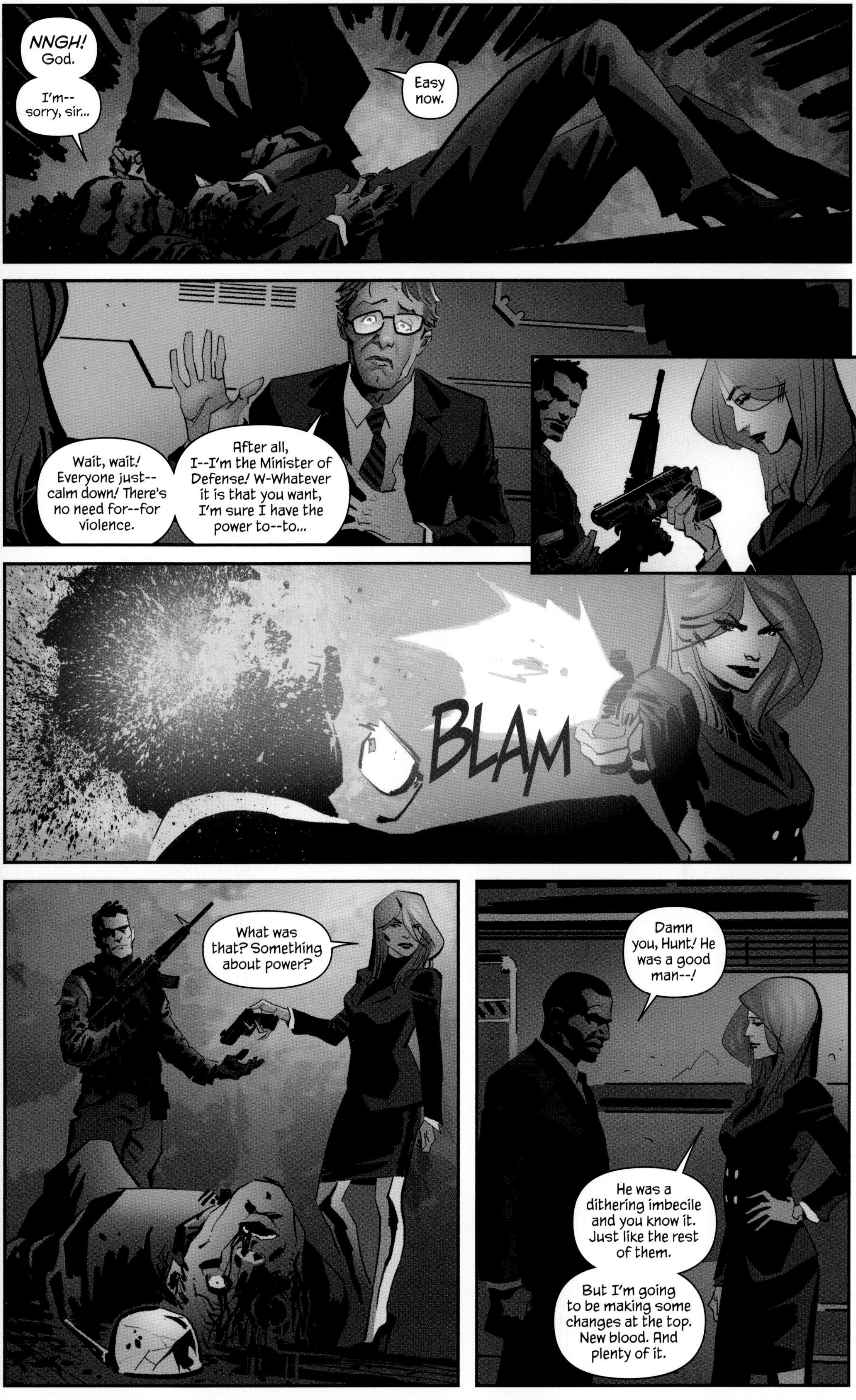
NNGH! God.
I'm-- sorry, sir...
Easy now.
Wait, wait! Everyone just-- calm down! There's no need for--for violence.
After all, I--I'm the Minister of Defense! W-Whatever it is that you want, I'm sure I have the power to--to...
BLAM
What was that? Something about power?
Damn you, Hunt! He was a good man--!
He was a dithering imbecile and you know it. Just like the rest of them.
But I'm going to be making some changes at the top. New blood. And plenty of it.

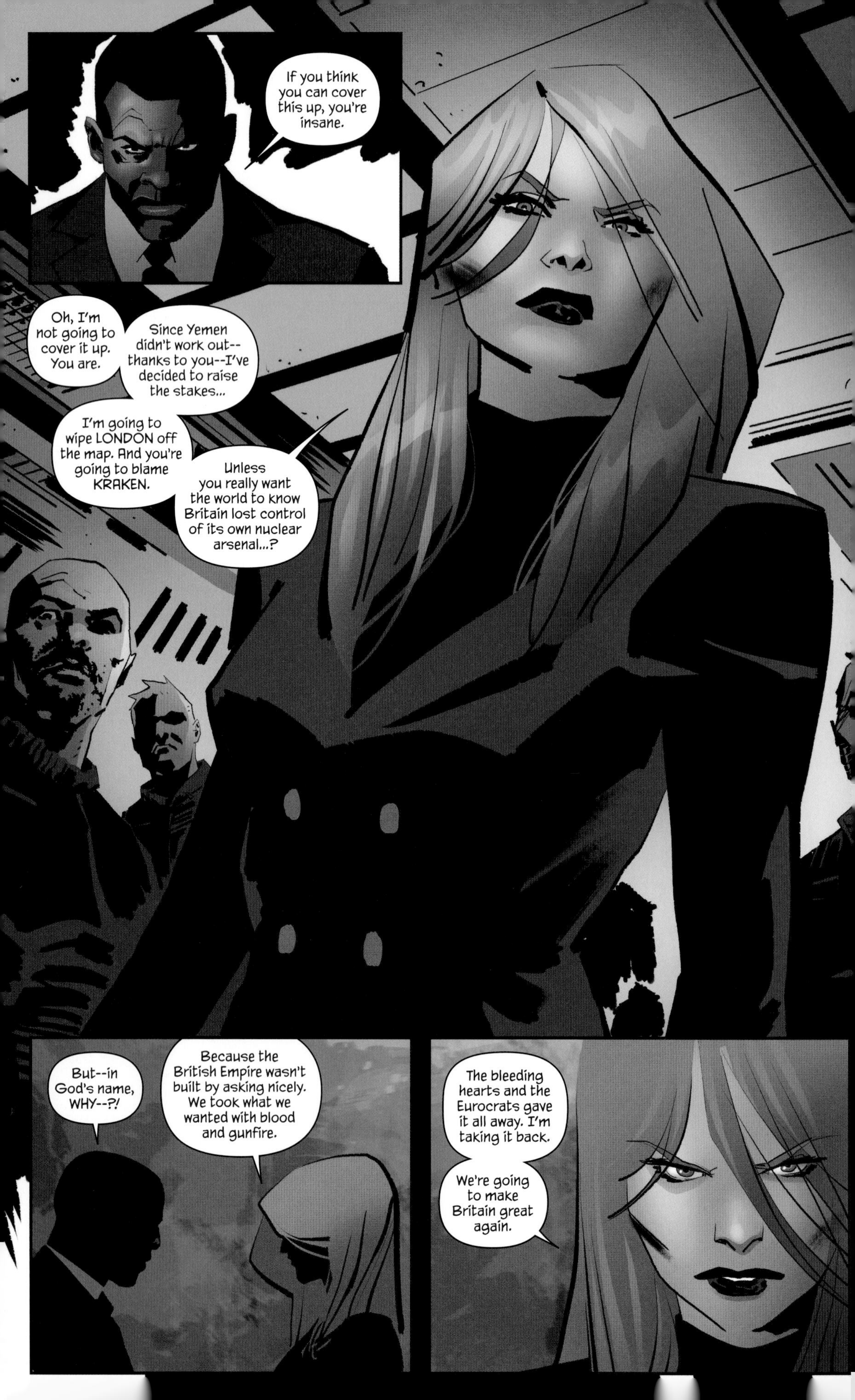
If you think you can cover this up, you're insane.
Oh, I'm not going to cover it up. You are.
Since Yemen didn't work out--thanks to you--I've decided to raise the stakes...
I'm going to wipe LONDON off the map. And you're going to blame KRAKEN.
Unless you really want the world to know Britain lost control of its own nuclear arsenal...?
But--in God's name, WHY--?!
Because the British Empire wasn't built by asking nicely. We took what we wanted with blood and gunfire.
The bleeding hearts and the Eurocrats gave it all away. I'm taking it back.
We're going to make Britain great again.

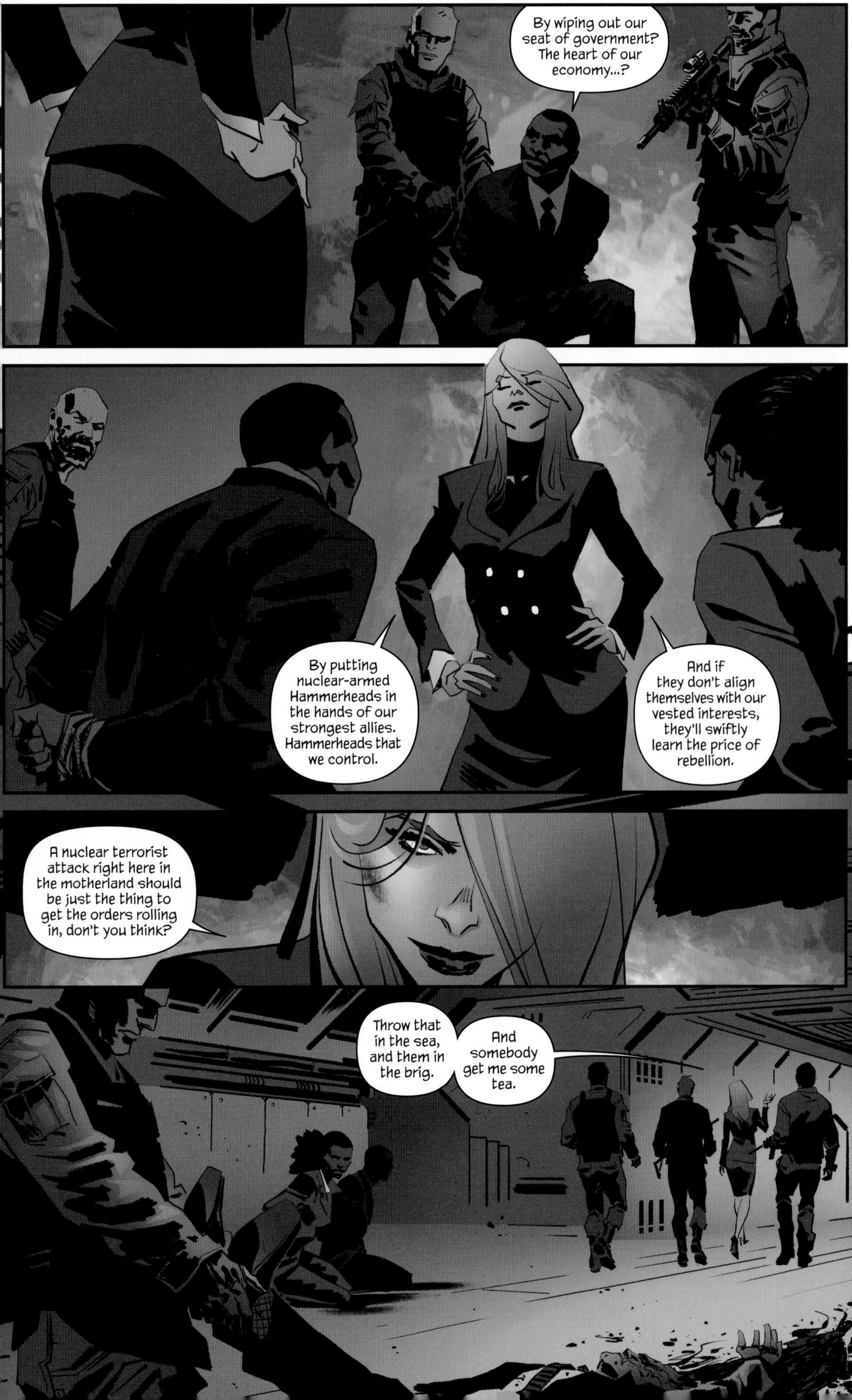
By wiping out our seat of government? The heart of our economy...?
By putting nuclear-armed Hammerheads in the hands of our strongest allies. Hammerheads that we control.
And if they don't align themselves with our vested interests, they'll swiftly learn the price of rebellion.
A nuclear terrorist attack right here in the motherland should be just the thing to get the orders rolling in, don't you think?
Throw that in the sea, and them in the brig.
And somebody get me some tea.

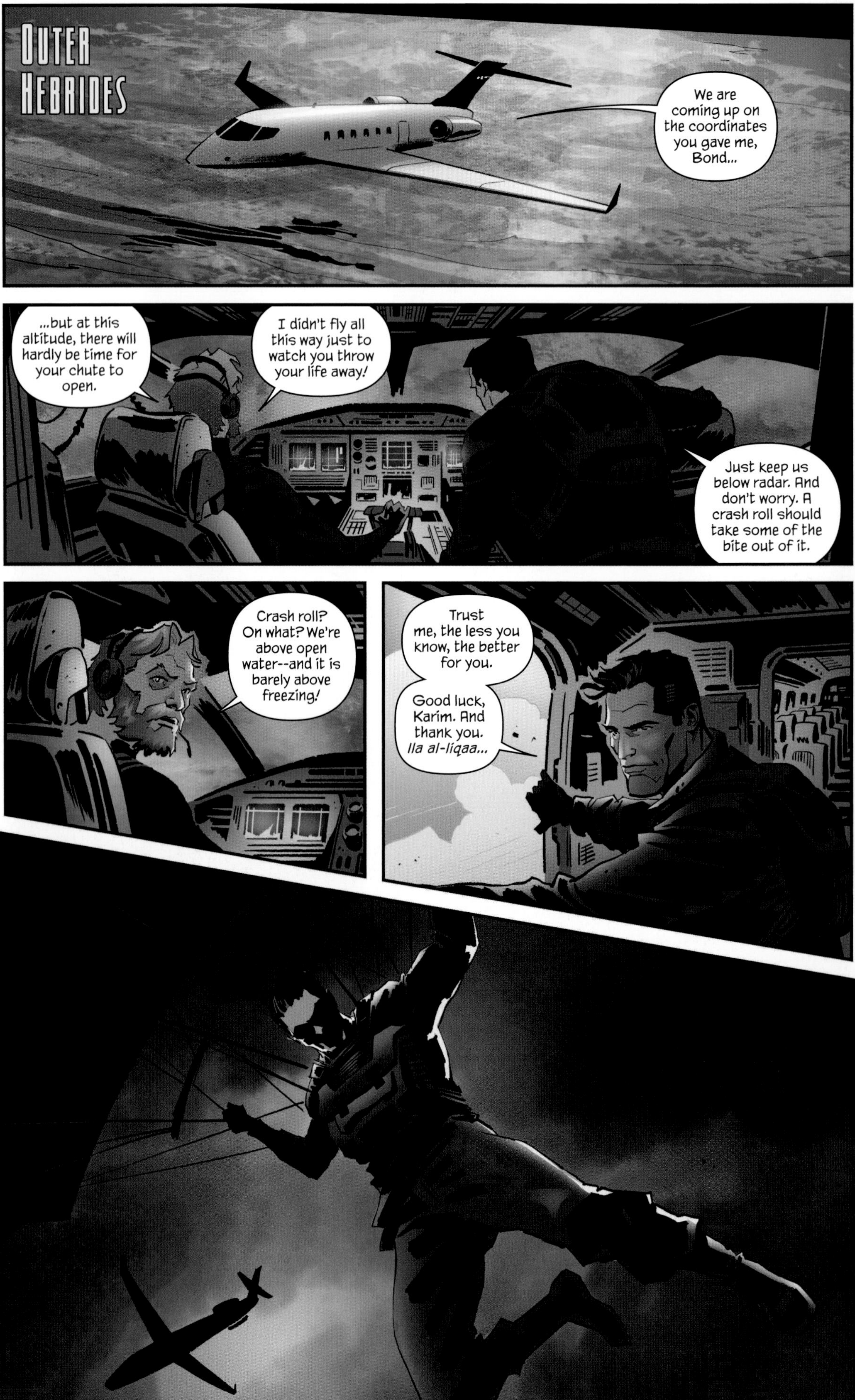
OUTER HEBRIDES
We are coming up on the coordinates you gave me, Bond...
...but at this altitude, there will hardly be time for your chute to open.
I didn't fly all this way just to watch you throw your life away!
Just keep us below radar. And don't worry. A crash roll should take some of the bite out of it.
Crash roll? On what? We're above open water--and it is barely above freezing!
Trust me, the less you know, the better for you.
Good luck, Karim. And thank you. *Ila al-liqaa...*

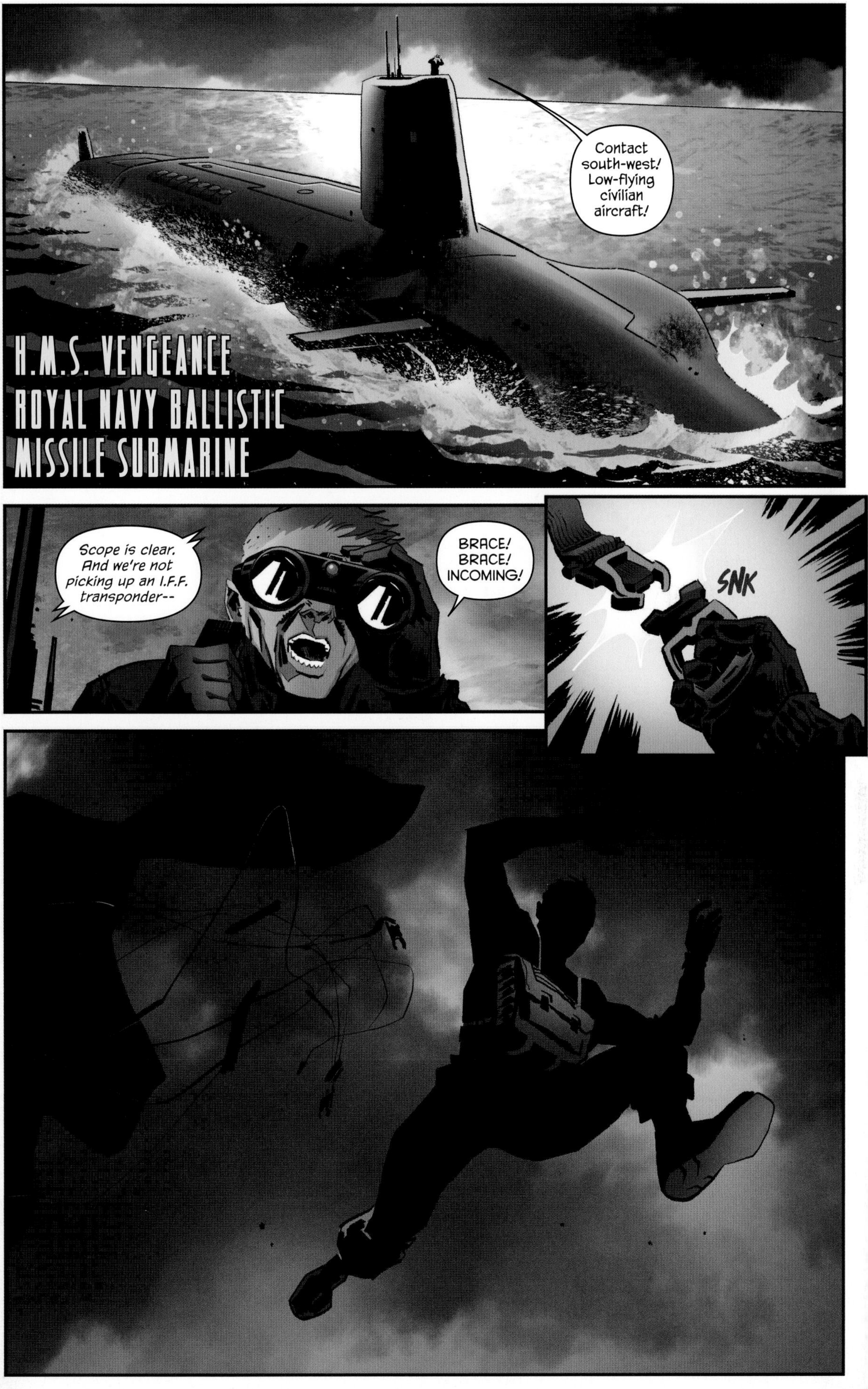
H.M.S. VENGEANCE
ROYAL NAVY BALLISTIC
MISSILE SUBMARINE
Contact south-west! Low-flying civilian aircraft!
Scope is clear. And we're not picking up an I.F.F. transponder--
BRACE! BRACE! INCOMING!
SNK

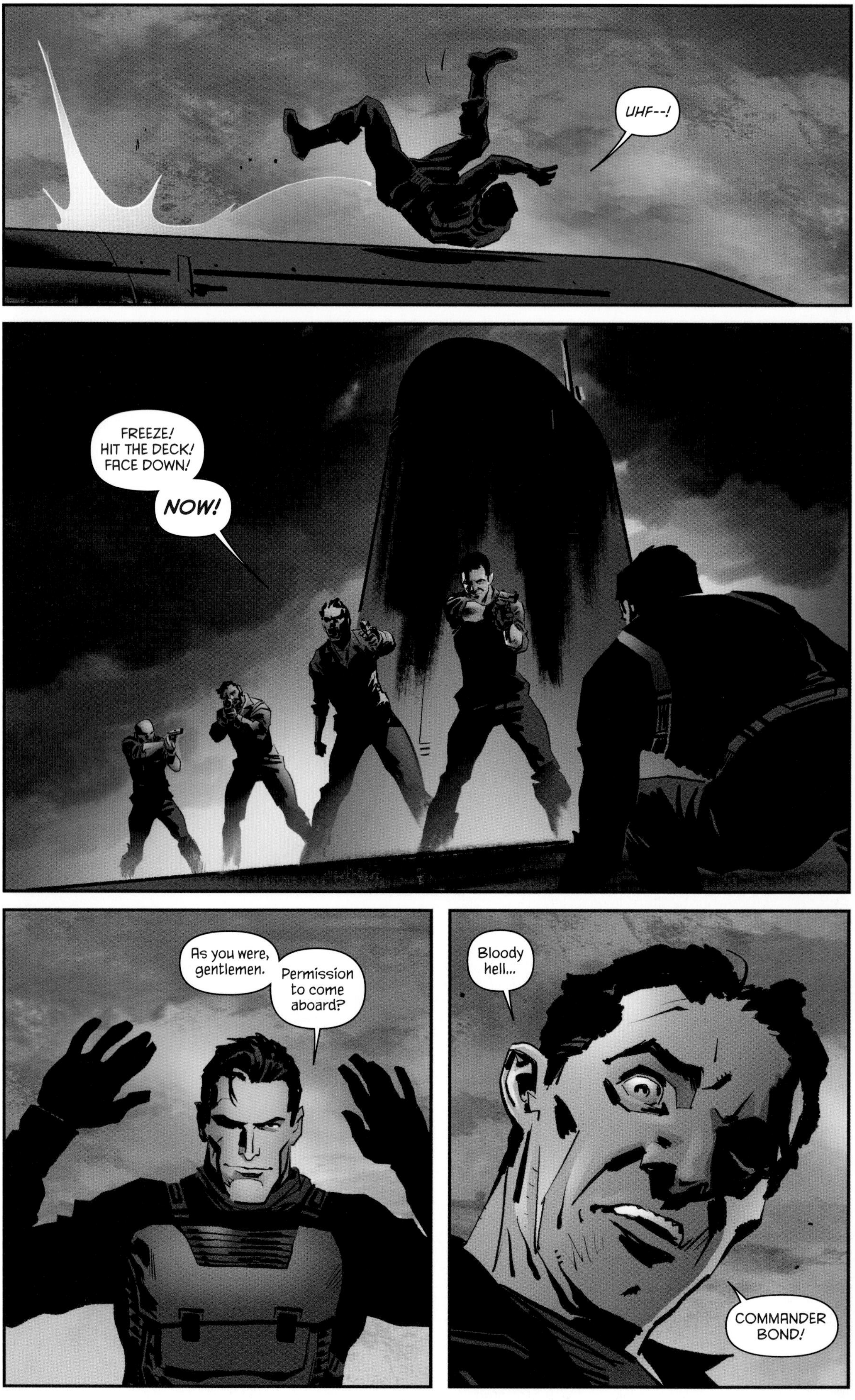
UHF--!
FREEZE! HIT THE DECK! FACE DOWN!
NOW!
As you were, gentlemen.
Permission to come aboard?
Bloody hell...
COMMANDER BOND!

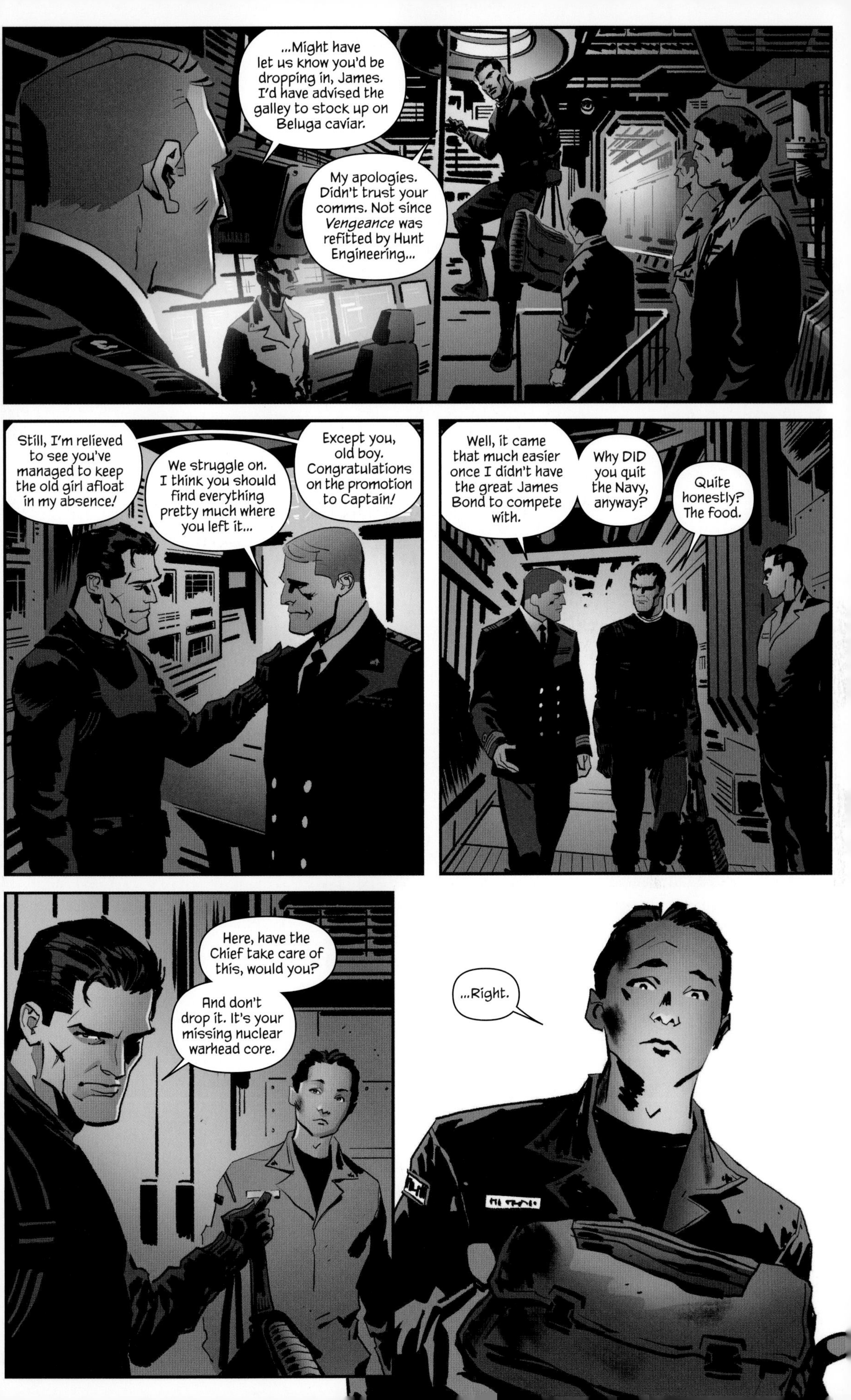
...Might have let us know you'd be dropping in, James. I'd have advised the galley to stock up on Beluga caviar.
My apologies. Didn't trust your comms. Not since *Vengeance* was refitted by Hunt Engineering...
Still, I'm relieved to see you've managed to keep the old girl afloat in my absence!
We struggle on. I think you should find everything pretty much where you left it...
Except you, old boy. Congratulations on the promotion to Captain!
Well, it came that much easier once I didn't have the great James Bond to compete with.
Why DID you quit the Navy, anyway?
Quite honestly? The food.
Here, have the Chief take care of this, would you?
And don't drop it. It's your missing nuclear warhead core.
...Right.

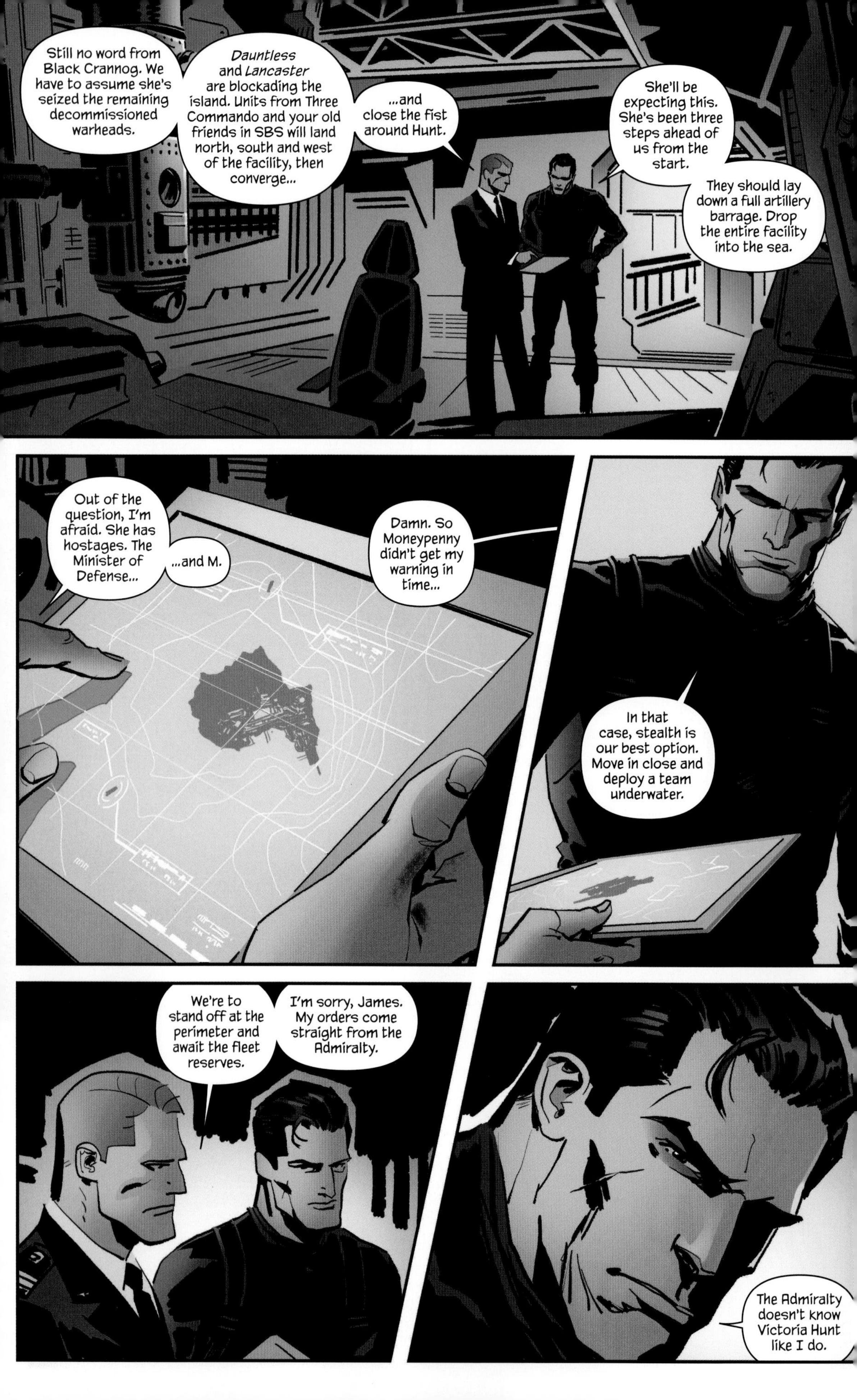
Still no word from Black Crannog. We have to assume she's seized the remaining decommissioned warheads.
Dauntless and *Lancaster* are blockading the island. Units from Three Commando and your old friends in SBS will land north, south and west of the facility, then converge...
...and close the fist around Hunt.
She'll be expecting this. She's been three steps ahead of us from the start.
They should lay down a full artillery barrage. Drop the entire facility into the sea.
Out of the question, I'm afraid. She has hostages. The Minister of Defense...
...and M.
Damn. So Moneypenny didn't get my warning in time...
In that case, stealth is our best option. Move in close and deploy a team underwater.
We're to stand off at the perimeter and await the fleet reserves.
I'm sorry, James. My orders come straight from the Admiralty.
The Admiralty doesn't know Victoria Hunt like I do.

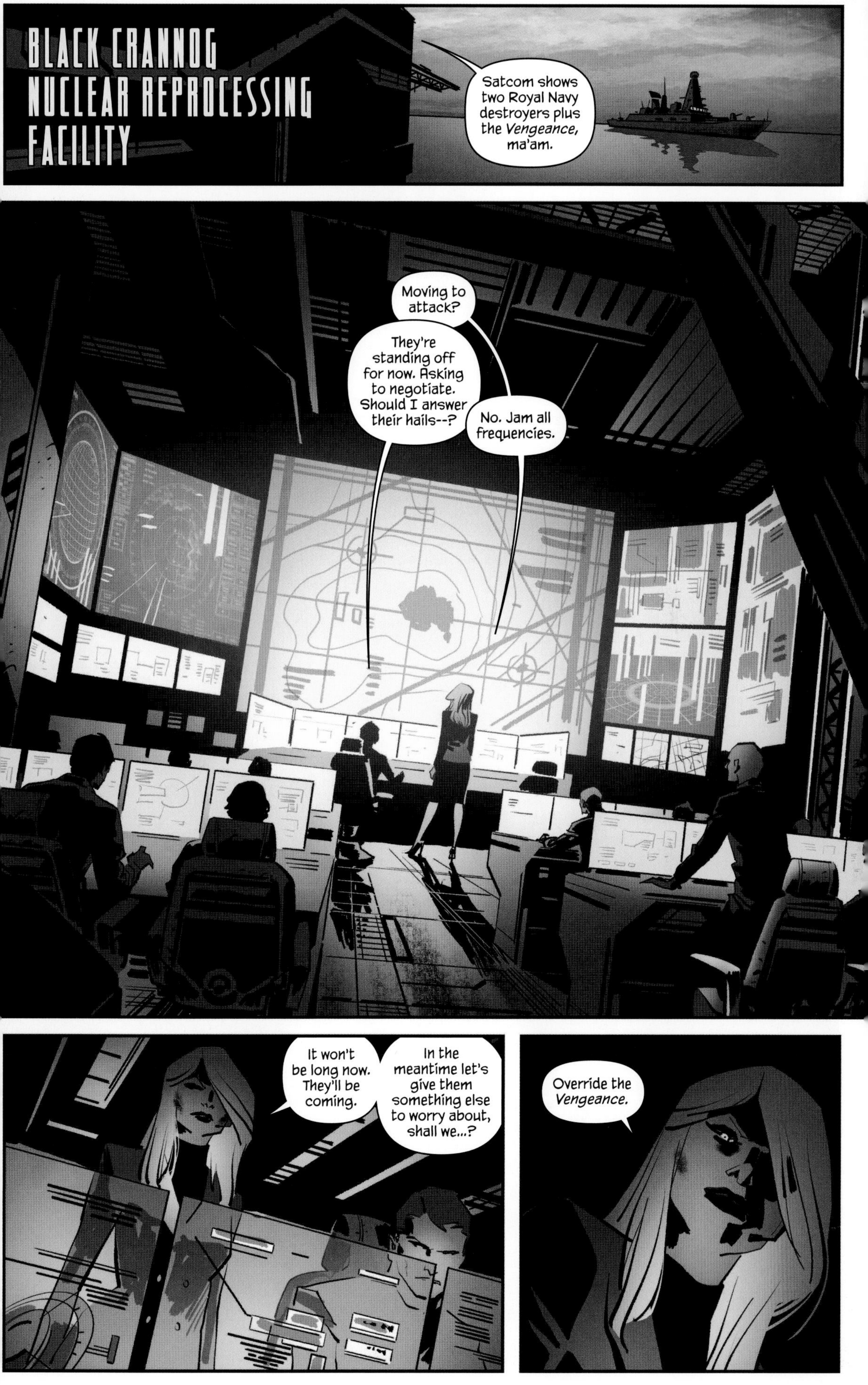
BLACK CRANNOG
NUCLEAR REPROCESSING
FACILITY
Satcom shows two Royal Navy destroyers plus the *Vengeance*, ma'am.
Moving to attack?
They're standing off for now. Asking to negotiate. Should I answer their hails--?
No. Jam all frequencies.
It won't be long now. They'll be coming.
In the meantime let's give them something else to worry about, shall we...?
Override the *Vengeance*.

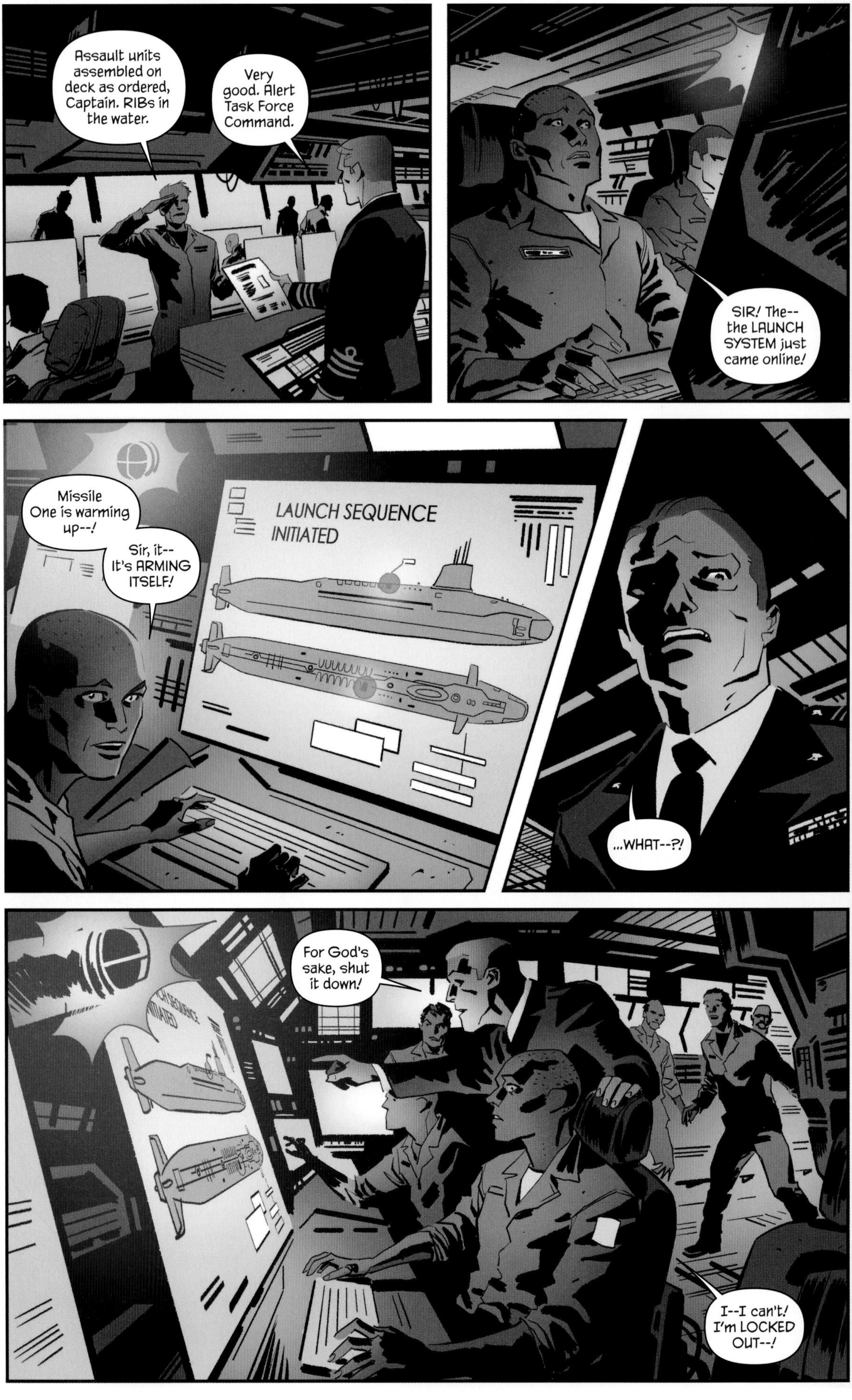

Assault units assembled on deck as ordered, Captain. RIBs in the water.
Very good. Alert Task Force Command.
SIR! The--the LAUNCH SYSTEM just came online!
Missile One is warming up--!
Sir, it--It's ARMING ITSELF!
LAUNCH SEQUENCE INITIATED
...WHAT--?!
For God's sake, shut it down!
I--I can't! I'm LOCKED OUT--!

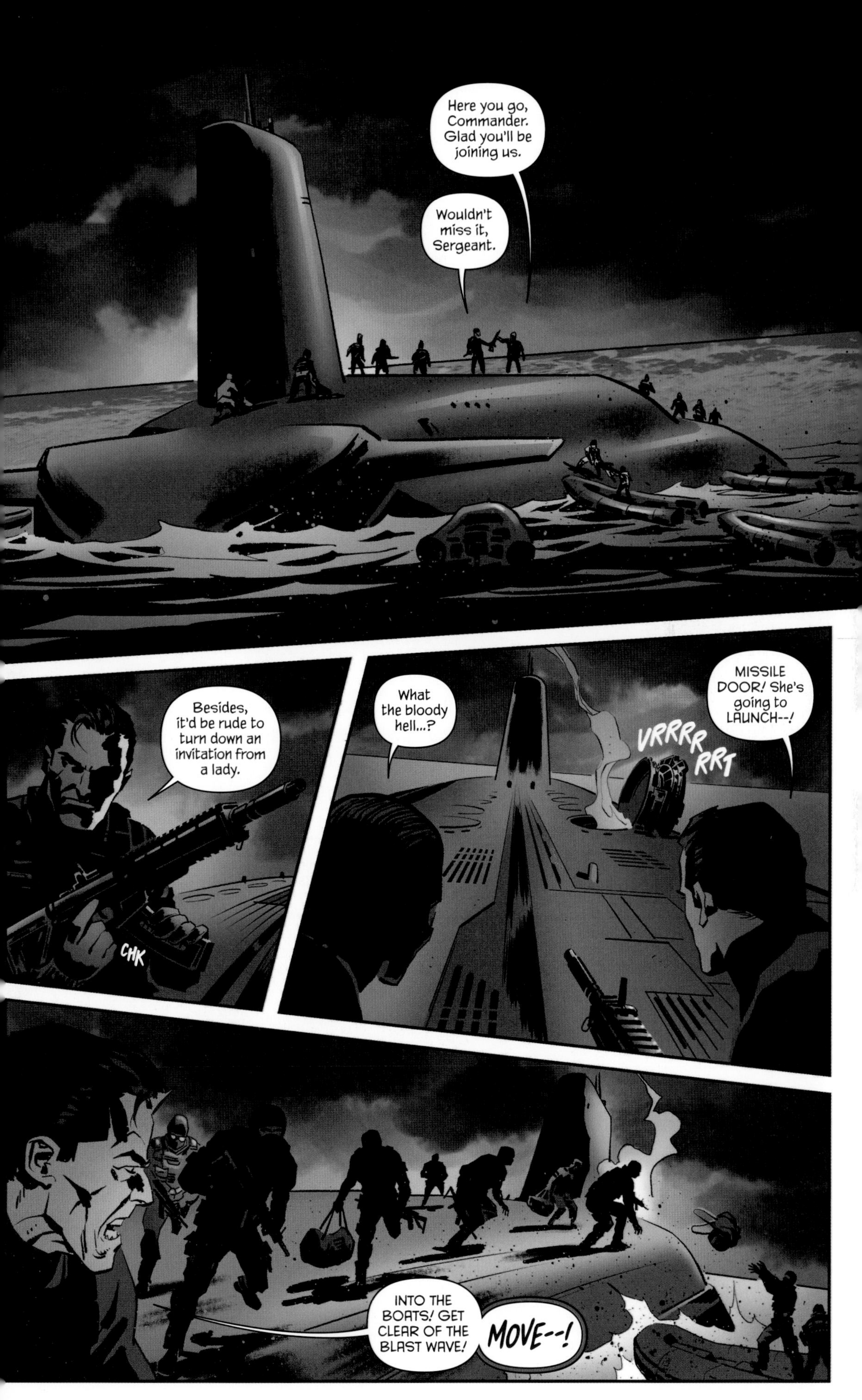
Here you go, Commander. Glad you'll be joining us.
Wouldn't miss it, Sergeant.
Besides, it'd be rude to turn down an invitation from a lady.
CHK
What the bloody hell...?
MISSILE DOOR! She's going to LAUNCH--!
VRRRRRRT
INTO THE BOATS! GET CLEAR OF THE BLAST WAVE!
MOVE--!

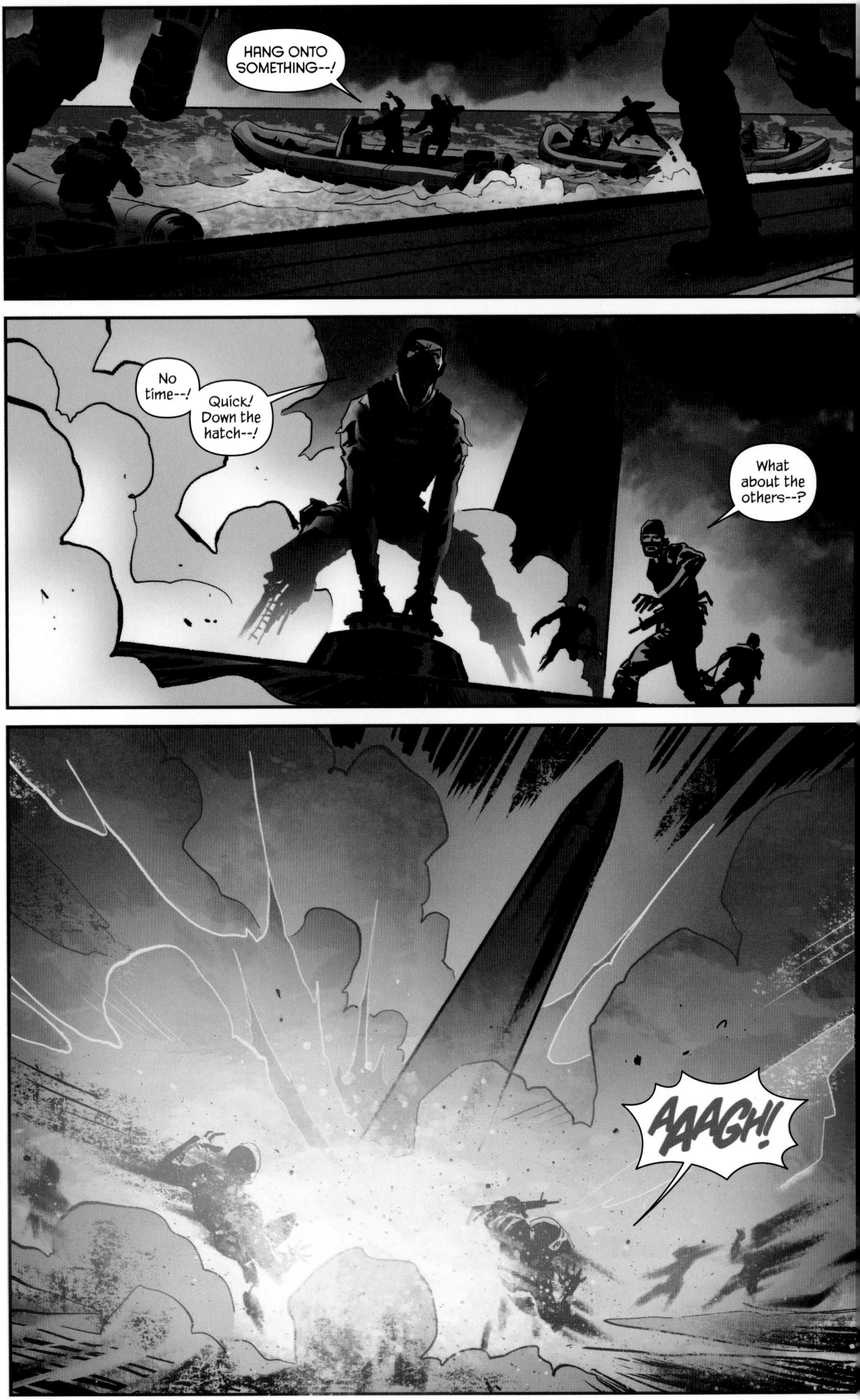
HANG ONTO SOMETHING--!
No time--!
Quick! Down the hatch--!
What about the others--?
AAAGH!

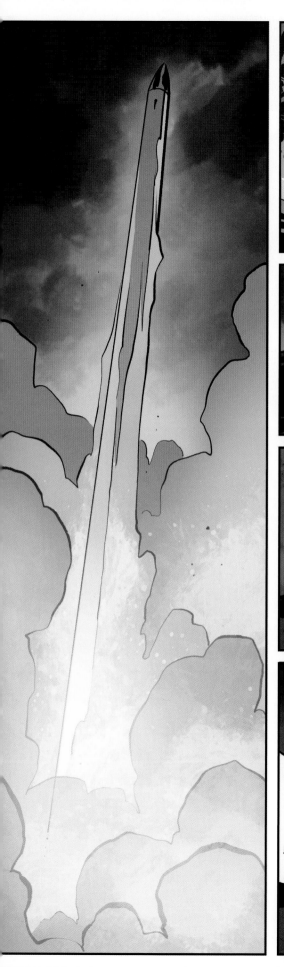

What are you all waiting for? Target that missile!

BRAKKA BRAKKA BRAKKA

...God help us all.

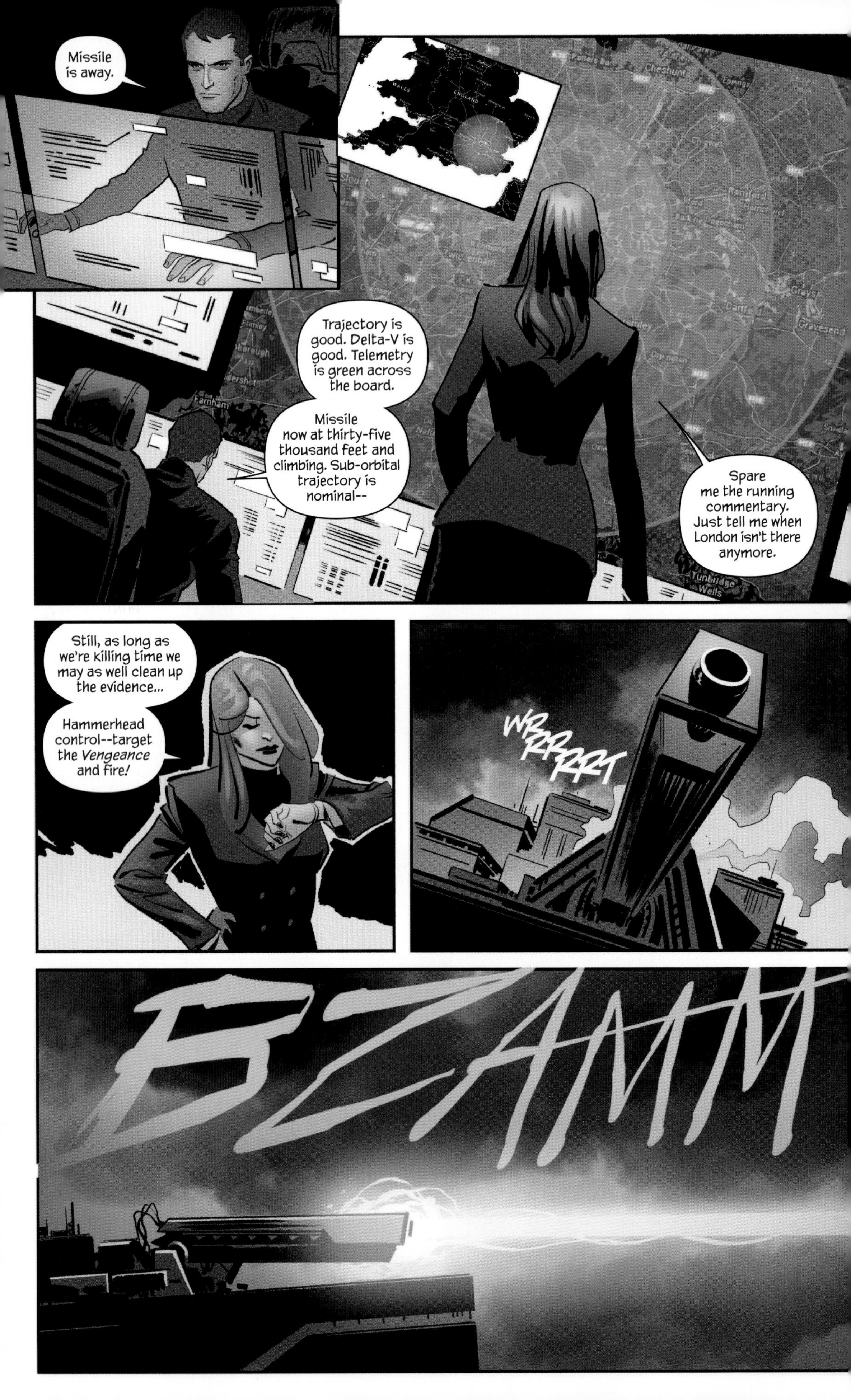
Missile is away.
WALES
ENGLAND
Cheshunt
Twickenham
Grays
Gravesend
Farnham
Tunbridge Wells
Trajectory is good. Delta-V is good. Telemetry is green across the board.
Missile now at thirty-five thousand feet and climbing. Sub-orbital trajectory is nominal--
Spare me the running commentary. Just tell me when London isn't there anymore.
Still, as long as we're killing time we may as well clean up the evidence...
Hammerhead control--target the *Vengeance* and fire!
WRRRRRT
BZAMM

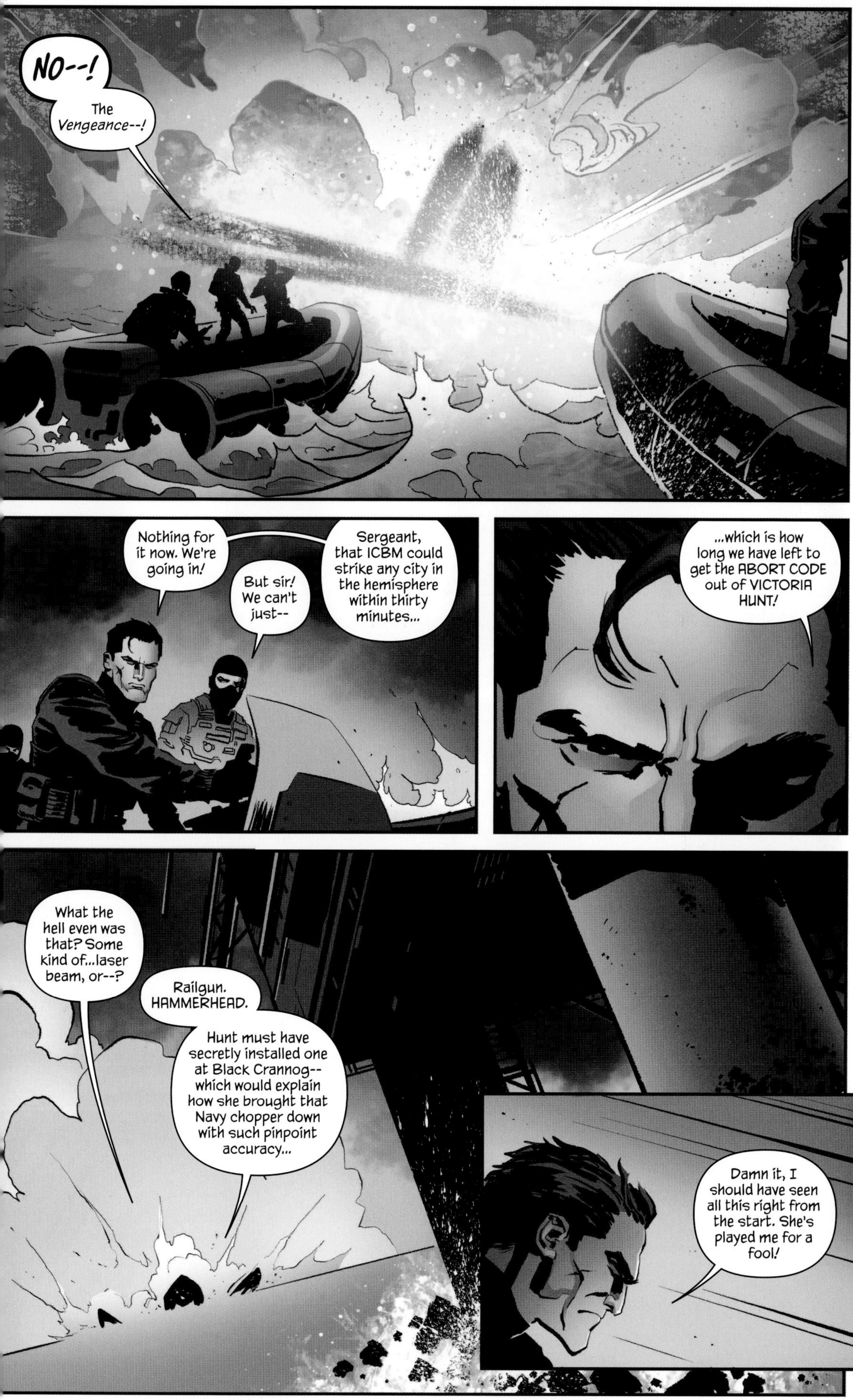
NO--!
The Vengeance--!
Nothing for it now. We're going in!
But sir! We can't just--
Sergeant, that ICBM could strike any city in the hemisphere within thirty minutes...
...which is how long we have left to get the ABORT CODE out of VICTORIA HUNT!
What the hell even was that? Some kind of...laser beam, or--?
Railgun. HAMMERHEAD.
Hunt must have secretly installed one at Black Crannog--which would explain how she brought that Navy chopper down with such pinpoint accuracy...
Damn it, I should have seen all this right from the start. She's played me for a fool!

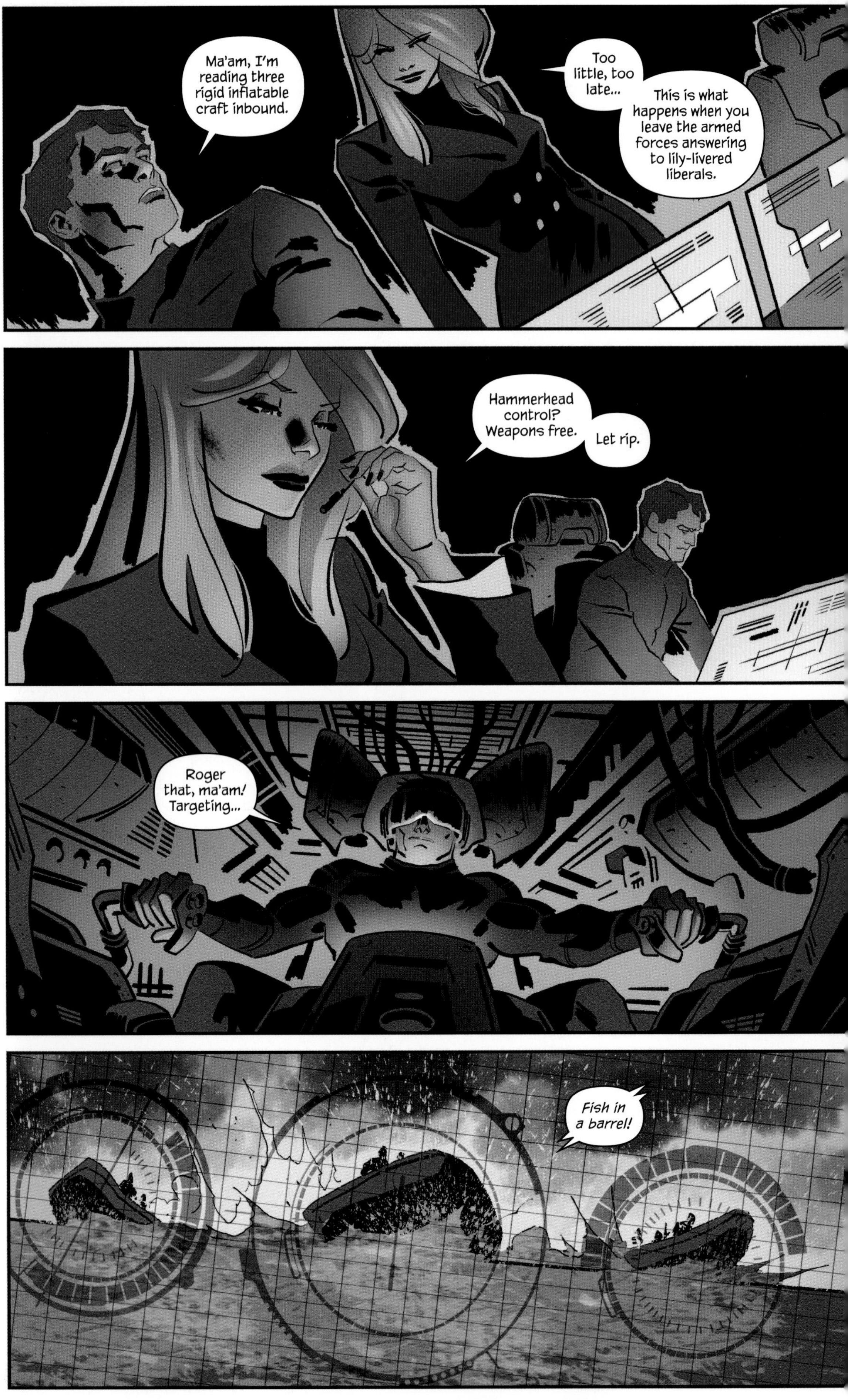
Ma'am, I'm reading three rigid inflatable craft inbound.
Too little, too late...
This is what happens when you leave the armed forces answering to lily-livered liberals.
Hammerhead control? Weapons free.
Let rip.
Roger that, ma'am! Targeting...
Fish in a barrel!

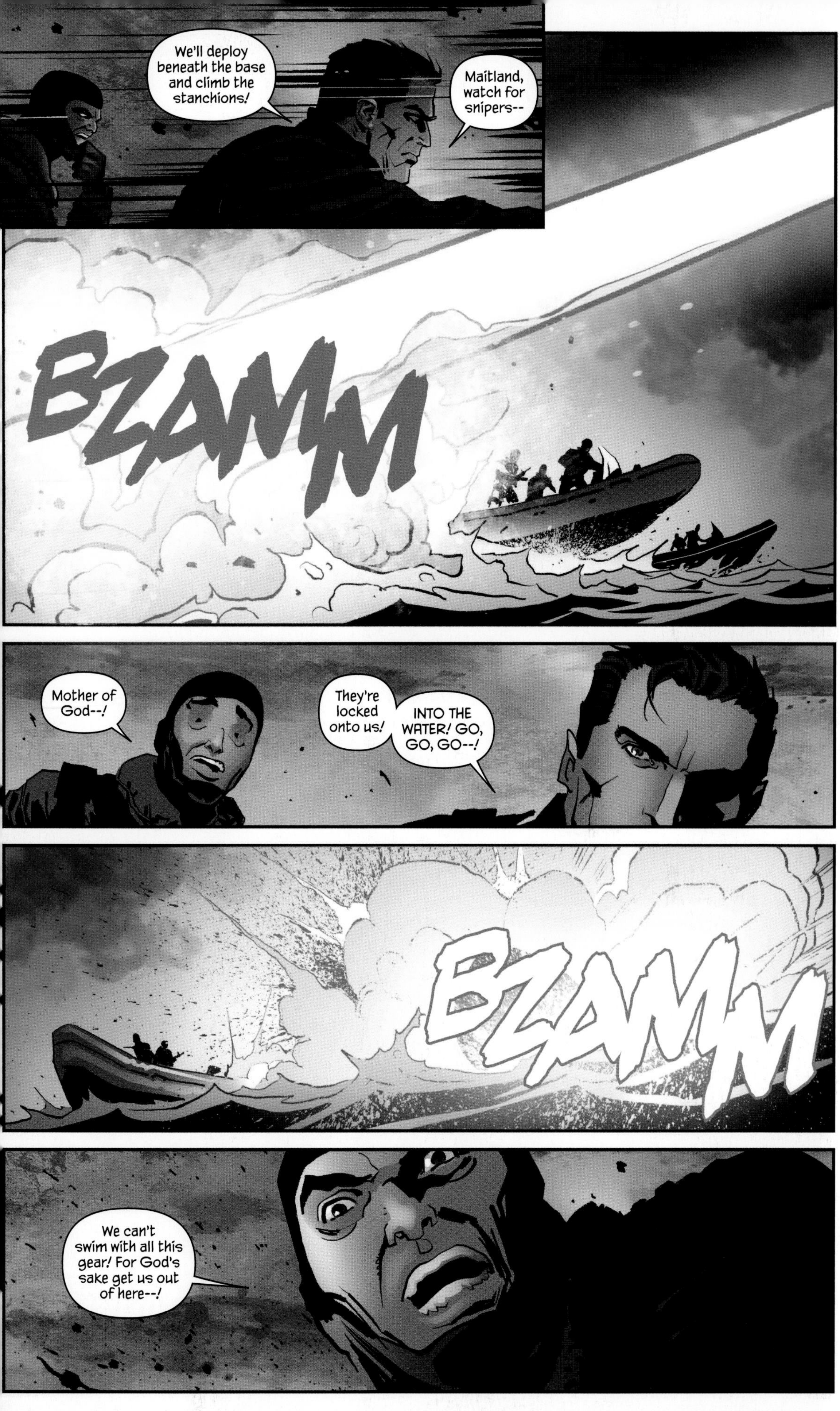
We'll deploy beneath the base and climb the stanchions!
Maitland, watch for snipers--
BZAMM
Mother of God--!
They're locked onto us!
INTO THE WATER! GO, GO, GO--!
BZAMM
We can't swim with all this gear! For God's sake get us out of here--!

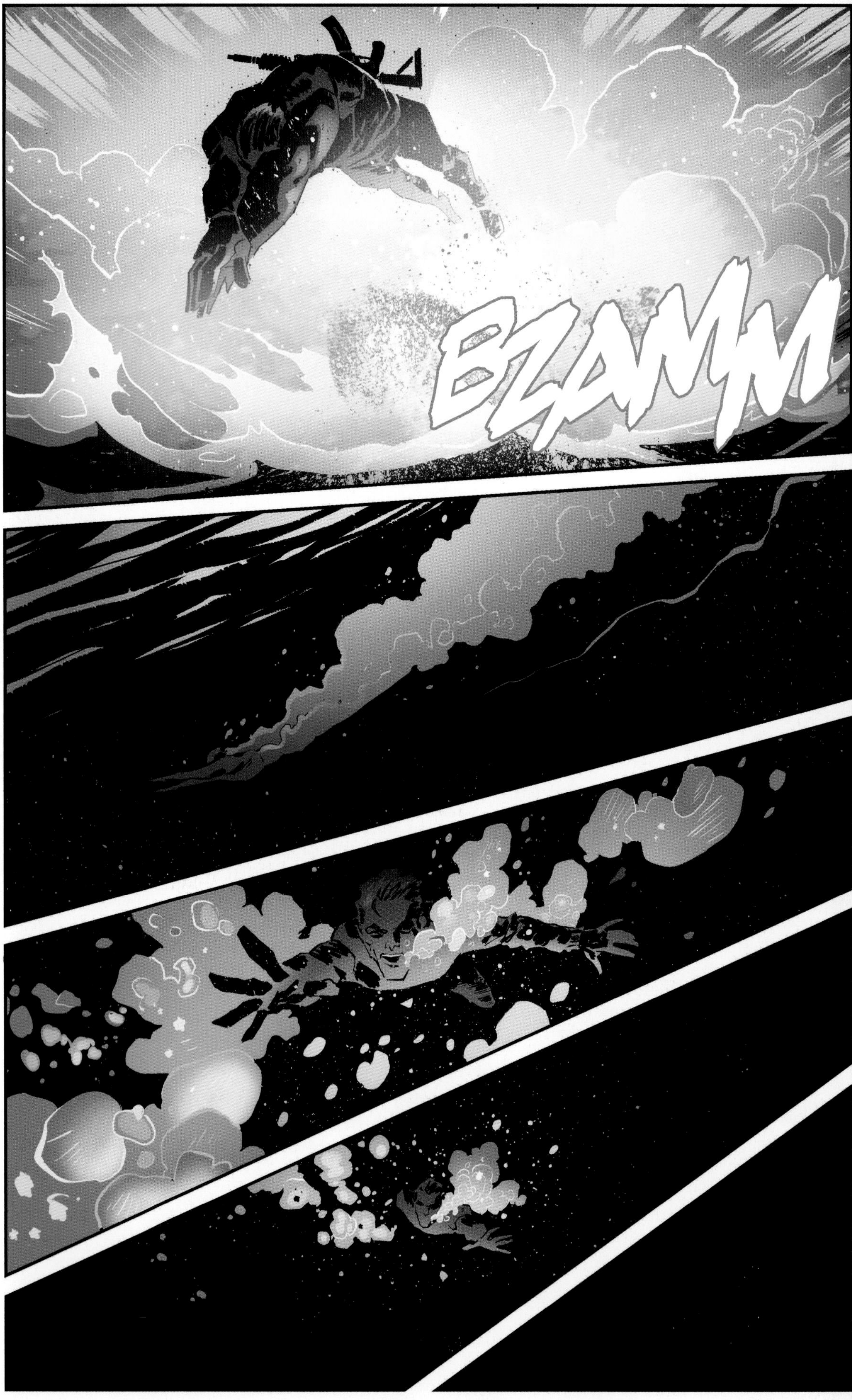
BZAMM

ISSUE 6

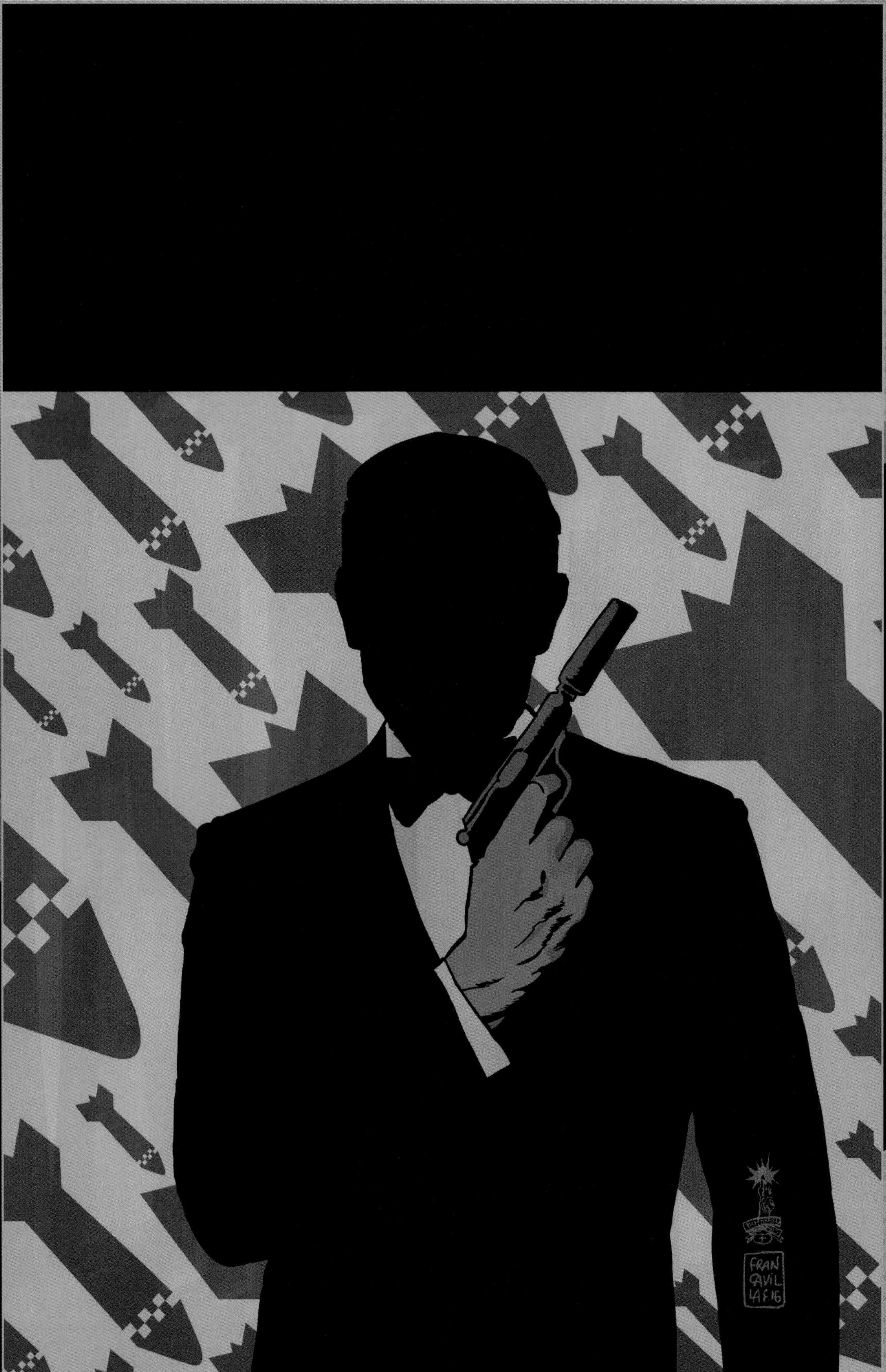
FRAN
CAVIL
LAF16

ISSUE 6 COVER
BY FRANCESCO FRANCAVILLA

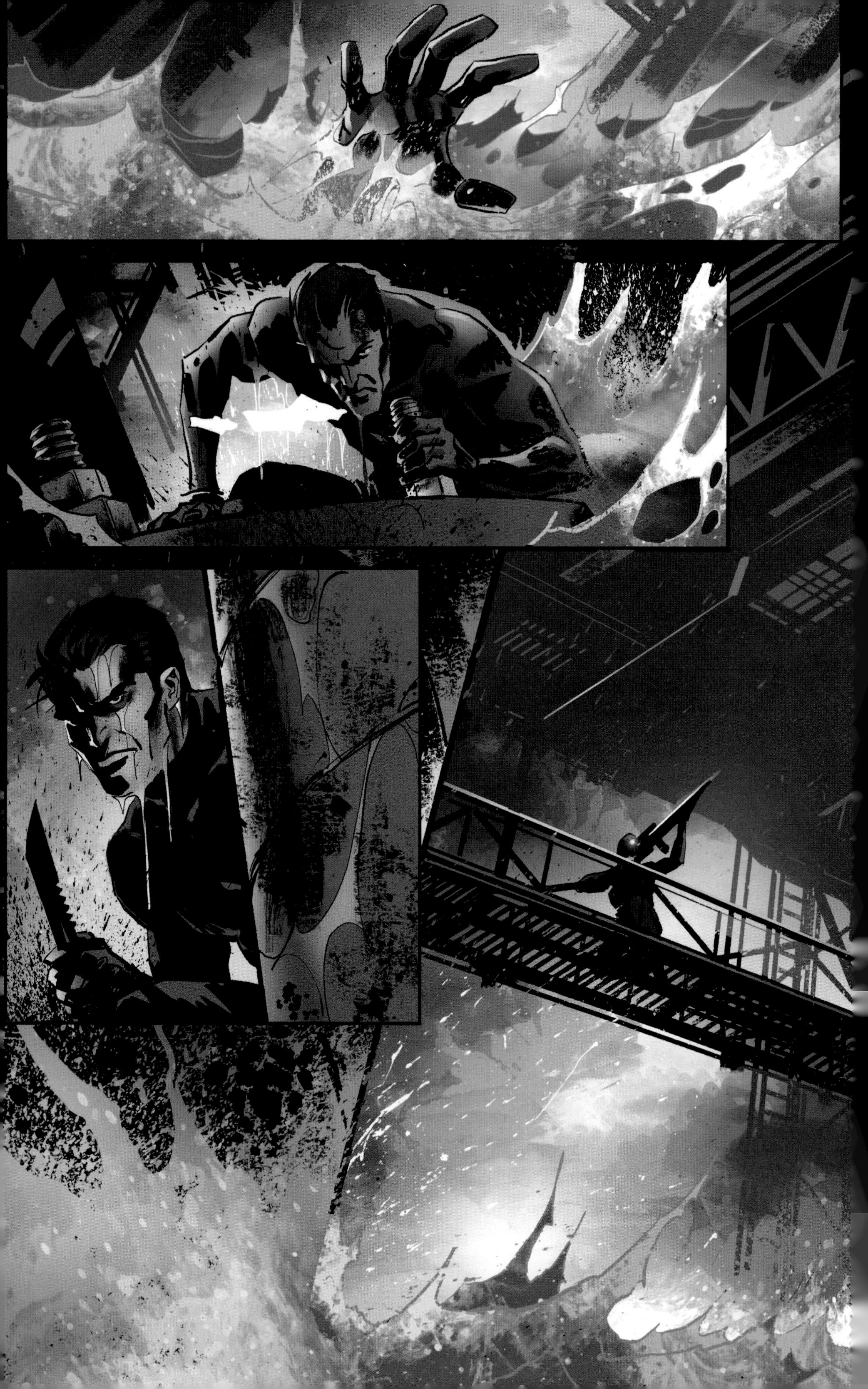

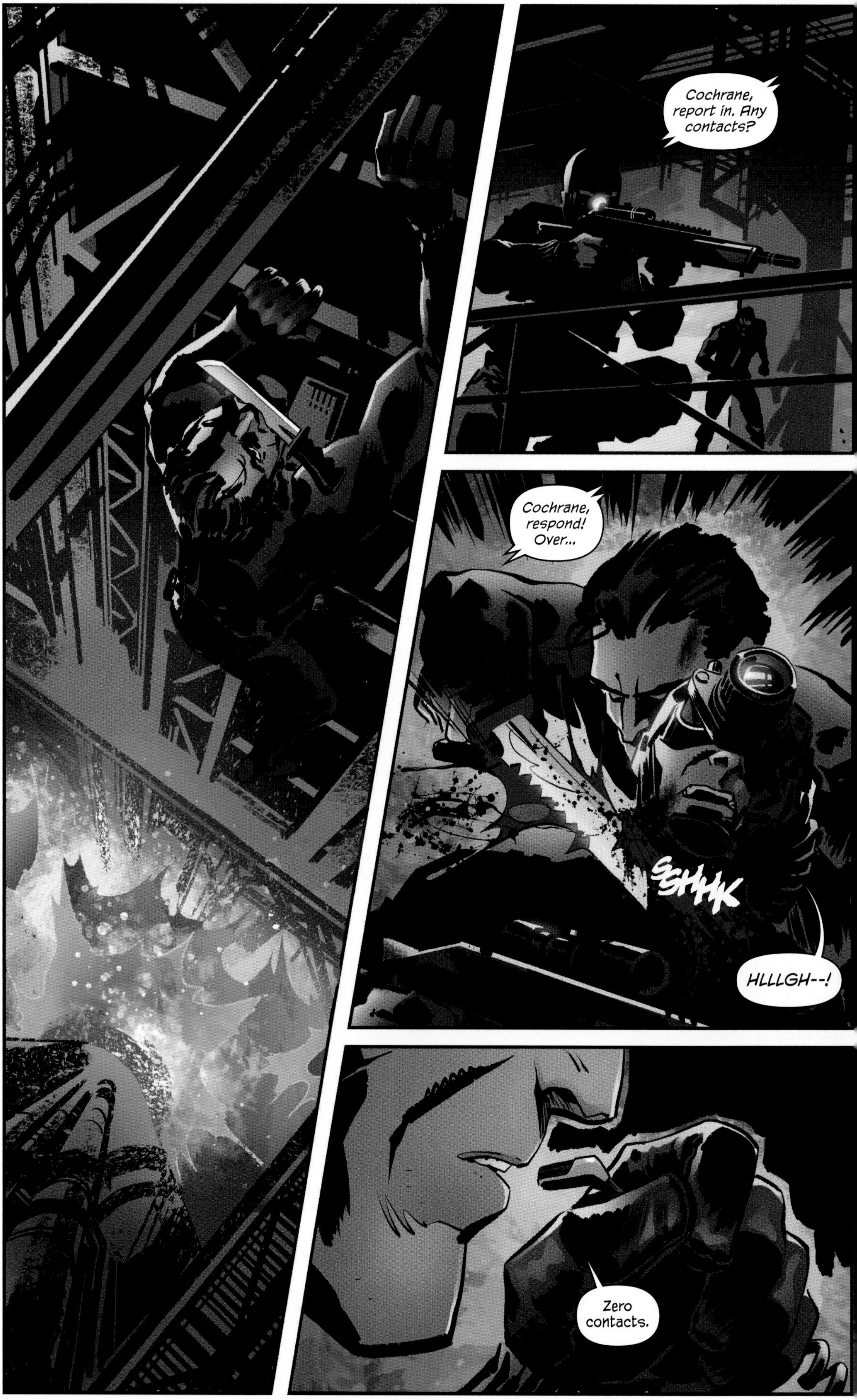
Cochrane, report in. Any contacts?
Cochrane, respond! Over...
SSHHK
HLLLGH--!
Zero contacts.

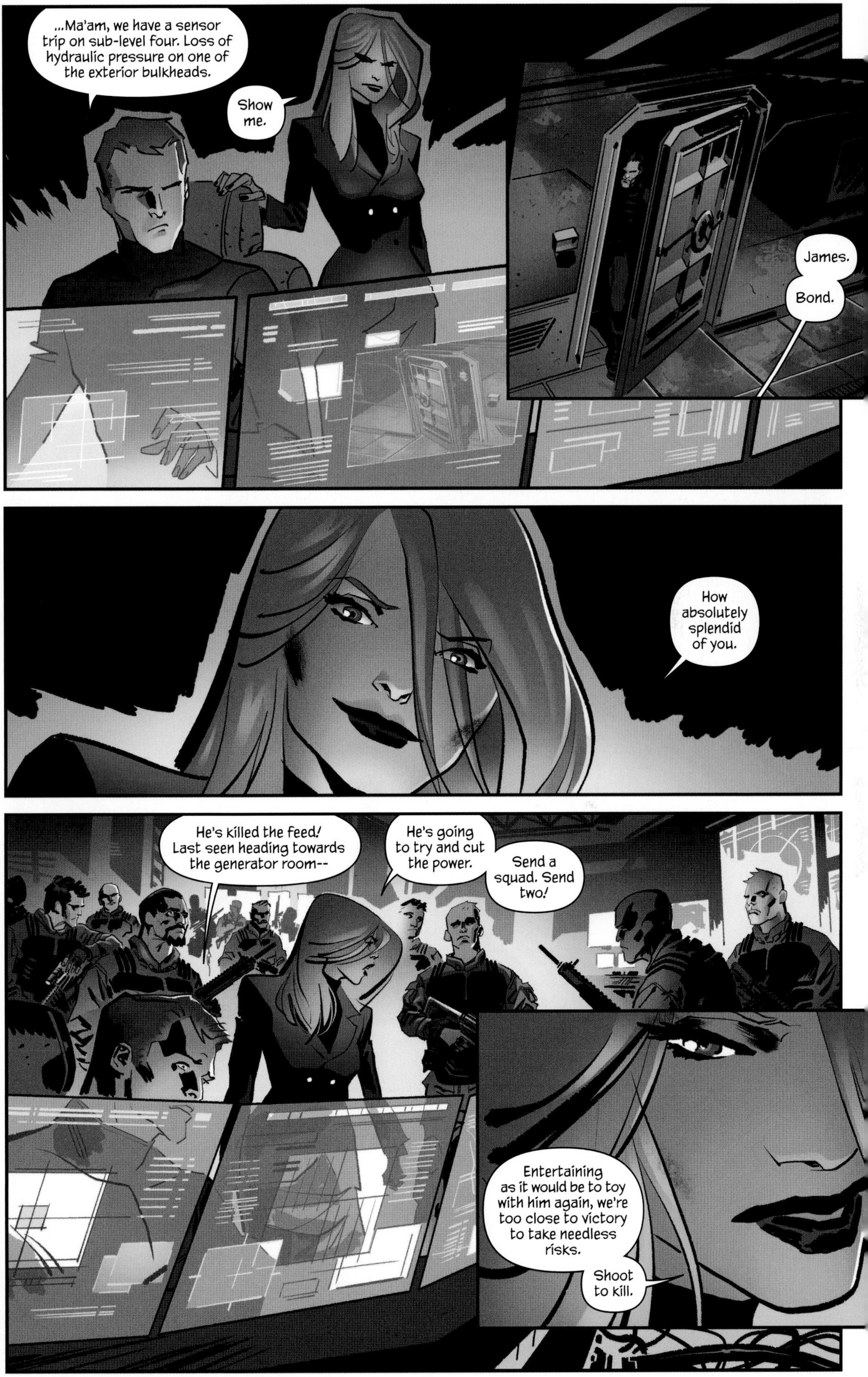
...Ma'am, we have a sensor trip on sub-level four. Loss of hydraulic pressure on one of the exterior bulkheads.
Show me.
James.
Bond.
How absolutely splendid of you.
He's killed the feed! Last seen heading towards the generator room--
He's going to try and cut the power.
Send a squad. Send two!
Entertaining as it would be to toy with him again, we're too close to victory to take needless risks.
Shoot to kill.

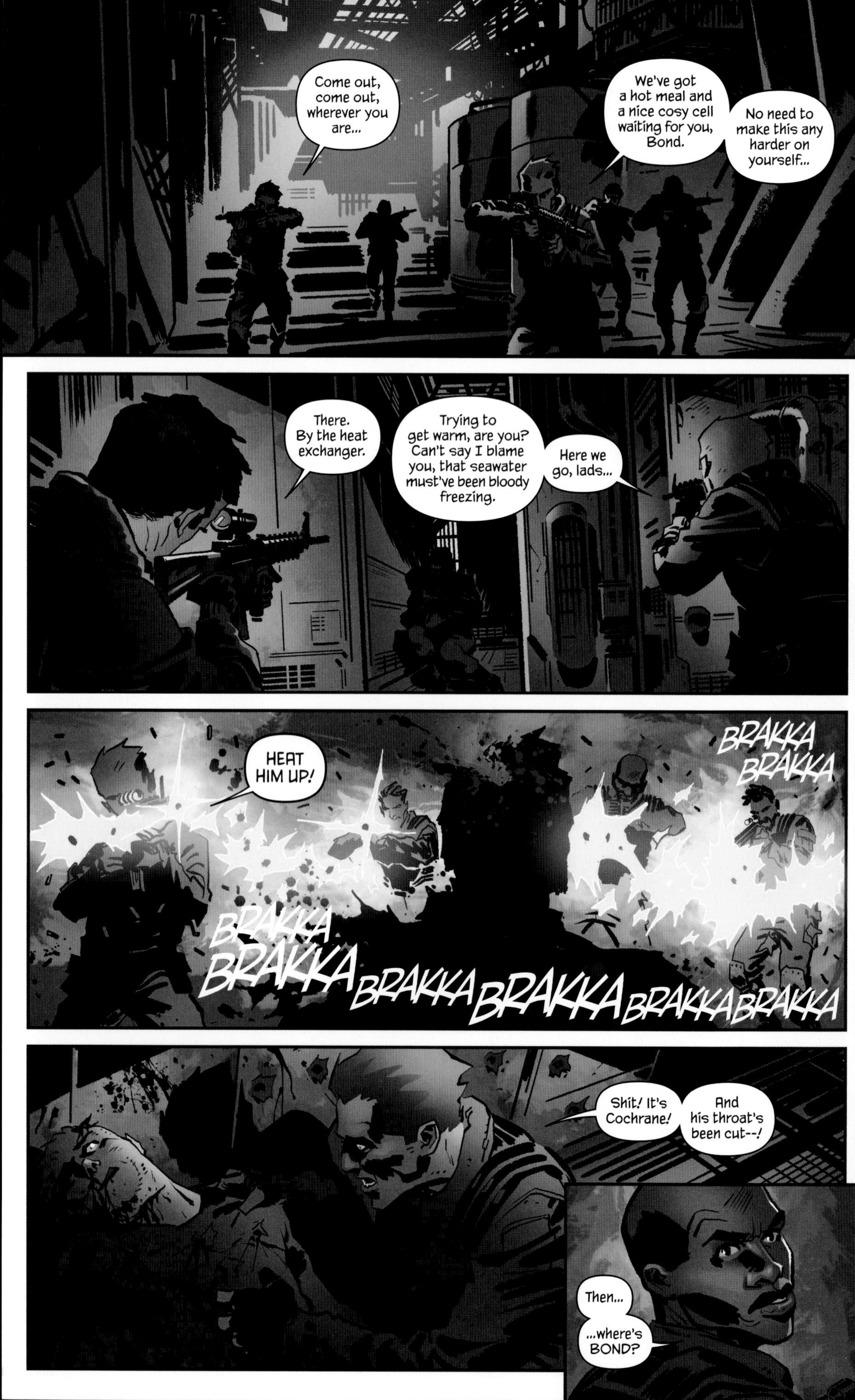
Come out, come out, wherever you are...
We've got a hot meal and a nice cosy cell waiting for you, Bond.
No need to make this any harder on yourself...
There. By the heat exchanger.
Trying to get warm, are you? Can't say I blame you, that seawater must've been bloody freezing.
Here we go, lads...
HEAT HIM UP!
BRAKKA BRAKKA
BRAKKA BRAKKA BRAKKA BRAKKA BRAKKA BRAKKA
Shit! It's Cochrane!
And his throat's been cut--!
Then...
...where's BOND?

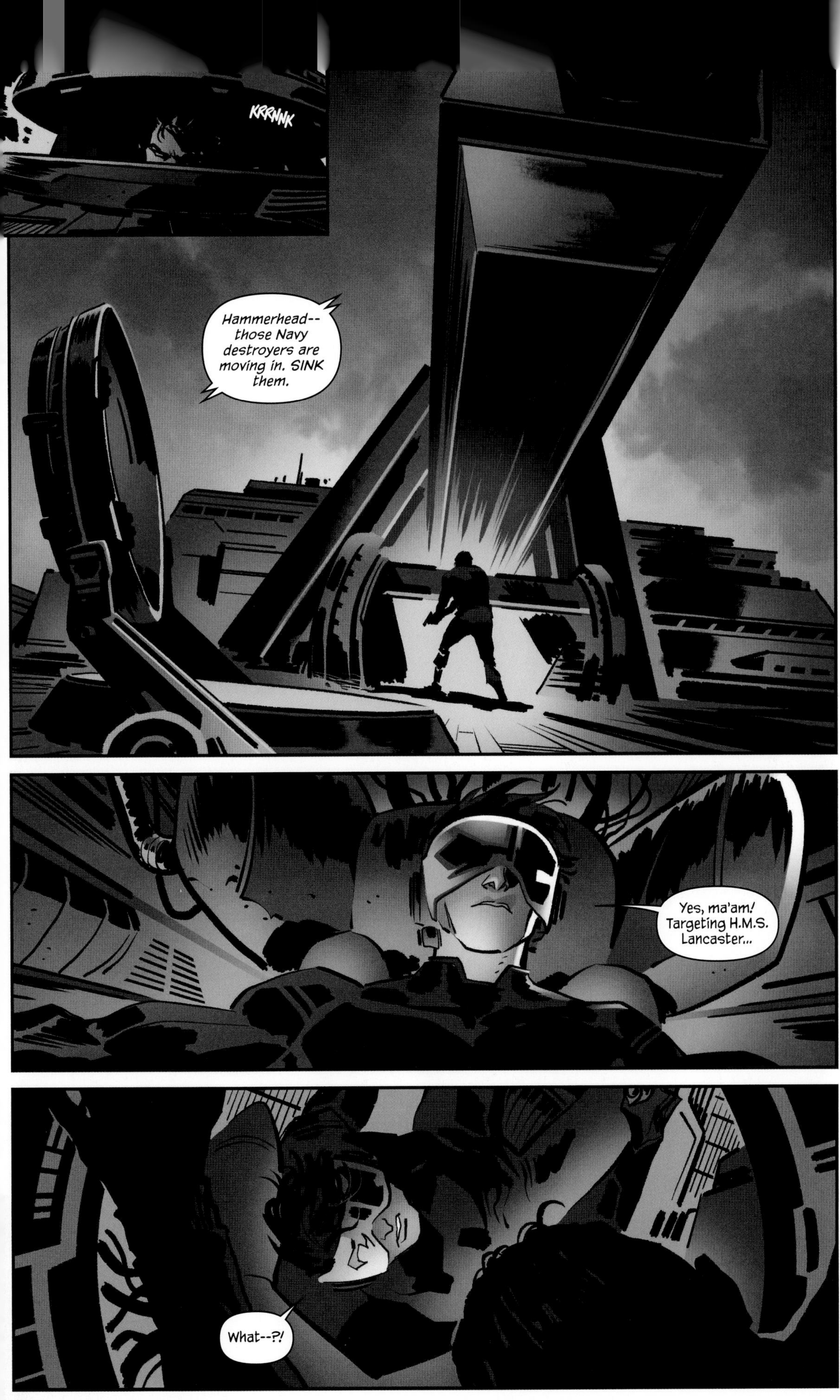
KRRNNK
Hammerhead-- those Navy destroyers are moving in. SINK them.
Yes, ma'am! Targeting H.M.S. Lancaster...
What--?!

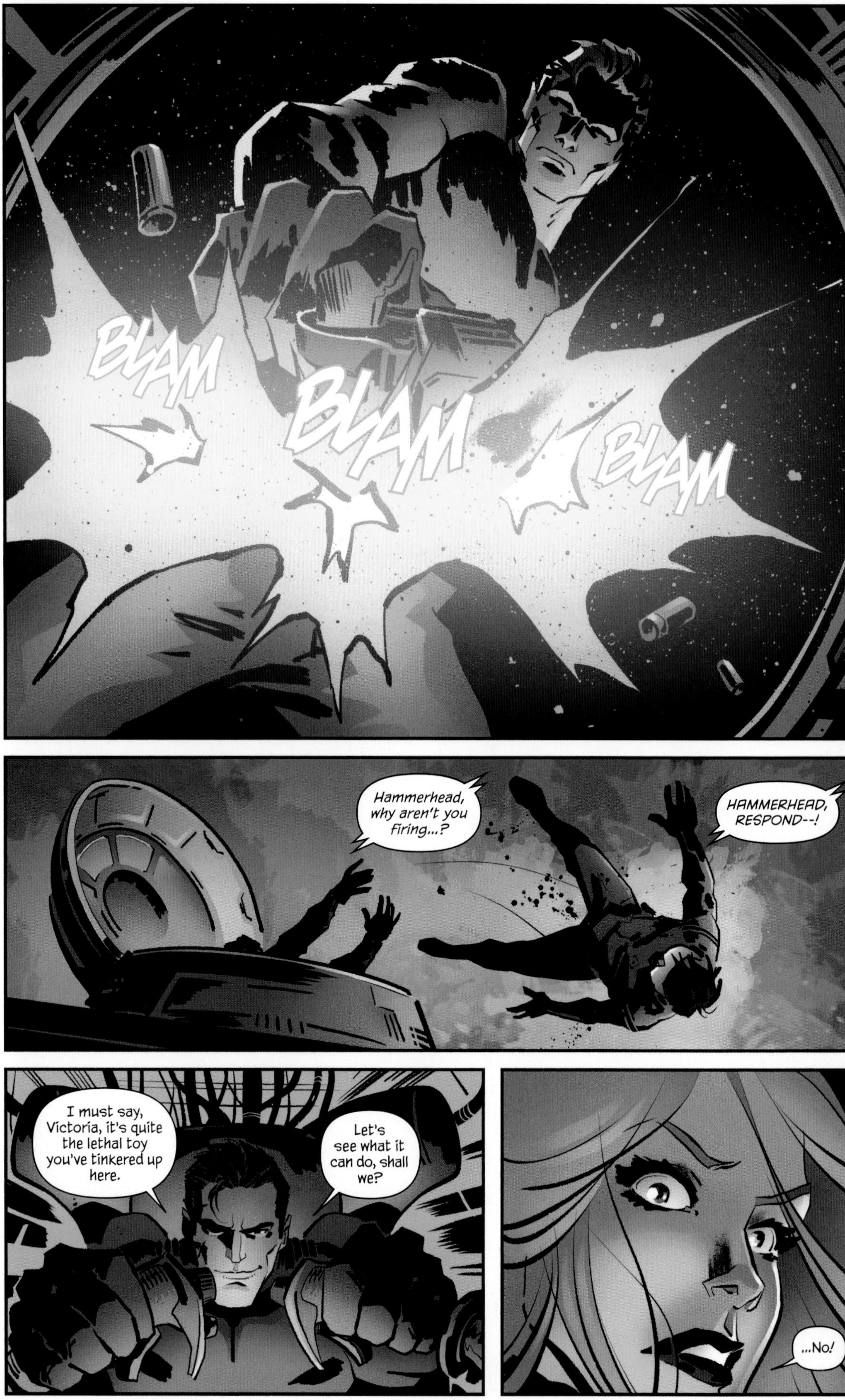
BLAM
BLAM
BLAM
Hammerhead, why aren't you firing...?
HAMMERHEAD, RESPOND--!
I must say, Victoria, it's quite the lethal toy you've tinkered up here.
Let's see what it can do, shall we?
...No!

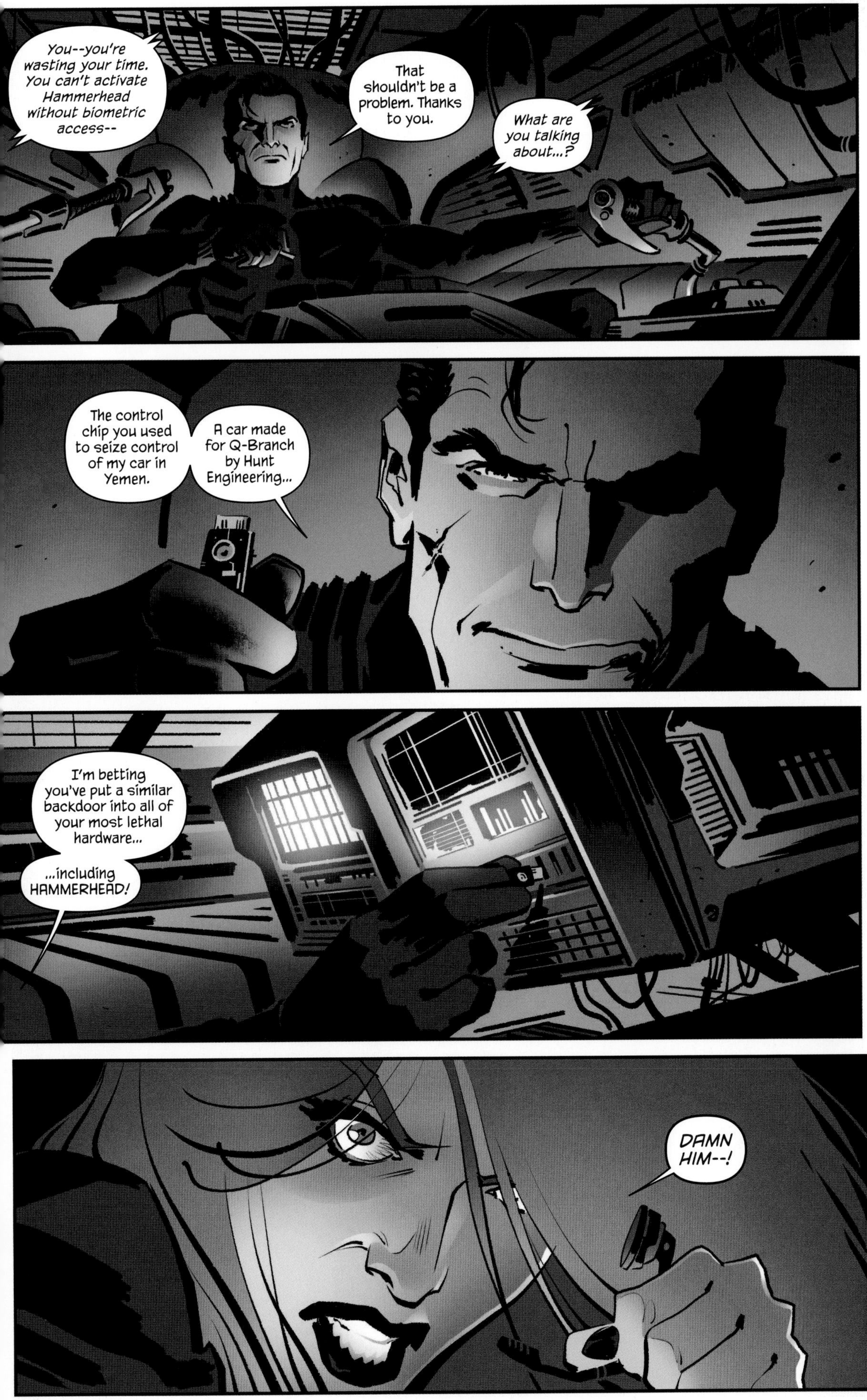
You--you're wasting your time. You can't activate Hammerhead without biometric access--
That shouldn't be a problem. Thanks to you.
What are you talking about...?
The control chip you used to seize control of my car in Yemen.
A car made for Q-Branch by Hunt Engineering...
I'm betting you've put a similar backdoor into all of your most lethal hardware...
...including HAMMERHEAD!
DAMN HIM--!

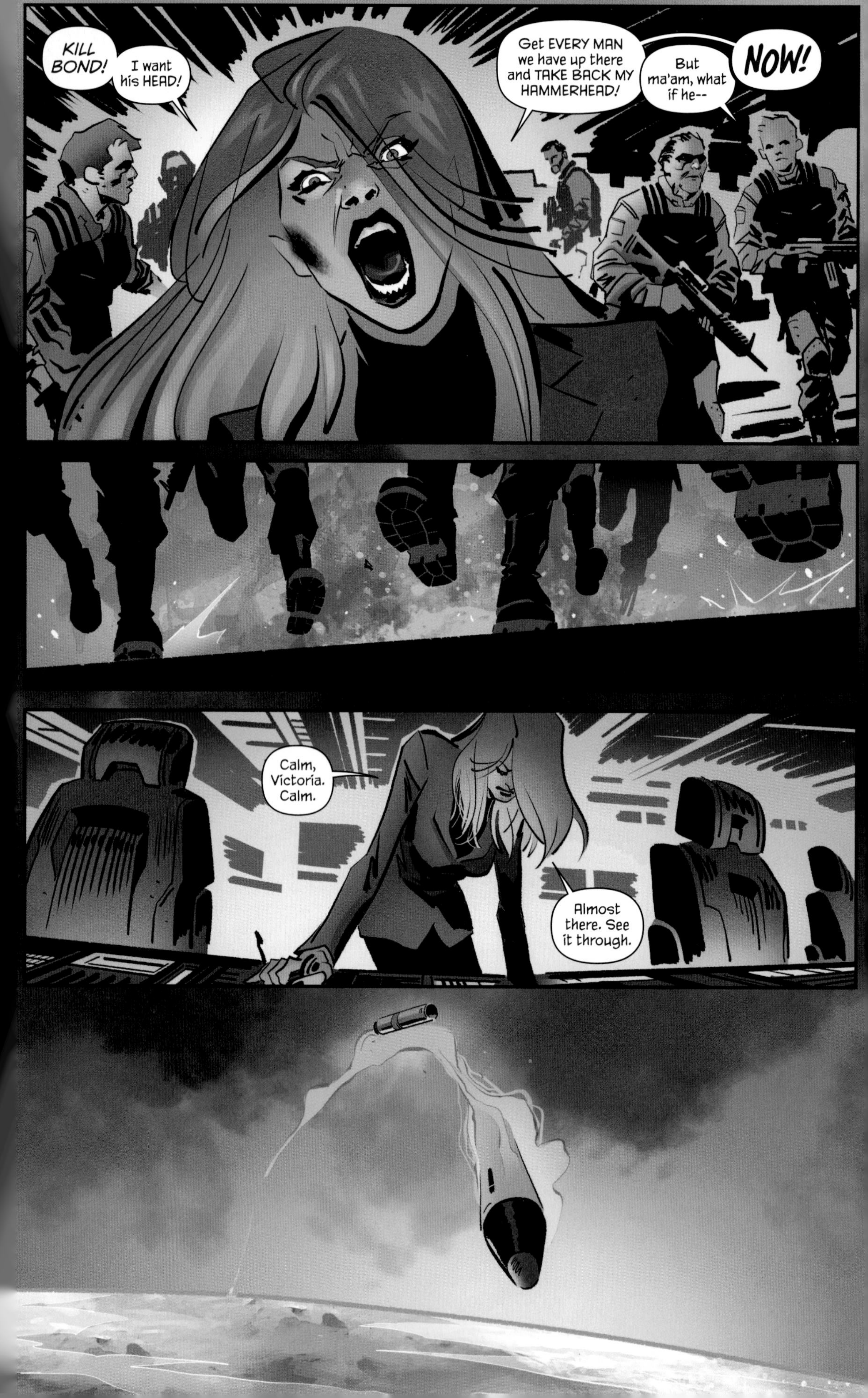
KILL BOND!
I want his HEAD!
Get EVERY MAN we have up there and TAKE BACK MY HAMMERHEAD!
But ma'am, what if he--
NOW!
Calm, Victoria. Calm.
Almost there. See it through.

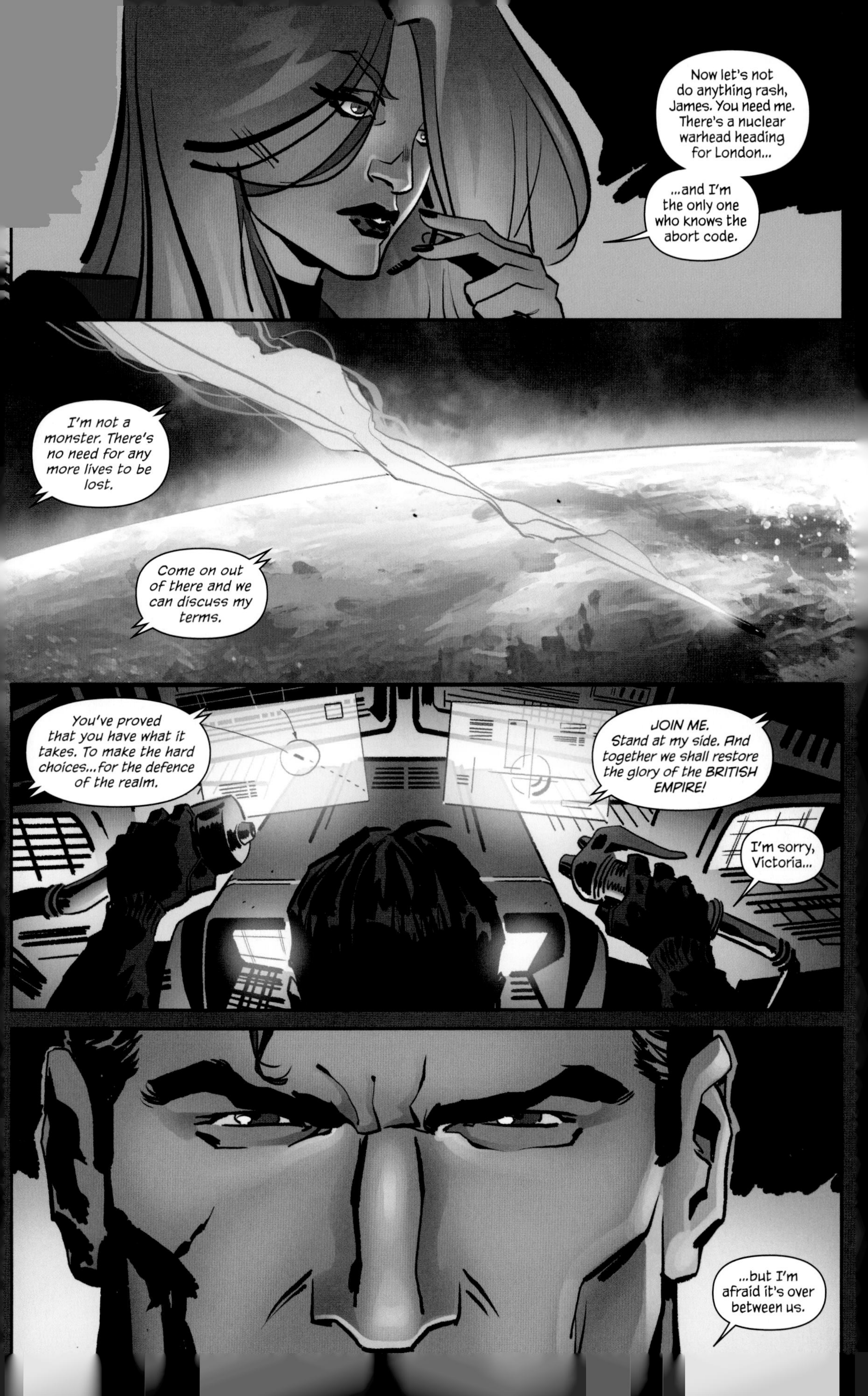
Now let's not do anything rash, James. You need me. There's a nuclear warhead heading for London...
...and I'm the only one who knows the abort code.
I'm not a monster. There's no need for any more lives to be lost.
Come on out of there and we can discuss my terms.
You've proved that you have what it takes. To make the hard choices...for the defence of the realm.
JOIN ME. Stand at my side. And together we shall restore the glory of the BRITISH EMPIRE!
I'm sorry, Victoria...
...but I'm afraid it's over between us.

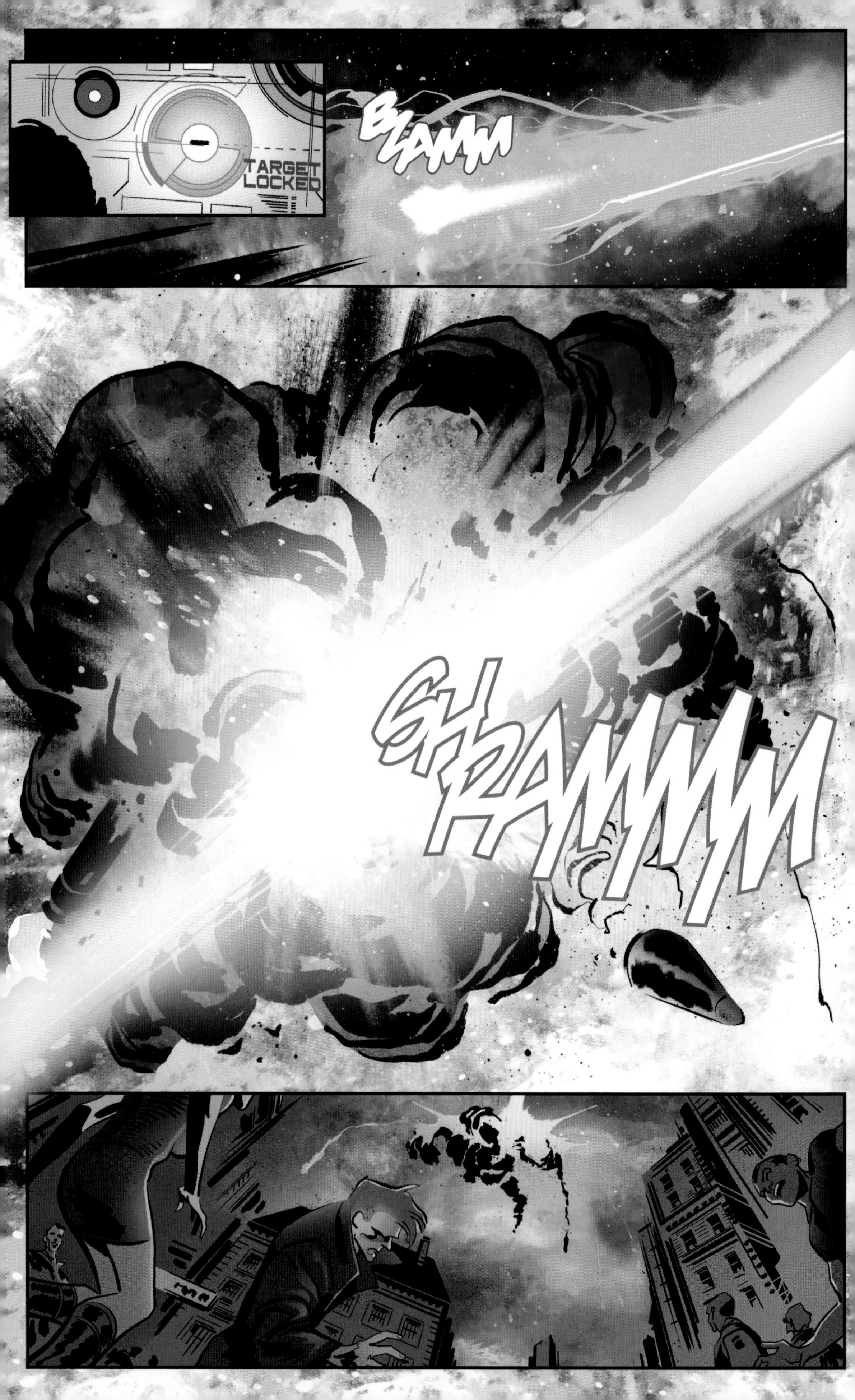
TARGET LOCKED
BLAMM
SHRAMMM

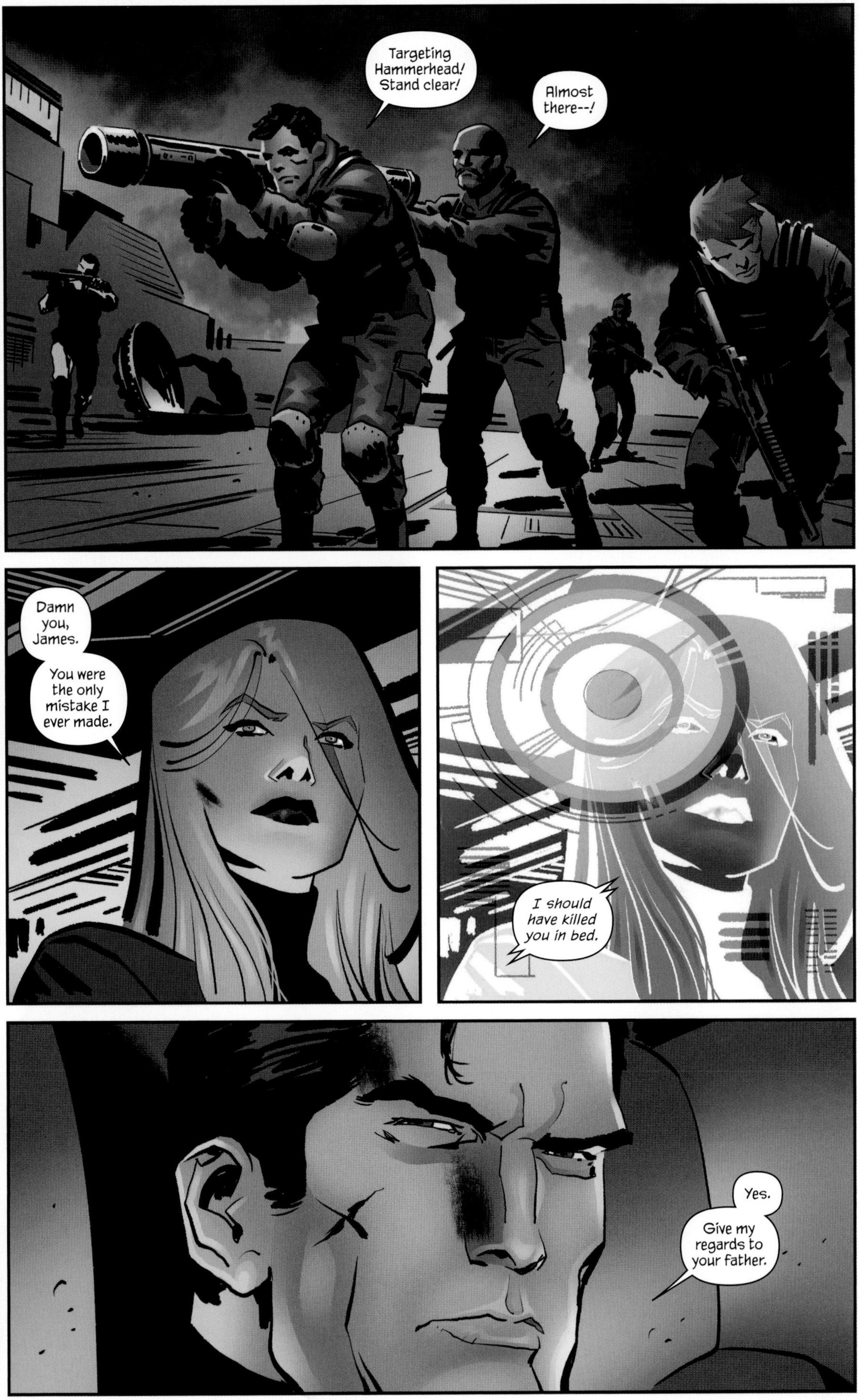
Targeting Hammerhead! Stand clear!
Almost there--!
Damn you, James.
You were the only mistake I ever made.
I should have killed you in bed.
Yes.
Give my regards to your father.

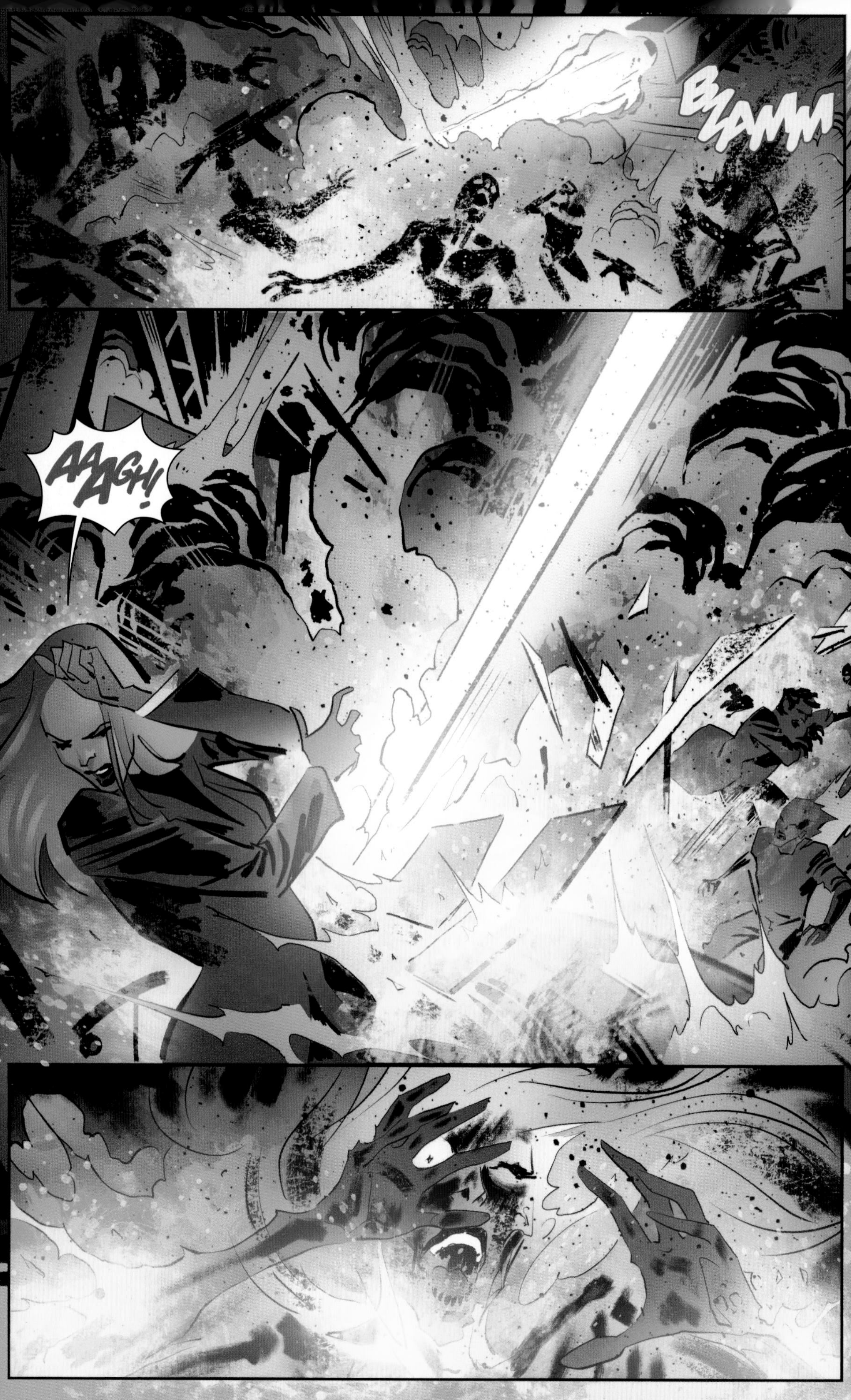
BLAMM
AAAGH!

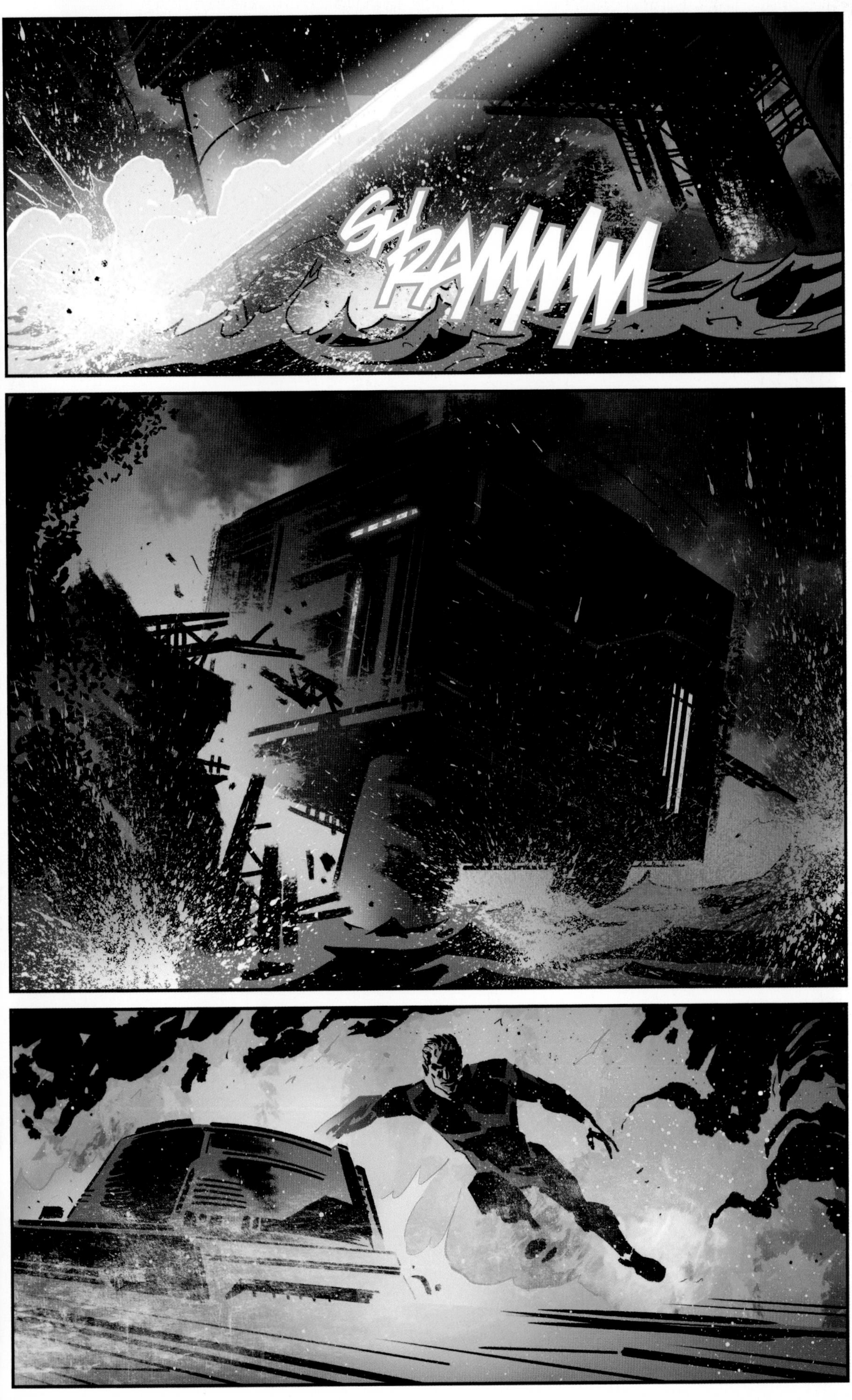
SHRAMMM

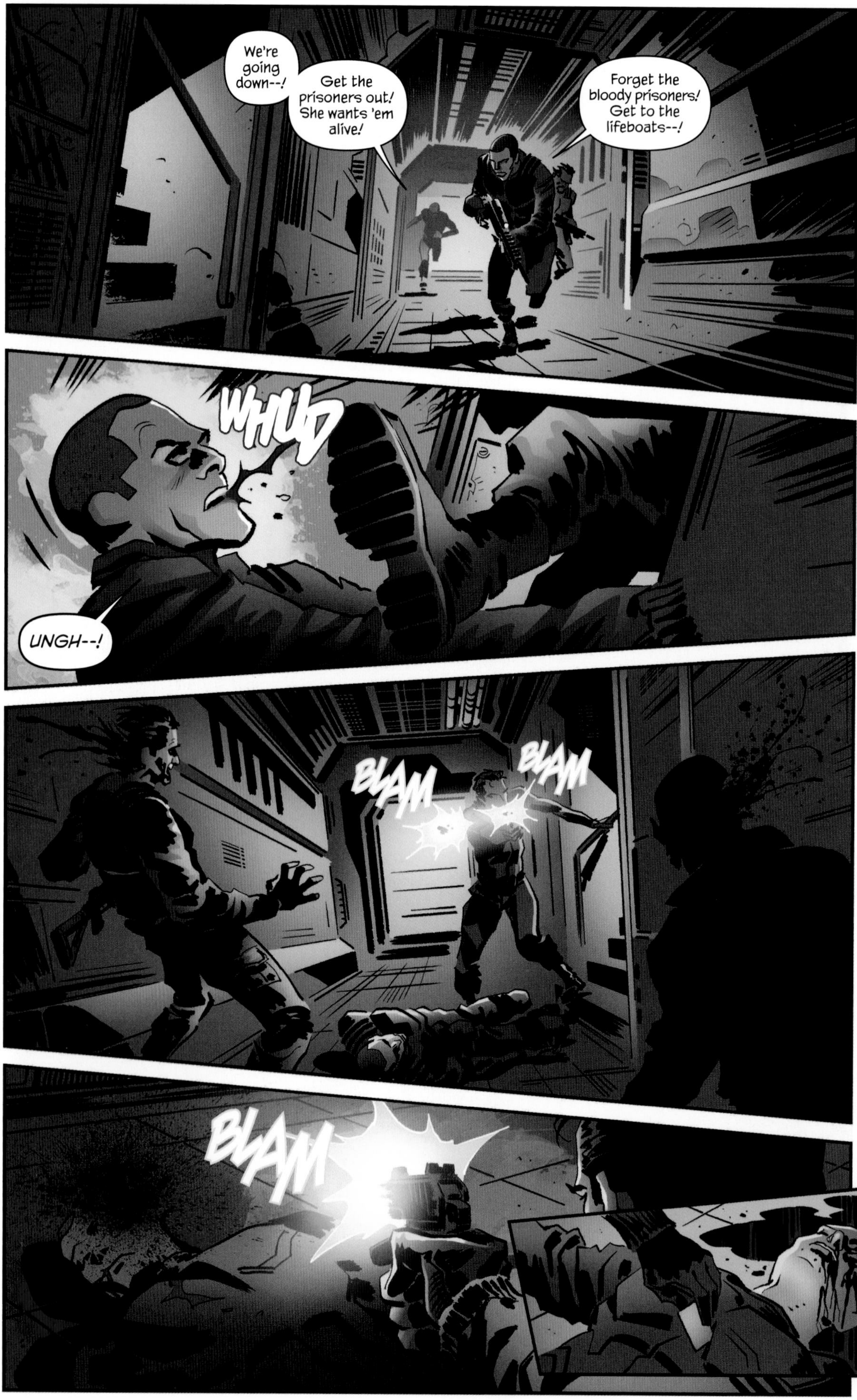
We're going down--!
Get the prisoners out! She wants 'em alive!
Forget the bloody prisoners! Get to the lifeboats--!
WHUD
UNGH--!
BLAM
BLAM
BLAM

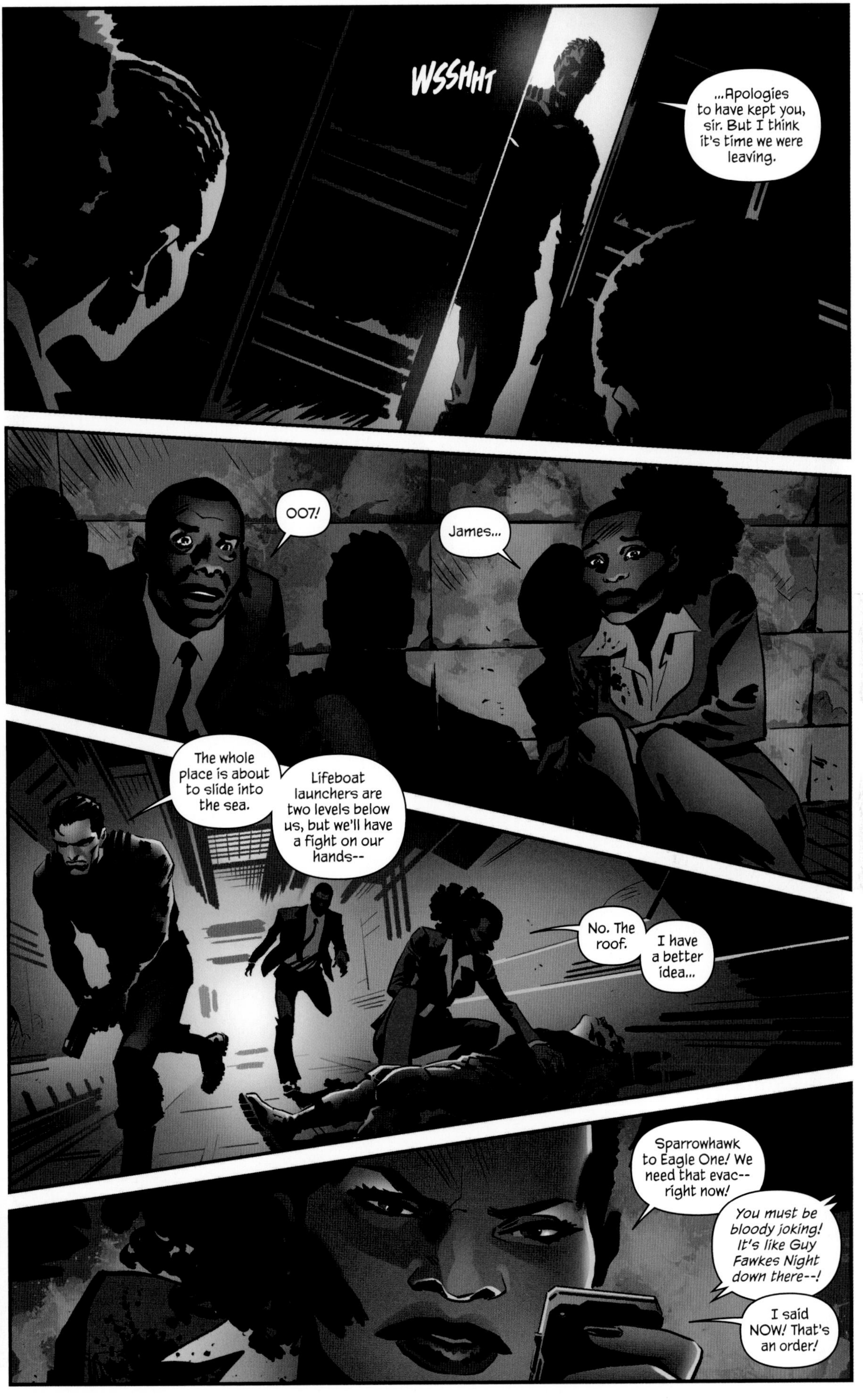
WSSHHT
...Apologies to have kept you, sir. But I think it's time we were leaving.
007!
James...
The whole place is about to slide into the sea.
Lifeboat launchers are two levels below us, but we'll have a fight on our hands--
No. The roof.
I have a better idea...
Sparrowhawk to Eagle One! We need that evac-- right now!
You must be bloody joking! It's like Guy Fawkes Night down there--!
I said NOW! That's an order!

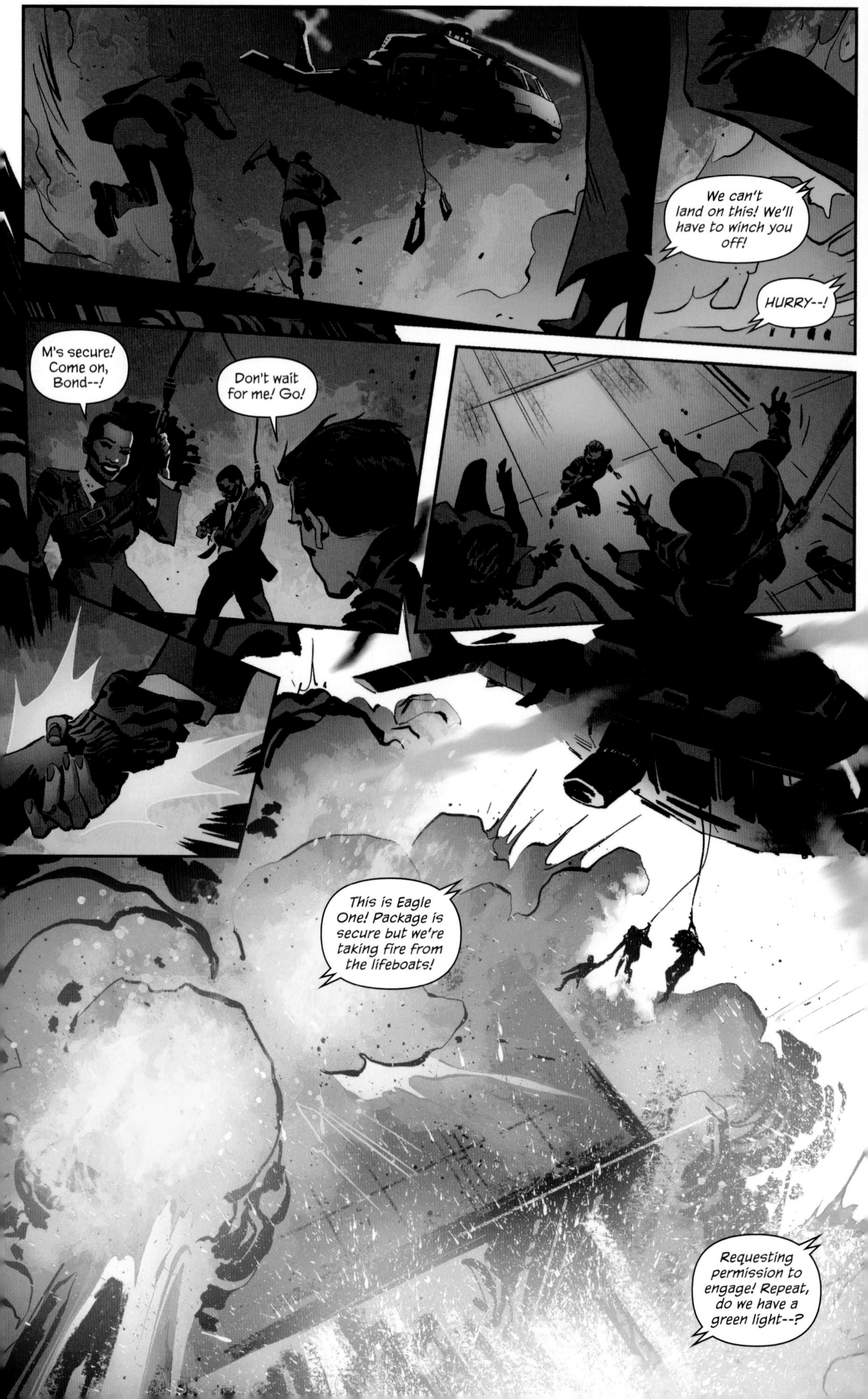
We can't land on this! We'll have to winch you off!
HURRY--!
M's secure! Come on, Bond--!
Don't wait for me! Go!
This is Eagle One! Package is secure but we're taking fire from the lifeboats!
Requesting permission to engage! Repeat, do we have a green light--?

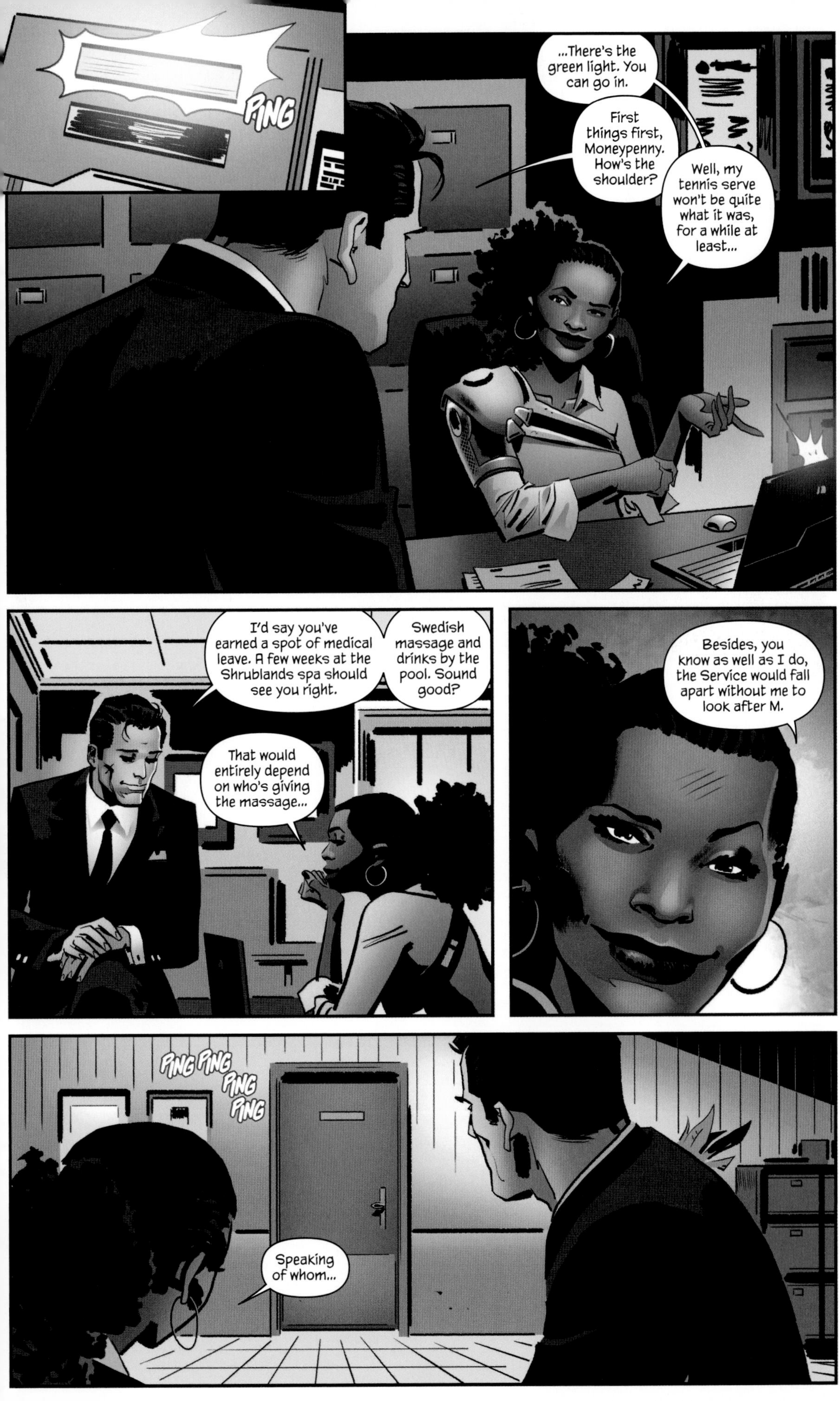
PING
...There's the green light. You can go in.
First things first, Moneypenny. How's the shoulder?
Well, my tennis serve won't be quite what it was, for a while at least...
I'd say you've earned a spot of medical leave. A few weeks at the Shrublands spa should see you right.
Swedish massage and drinks by the pool. Sound good?
That would entirely depend on who's giving the massage...
Besides, you know as well as I do, the Service would fall apart without me to look after M.
PING PING PING PING
Speaking of whom...

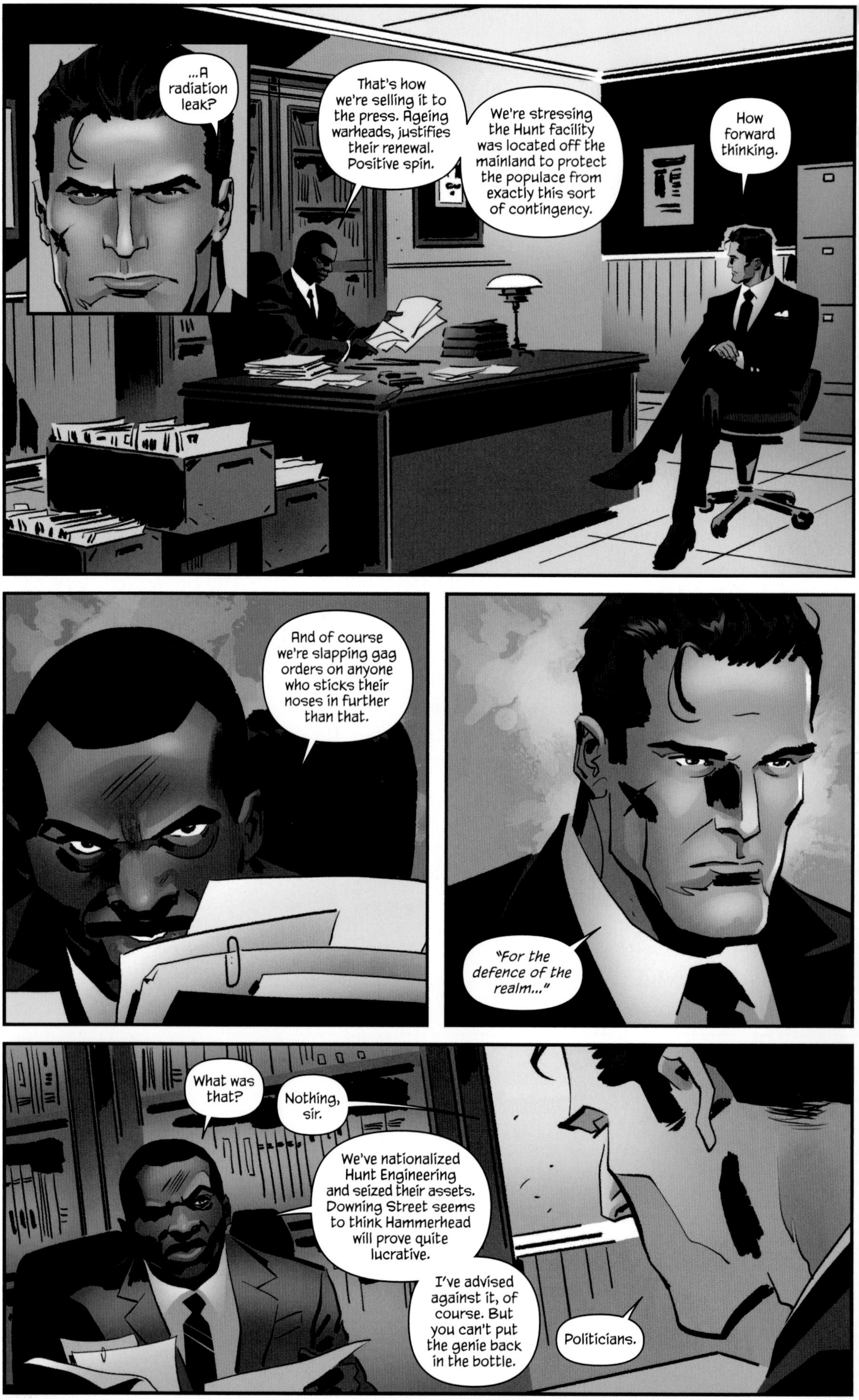
...A radiation leak?
That's how we're selling it to the press. Ageing warheads, justifies their renewal. Positive spin.
We're stressing the Hunt facility was located off the mainland to protect the populace from exactly this sort of contingency.
How forward thinking.
And of course we're slapping gag orders on anyone who sticks their noses in further than that.
"For the defence of the realm..."
What was that?
Nothing, sir.
We've nationalized Hunt Engineering and seized their assets. Downing Street seems to think Hammerhead will prove quite lucrative.
I've advised against it, of course. But you can't put the genie back in the bottle.
Politicians.

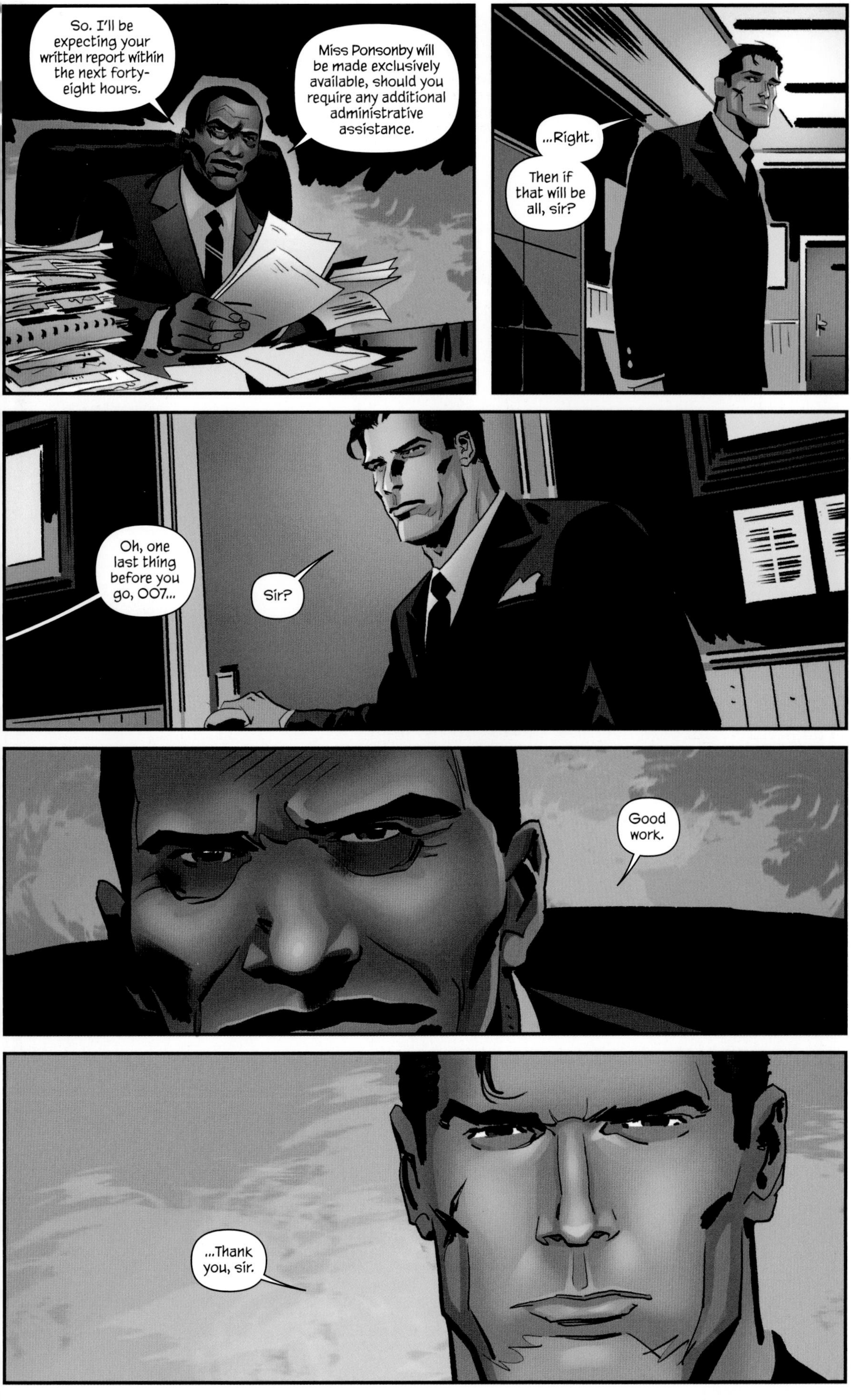
So. I'll be expecting your written report within the next forty-eight hours.
Miss Ponsonby will be made exclusively available, should you require any additional administrative assistance.
...Right.
Then if that will be all, sir?
Oh, one last thing before you go, 007...
Sir?
Good work.
...Thank you, sir.

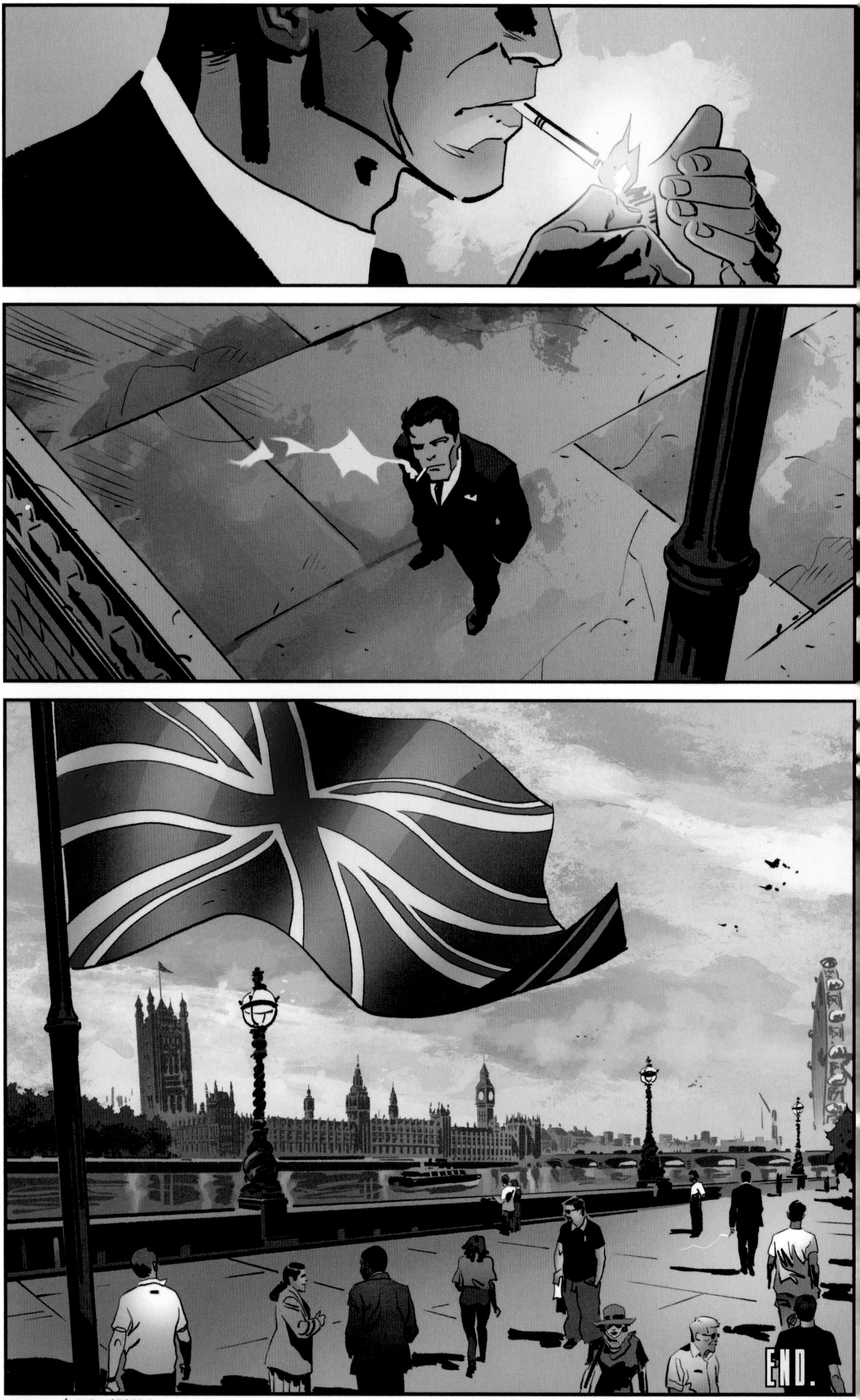
END.

DIGGLE / CASALANGUIDA

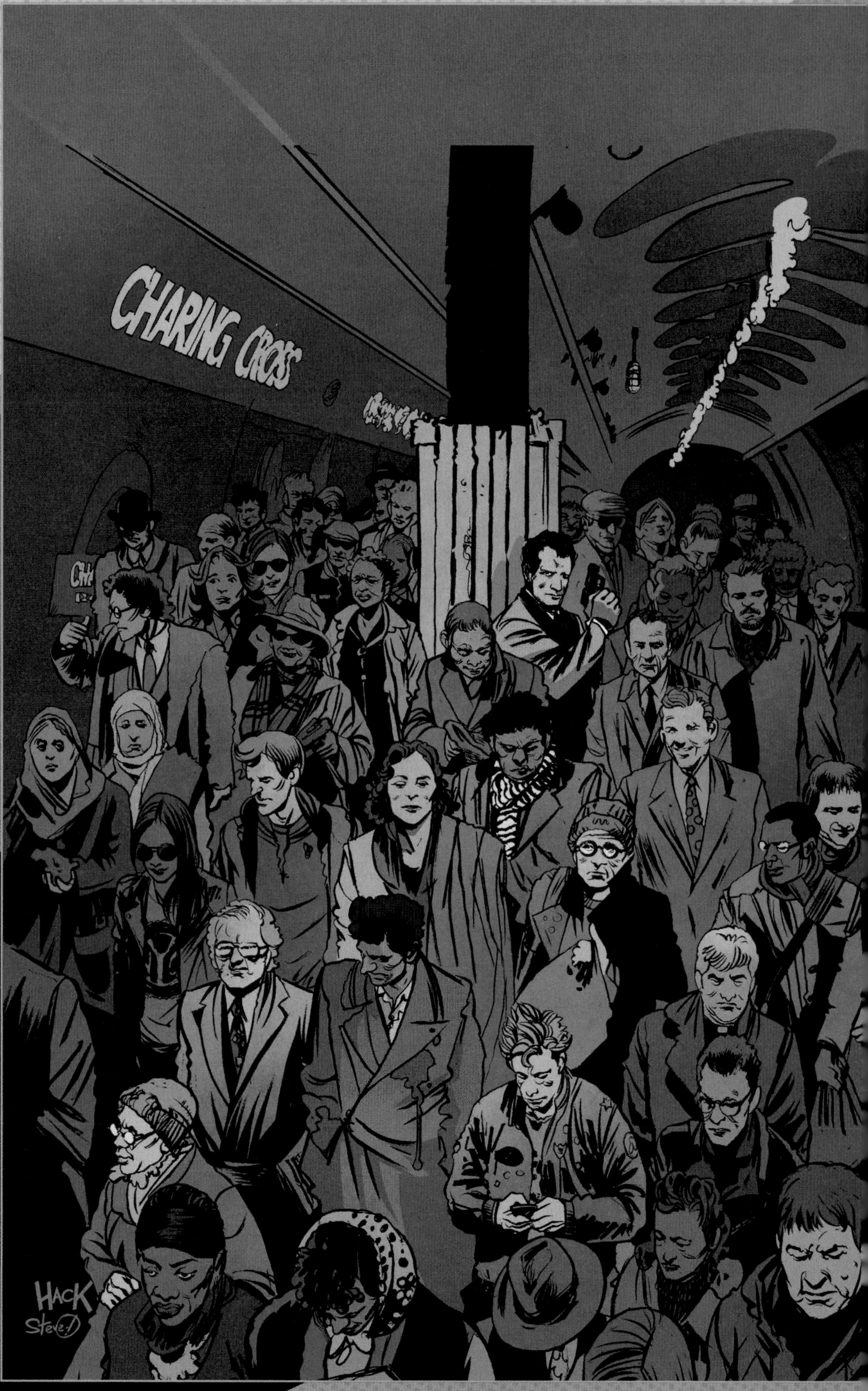
CHARING CROSS
HACK

ISSUE 1 VARIANT COVER
BY ROBERT HACK

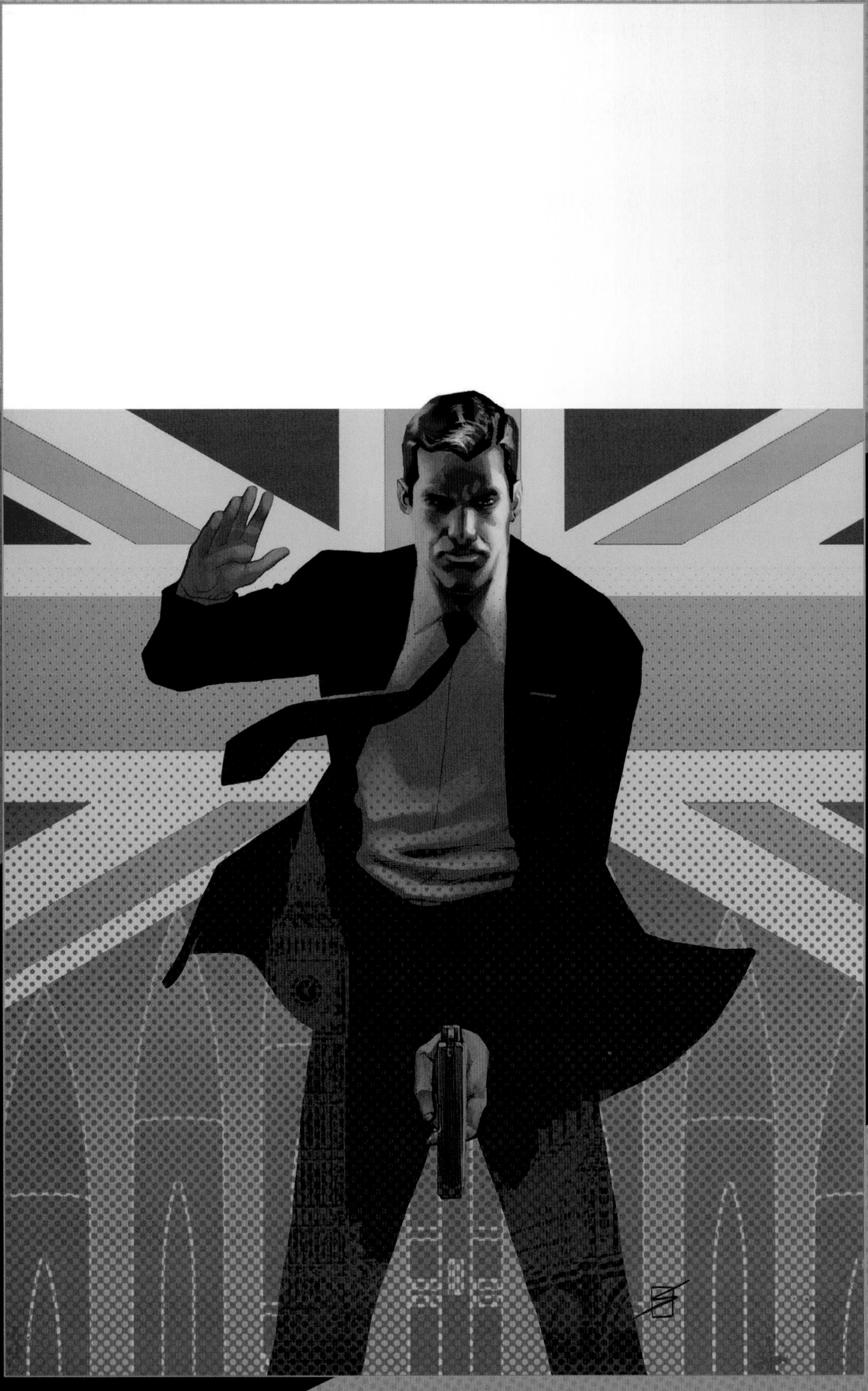

ISSUE 1 VARIANT COVER
BY RON SALAS

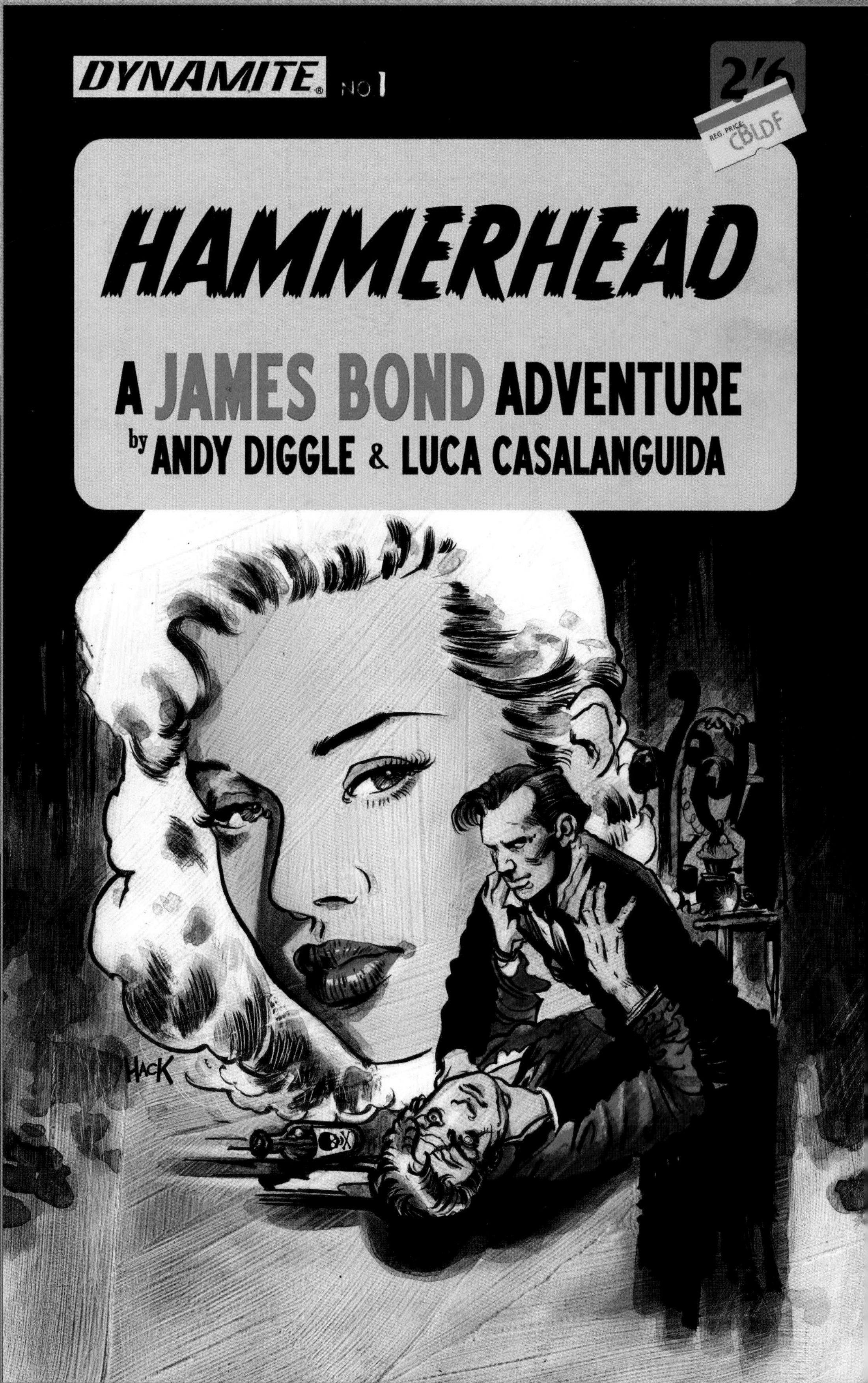
DYNAMITE
NO 1
2/6
REG. PRICE
CBLDF
HAMMERHEAD
A JAMES BOND ADVENTURE
by ANDY DIGGLE & LUCA CASALANGUIDA
HACK

ISSUE 1 "COMIC BOOK LEGAL DEFENSE FUND"
VARIANT COVER BY ROBERT HACK

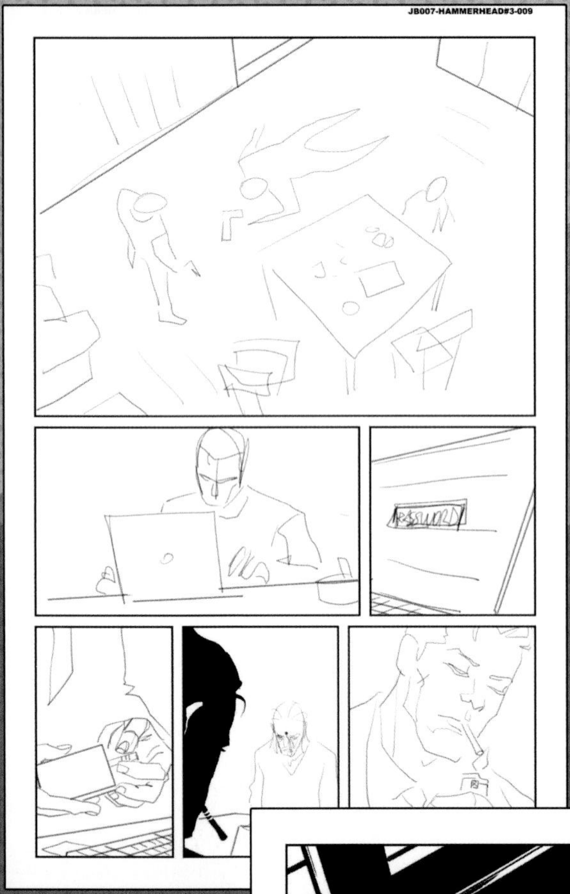
JB007-HAMMERHEAD#3-009

ISSUE 3 PAGE 9
LAYOUT STAGE

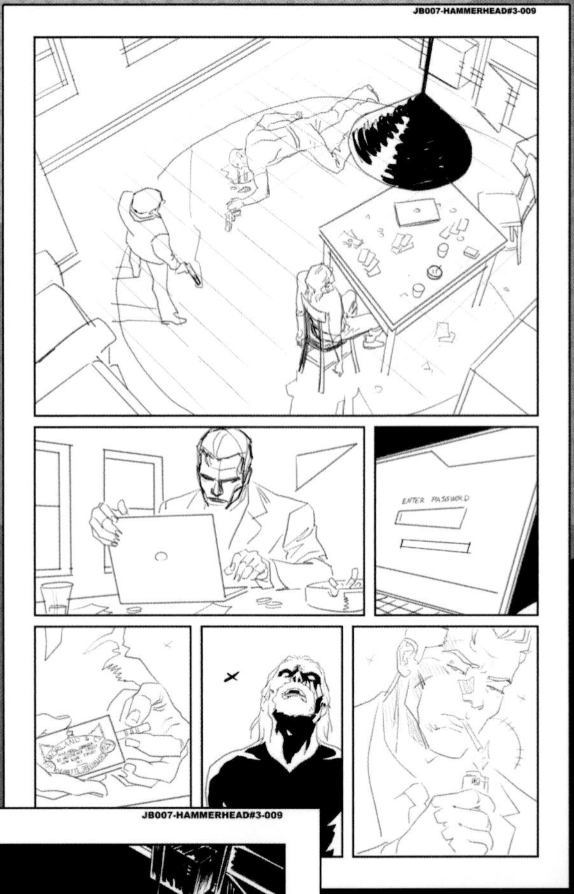
JB007-HAMMERHEAD#3-009
ENTER PASSWORD

ISSUE 3 PAGE 9
PENCIL STAGE

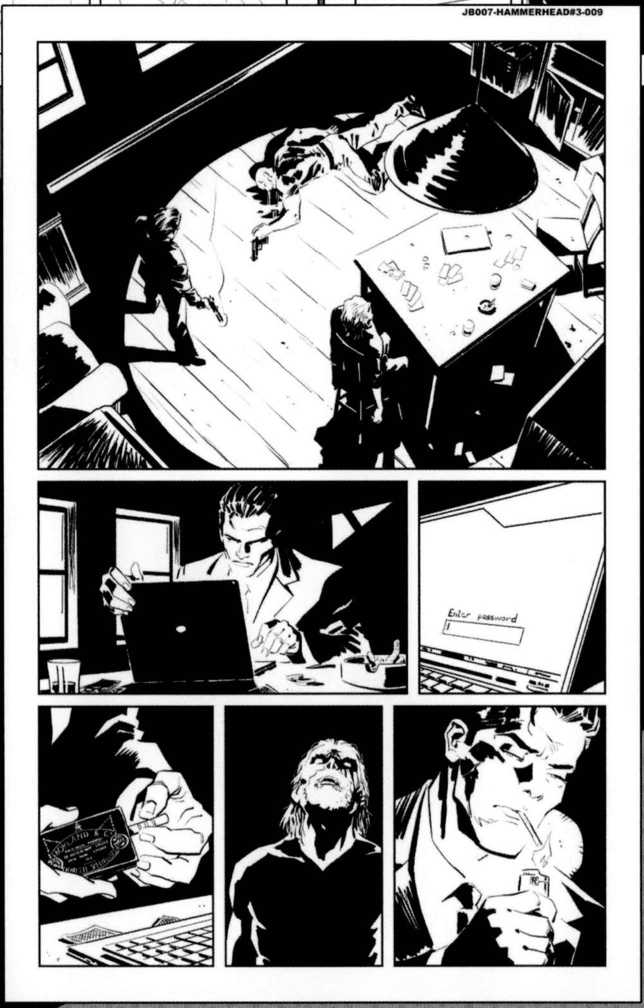
JB007-HAMMERHEAD#3-009
Enter password

ISSUE 3 PAGE 9 FINAL INK STAGE
(ALL ART BY LUCA CASALANGUIDA)

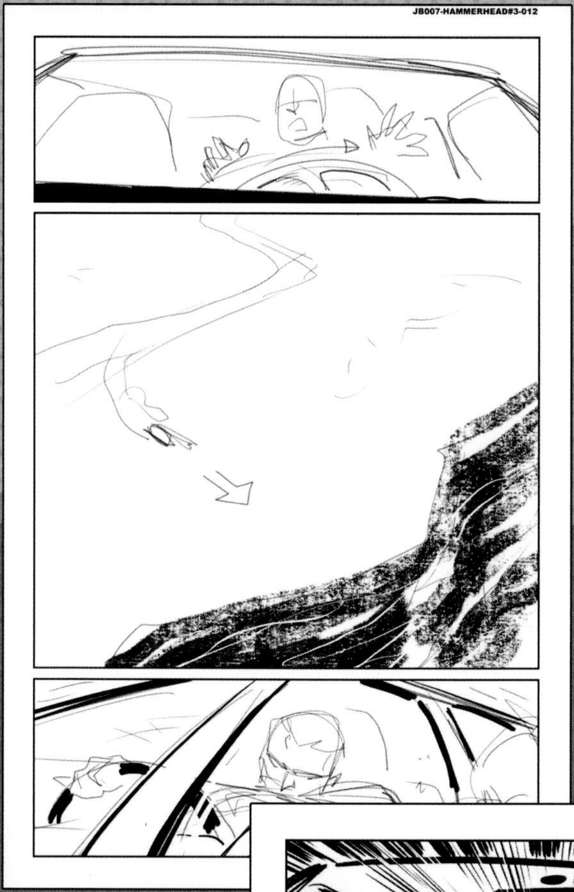
JB007-HAMMERHEAD#3-012

ISSUE 3 PAGE 12
LAYOUT STAGE

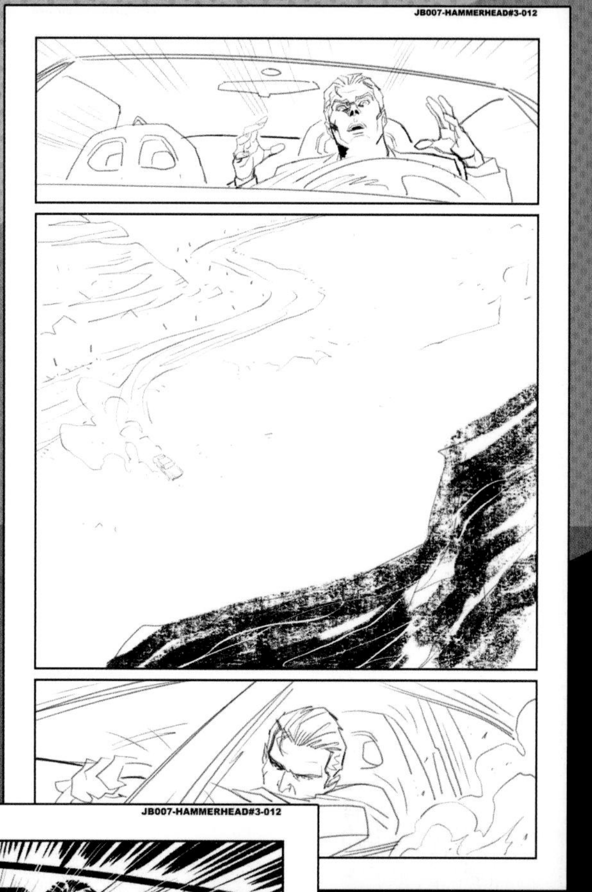
JB007-HAMMERHEAD#3-012

ISSUE 3 PAGE 12
PENCIL STAGE

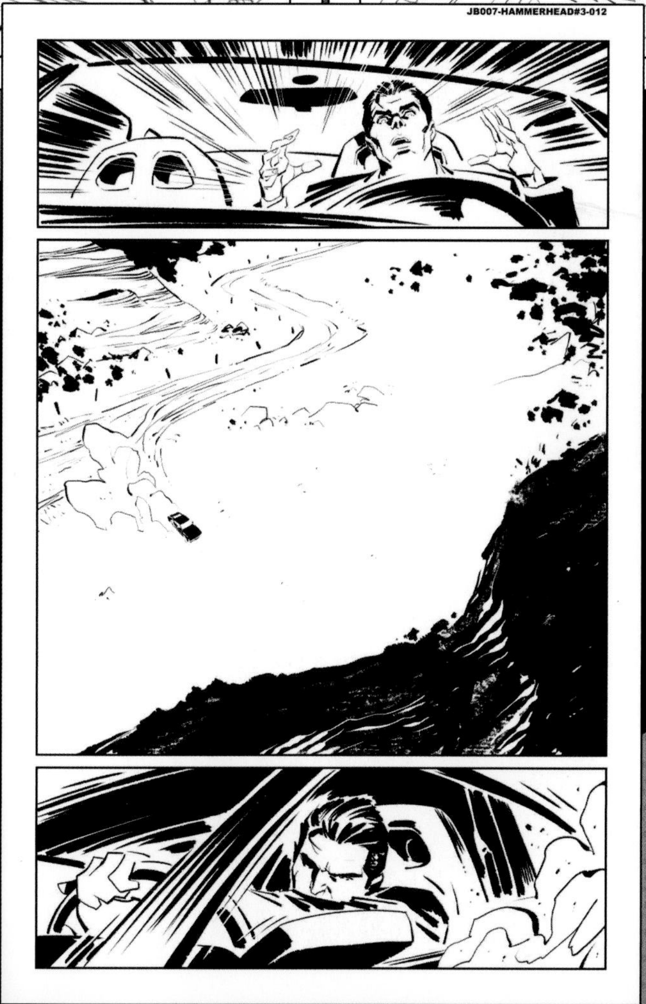
JB007-HAMMERHEAD#3-012

ISSUE 3 PAGE 12 FINAL INK STAGE
(ALL ART BY LUCA CASALANGUIDA)

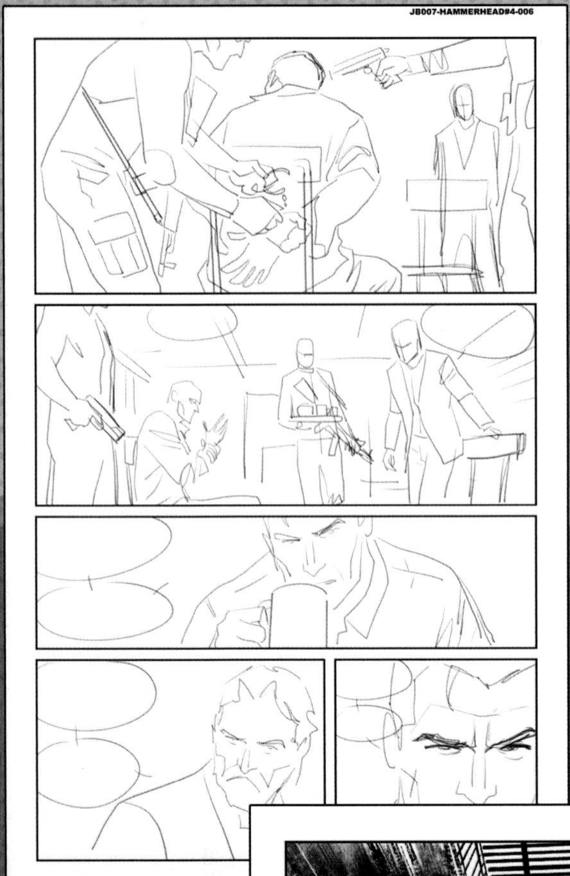
JB007-HAMMERHEAD#4-006

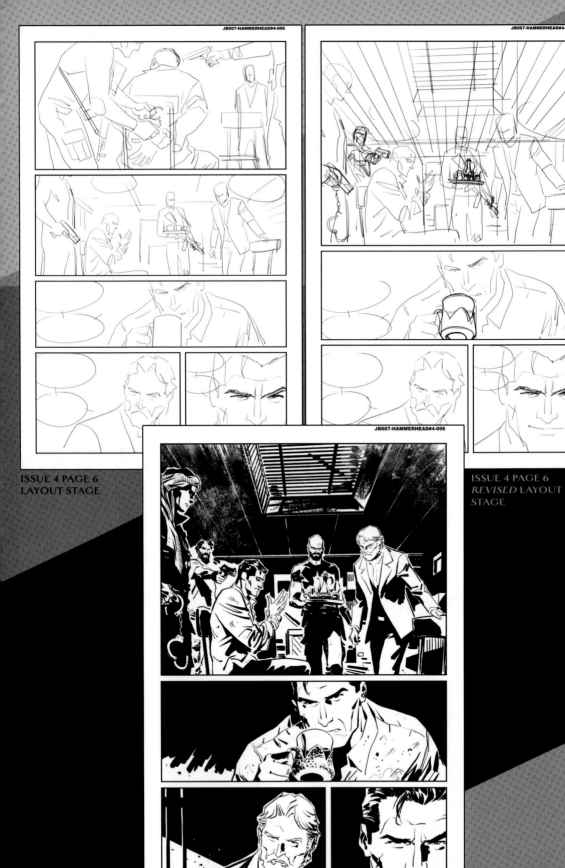

ISSUE 4 PAGE 6
LAYOUT STAGE

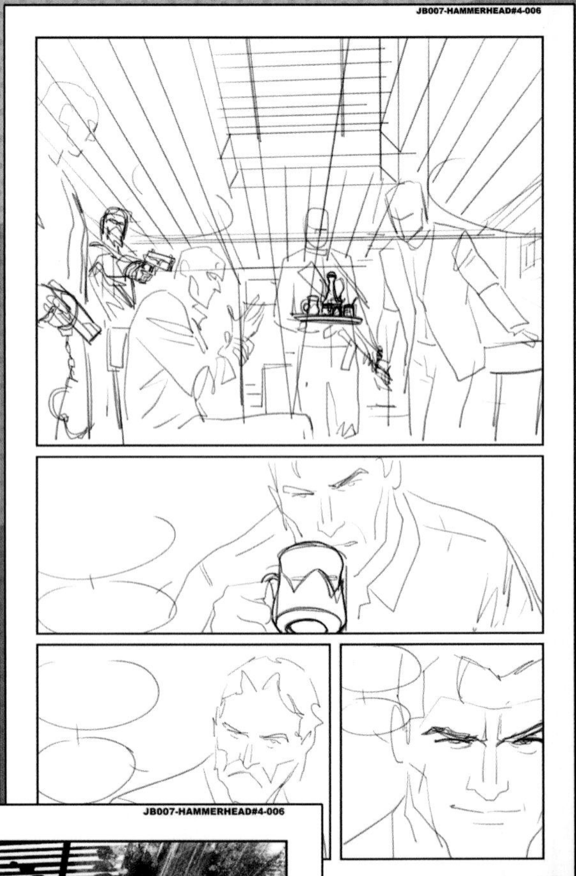
JB007-HAMMERHEAD#4-006

ISSUE 4 PAGE 6
REVISED LAYOUT
STAGE

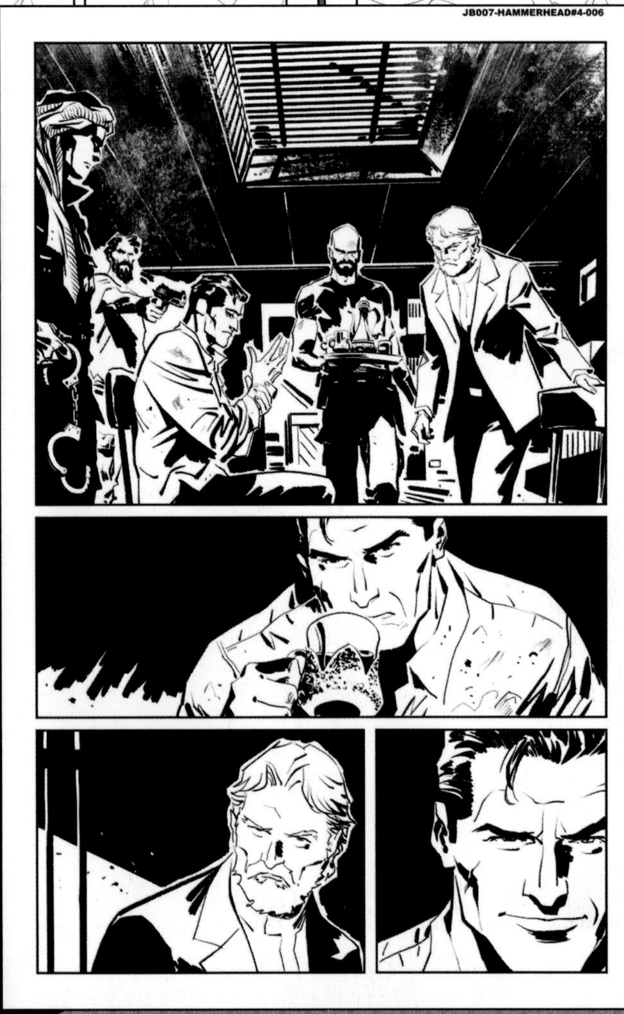
JB007-HAMMERHEAD#4-006

ISSUE 4 PAGE 6 FINAL INK STAGE
(ALL ART BY LUCA CASALANGUIDA)

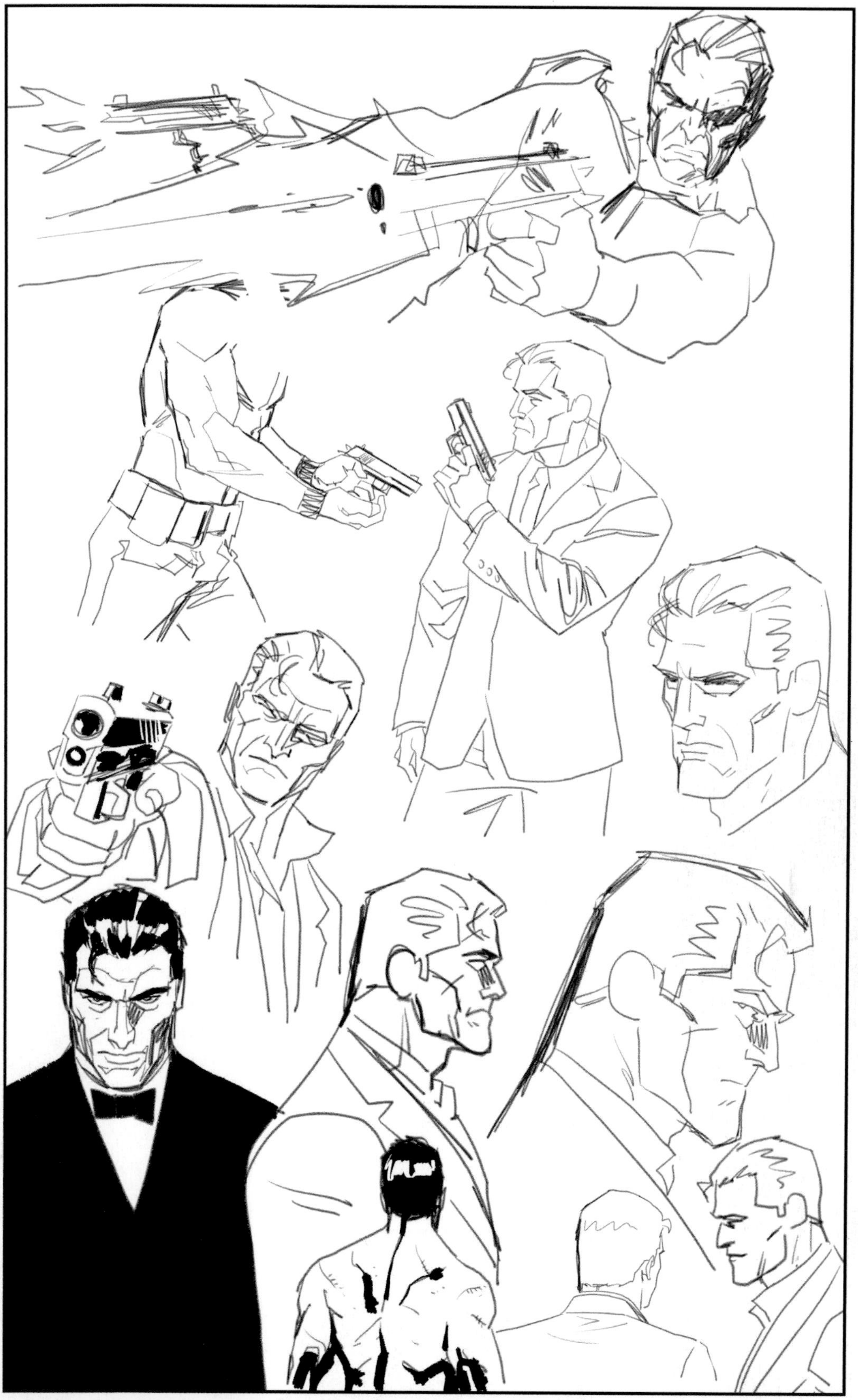

JAMES BOND CHARACTER SKETCHES
BY LUCA CASALANGUIDA

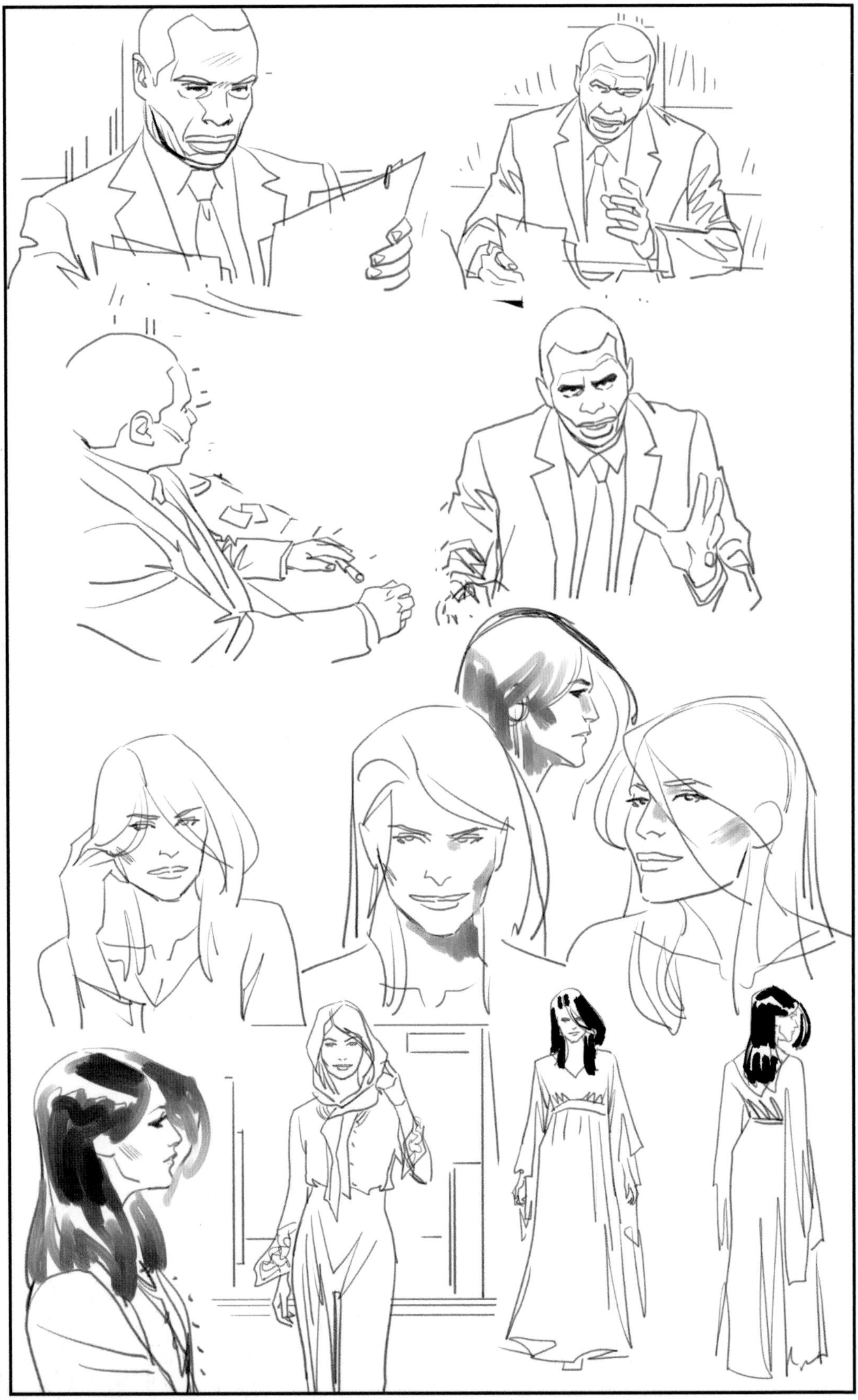

M AND *KRAKEN* CHARACTER SKETCHES
BY LUCA CASALANGUIDA